The Tudors by Numbers

The Tudors by Numbers

The Stories and Statistics Behind England's Most Infamous Royal Dynasty

Carol Ann Lloyd

First published in Great Britain in 2023 by
Pen & Sword History
An imprint of Pen & Sword Books Limited
Yorkshire – Philadelphia

Copyright © Carol Ann Lloyd 2023

ISBN 978 1 39906 294 7

The right of Carol Ann Lloyd to be identified as
Author of this Work has been asserted by her in accordance
with the Copyright, Designs and Patents Act 1988.

A CIP catalogue record for this book is
available from the British Library

All rights reserved. No part of this book may be reproduced or
transmitted in any form or by any means, electronic or mechanical
including photocopying, recording or by any information storage and
retrieval system, without permission from the Publisher in writing.

Typeset by Mac Style
Printed in the UK by CPI Group (UK) Ltd, Croydon, CR0 4YY.

Pen & Sword Books Limited incorporates the imprints of After
the Battle, Atlas, Archaeology, Aviation, Discovery, Family History,
Fiction, History, Maritime, Military, Military Classics, Politics,
Select, Transport, True Crime, Air World, Frontline Publishing, Leo
Cooper, Remember When, Seaforth Publishing, The Praetorian Press,
Wharncliffe Local History, Wharncliffe Transport, Wharncliffe True
Crime and White Owl.

For a complete list of Pen & Sword titles please contact

PEN & SWORD BOOKS LIMITED
47 Church Street, Barnsley, South Yorkshire, S70 2AS, England
E-mail: enquiries@pen-and-sword.co.uk
Website: www.pen-and-sword.co.uk
or
PEN AND SWORD BOOKS
1950 Lawrence Rd, Havertown, PA 19083, USA
E-mail: Uspen-and-sword@casematepublishers.com
Website: www.penandswordbooks.com

*To Grandma Helen, who inspired me to
follow my dream of going to England.*

Contents

Acknowledgements		xi
Introduction		xiv
Chapter 1	**1 Rose**	1
	The Roses Take Centre Stager	1
	The Story of a Rose by the Numbers	3
	3 Wives and 2 Sides	4
	14 Years spent in Exile	6
	21 Days and the Beginning of the Reign	7
	1 Wedding of Roses	8
	2 Pretenders	11
	Numbers and the Rose	16
Chapter 2	**2 Crowned Queens**	19
	The Queen is Dead, Long Live the Queen	19
	The Story of 2 Crowned Queens	20
	0 Queens Crowned Before the Tudors	21
	3 Succession Acts of Henry VIII	22
	2 Reimagined Coronations	24
	42 Percent of the Tudor Dynasty Ruled by a Queen	28
	100 Percent of Dynasties after the Tudors with a Queen	30
	Numbers and Queens	31
Chapter 3	**We 3 Kings**	34
	Birth of a Prince	34
	The Story of 3 Tudor Kings	35

	1 Traditional Royal Succession	35
	3 Religions for 3 Kings	36
	7 Consorts Among 3 Kings	40
	68 Years of Tudor Kings	43
	Numbers and Kings	47
Chapter 4	**4 Cornerstones of Elizabeth I's Success**	49
	Heart and Stomach of a king	49
	A Foundation of 4 Cornerstones	50
	45 Years with a Cecil at the Heart of Government	51
	25 Progresses: The Queen on the Road	55
	0 Masters: The Marriage Game	58
	2 Queens, 1 Crown: The Queen of Scots	61
	Numbers and Elizabeth's Reign	64
Chapter 5	**5 Tudor Monarchs (Or is that 6??)**	66
	The Search for 'Heires Males'	66
	Were There 5 or 6 Tudor Monarchs?	67
	2 Previous Tudor Transitions	68
	2 Versions of the Devise for the Succession	69
	13 Days: Who was Queen?	70
	2 Proclamations, 2 Queens	77
	9 Women Who Could be Heirs to the Throne	78
	Numbers and Monarchs	79
Chapter 6	**6 Very Different Wives**	81
	The Marrying Game	81
	How the Six Wives Shaped Henry VIII's Reign	82
	70 Percent of the Reign with Katherine and Anne	82
	And Baby Makes 3	88
	2 Weddings, An Annulment, and a Child Bride	90
	3½ Years of Bachelor Life	95
	Once, Twice, 3 Times a (Married) Lady	96
	Numbers and Wives	98

Chapter 7	**7 Coronations**	99
	The Crown, Once Worn	99
	The Story of 7 Tudor Coronations	100
	1 Joint Coronation	101
	2 Kings Crowned Alone	102
	2 Queens Consort Crowned Individually	104
	2 Successive Regnant Queens Crowned	108
	Bonus: 1 Possible Battlefield Coronation	112
	Numbers and Coronations	112
Chapter 8	**8 Royal Road Trips**	114
	The Court on the Move	114
	8 Royal Road Trips that Shaped the Dynasty	115
	1 Progress to Kick Things Off	116
	1 Over the Top International Event	118
	1 Missed Meeting for Henry and 1 Big Problem for Catherine Howard	119
	2 Youthful Progresses of Edward VI	121
	2 Become 1: Mary's Marriage Progress	123
	1 Queen with Many Progresses	125
	19 Days at Kenilworth	125
	1 Final Progress of the Tudor Dynasty	128
	Numbers and Progresses	130
Chapter 9	**9 Ways the Tudors Changed Everything**	131
	The Difference a Dynasty Makes	131
	The Story of 9 Ways the Tudors Changed Everything	132
	3 Meals: The Tudors and Breakfast	133
	1 Toilet: First Flush in England	134
	6 Permanent Outdoor Theatres	135
	200,000 People Living in London in 1600	137
	1 Central Location for Commerce: The Royal Exchange	138
	1 Iconic Kingly Image (Thanks to Henry and Holbein)	140

	800 (approximately) Monasteries Dissolved in the Reign of Henry VIII	142
	4 English Translations of the Bible	144
	1 New (and Changing) 'State" Church, and Some Other Options	146
	Numbers and Changes	148
Chapter 10	**Top 10 Tudor Secrets and Surprises**	149
	The End of the Tudor Dynasty	149
	The Top 10 Tudor Surprises	150
	2 Bookends of the Dynasty: Margaret Beaufort and Elizabeth I	150
	3 or 5: Katherine of Aragon's Place in Tenure as Queen Consort	152
	6 'Other' Marriages	153
	5,000 Calories in 2 Meals	155
	56 Years After the Wars of the Roses, the Final 'Yorkist Pretender' Was Executed	156
	1 Tudor Monarch Left a Diary	157
	7, as in 007: John Dee and James Bond	158
	2 Hours of Prep Time for Elizabeth Every Morning	159
	1 Bath a Month, Whether She Needed it or Not	160
	3 Recent Discoveries about the Tudors	162
	Numbers and Surprises	163

Notes   165
Bibliography   177
Index   187

Acknowledgements

Tudors by the Numbers has been a journey for the ages! I've carried the idea with me for many years, chatting with friends and colleagues, speaking to history-based groups around the country, and thinking about how to tell these stories. This book represents the realisation of a dream: to publish a book about Tudor history!

I so appreciate the kind help of various libraries and librarians. I was able to go to London to visit the British Library and National Archives (UK). The staff was endlessly helpful and patient in both locations, guiding a new researcher through such challenging tasks as scanning my card correctly through the door. To be in the presence of documents and artifacts I have only imagined exceeded my expectations.

In addition, my heartfelt thanks to the wonderful people at Folger Shakespeare Library in Washington, DC. It was my home away from home as an employee for years, and now it's my other home as a reader. Through the challenges of a pandemic and massive reconstruction project, the Library staff have continued to make resources available and have provided such creative support as The Armchair Radio Reference (Half) Hour.

I am so grateful for the historians who have come on my podcast and explored the Tudors and other historic figures with me. Their generosity in sharing expertise and wisdom is truly inspiring. I find it magical that I am having conversations with people whose books have filled my shelves and my mind for all these years.

I appreciate Pen & Sword Books and their staff for helping me shape and share this book. Many, many thanks to Jonathan Wright, Danna Messer, Laura Hirst, Charlotte Mitchell, and everyone there for walking me through the process, answering my questions, and offering encouragement and support.

Of course, none of this would have happened without a strong support base. I cannot thank my friend and colleague Lindsey Lindstrom adequately for the support she has offered. From discussing ideas to reading drafts to offering spot-on advice to being a cheerleader, she is the foundation of the book, the podcast, and so many other things.

Finally, I owe everything I am able to do to my family. I have been inspired by the strong women in my life, from a great grandmother (Elise Chamberlain Carroll) who wrote books and taught college courses, to a grandmother (Helen Carroll Lloyd) who travelled the world and taught me I could do the same, to a mother (Karen Nelson Lloyd) who responded to every challenge with grace and brilliance. I am the result of their efforts. Finally, I thank my husband Marv for his patience when books and papers filled every inch of every table in the house. I thank my daughter Chelsea and son-in-law Lance for their support and encouragement. And I thank my two wonderful granddaughters, Elise and Olivia, for reminding me of the power of the past and the future as they keep me grounded in the present.

She shall be, to the happiness of England,
An aged princess; many days shall see her,
And yet no day without a deed to crown it.
Would I had known no more! But she must die,
She must, the saints must have her; yet a virgin,
A most unspotted lily shall she pass
To the ground, and all the world shall mourn her.
Shakespeare, *Henry VIII*

Introduction

Edward III is often described as an ideal medieval King. He was a great warrior and won many battles in France. He responded well to domestic issues like the plague and kept his country steady. And he provided for the future with a son, and a son ... in fact, with five sons who lived to adulthood.

His eldest son and heir preceded him in death, so his grandson succeeded him as Richard II when only 10 years old. After an uneven reign, Richard was challenged by Henry Bolingbroke, another grandson of Edward III. Bolingbroke was the son of John of Gaunt, himself an ambitious son of Edward III, who had three wives and three families, two of whom, the Lancastrians and the Beauforts, shaped English history through the fifteenth century. Bolingbroke forced Richard II to abdicate and became Henry IV, putting the Lancaster family on the throne.

That worked extremely well through the years of Henry V, a model king like Edward III. Unfortunately, he died young and left his throne, as well as the inheritance of the French throne, to his baby son. Henry VI was surrounded by ministers with differing agendas, and as he grew up he wasn't able to manage them. Eventually, other descendants of Edward III, through the House of York, challenged the leadership and then the rule of Henry VI. Edward, Duke of York, became Edward IV after defeating King Henry's forces in 1461. The battles continued, with Henry VI regaining on the throne in 1470 and Edward IV taking it back in 1471. After Edward's death in 1483, everyone expected his son to become Edward V. Richard, Duke of Gloucester, ended up taking the throne instead as Richard III.

Henry Tudor was born in 1457 and grew up in the midst of these battles for the throne. Through his mother, Margaret Beaufort, he had a claim to the English crown. The chaos surrounding Richard, who was viewed as a usurper by many contemporaries, presented an opening for Henry, who mustered some support from French mercenaries and English nobles not happy with Richard's reign. He landed at Mill Bay in Wales and made his way into England, meeting Richard's forces at Bosworth in the Midlands. After an unlikely victory against Richard, Henry was faced with an even bigger task: creating a new dynasty.

This is the story of that dynasty. It's the story of an unlikely king who was able to convince his people that the need for fighting for the crown was over because he had resolved the conflict. It's the story of a king who married six times in search of a son. It's the story of two women who changed the monarchy by becoming the first two crowned regnant queens in English history.

The Tudors came out of the so-called Wars of the Roses, creating the Tudor rose and the Tudor mystique. But it wasn't easy. Their story is a story of numbers.

Chapter One

1 Rose

Henry VII created a symbol for his dynasty that was so simple and yet so powerful that it would provide an anchor for his reign, for the dynasty, and for the reimagination of the English monarchy. One rose of two colours, one monarchy of two families. One future.

The Roses Take Centre Stage

In 1592,[1] crowds jammed into the Rose theatre in London. They were there to see a new play by an up-and-coming playwright, William Shakespeare. While the play was new, the story was not. The tale of the wars that had rocked the kingdom just 150 years ago was well known.

Richard Plantagenet (Duke of York) has been arguing with the earl of Somerset over the law. Plantagenet challenges his friends to choose his side:[2]

Plantagenet:
> *Since you are tongue-tied and so loath to speak,*
> *In dumb significants proclaim your thoughts:*
> *Let him that is a trueborn gentleman*
> *And stands upon the honor of his birth,*
> *If he suppose that I have pleaded truth,*
> *From off this brier pluck a white rose with me.*

Challenge delivered dramatically by Plantagenet plucking a white rose. Then Somerset, who is associated with the House of Lancaster, responds.

Somerset:

> *Let him that is no coward nor no flatterer,*
> *But dare maintain the party of the truth,*
> *Pluck a red rose from off this thorn with me.*

Others eagerly jump in. Neville, Earl of Warwick, rushes to support Plantagenet.

Warwick:

> *I love no colours; and without all colour*
> *Of base insinuating flattery,*
> *I pluck this white rose with Plantagenet.*

And now Suffolk, a known Lancastrian supporter, gets in on the action as well.

Suffolk:

> *I pluck this red rose with young Somerset,*
> *And say withal I think he held the right.*

And there it is. The series of battles that so devastated the country portrayed with red and white roses. The play was a popular one at that time.[3] The Tudor rose, with its joined red and white petals, was the primary symbol of the Tudor dynasty and the inevitable conclusion of battles and questions about who should be the king. The marriage between the Houses of Lancaster and York combined the fighting families into one, and was demonstrated by the combination of the two emblems into one: the Tudor rose.

Since the first days of Henry VII's reign, he had worked to associate the red rose with the house of Lancaster and the white rose with the house of York. It had taken some manipulation – the white rose was only one of the Yorkist emblems, and the red rose hadn't been associated with the Lancastrians for more than a century. But Henry VII had based his dynasty on the powerful visual image of red and white roses coming together into one, with the emergence of the Tudor rose symbolizing the end of the disputes for the crown.

But is there more to the story? Did Henry VII really end the Wars of the Roses by marrying Elizabeth of York, daughter of Edward IV, and creating the Tudor dynasty?

Let's find out. Let's roll the numbers!

The Story of a Rose by the Numbers

The numbers tell us that the path to one single rose and the establishment of the Tudor dynasty was a long and treacherous road made up of many complications.

The numbers tell us the real story of the beginning of the Tudor Dynasty. The most important number in Henry VII's narrative is one. He based his claim and the establishment of his dynasty on there being:

- one heir to the Lancastrian claim to the throne: Henry himself
- one heir to the Yorkist claim to the throne: Elizabeth of York
- one marriage that united those two claimants
- one option for king, based on the above.

So, the question of who should be rightful king of England, which had rocked the country since 1399 when Richard II had been deposed, all came down to one man in 1485: Henry Tudor.

Henry needed to tell his story. He decided to do so with red and white roses.

The white rose had a long history with Edward IV. It's found on his manuscripts and features prominently in his genealogical roll, which was probably created to celebrate his coronation as King of England. After all, he had not inherited the throne from a royal father; instead, he had seized it from an anointed king in battle. To demonstrate the superiority of his family claim to the throne, his supporters created an elaborate genealogical roll filled with symbols to validate his divine right to the throne: three suns representing the holy trinity and white roses. Perpetuating the story that Elizabeth's two brothers had died during the reign of Richard III, Henry recognised Elizabeth as the heir to the Yorkist claim. He seized on the white rose and passed the symbol on to Edward's eldest daughter.

The red rose proved a trickier problem. A few previous Lancastrians had used a gold rose, but not consistently. Henry Tudor's Lancastrian predecessor, Henry VI, had used the antelope. Henry Tudor himself had initially used the symbol of the red dragon of Wales, associating himself with the mythical British King Cadwalladr. We don't see any evidence of Henry using the red rose before Bosworth. But once he was king, he realised the power of symbolism and settled upon something that would allow him to put his stamp on the country forever. It was a masterstroke. The combination of the red and white rose was powerful in its simplicity and effective in its message. The king then went about carving that rose into buildings, emblazoning it on royal documents, and including it in portraits.

That was his math: 1 (red rose) + 1 (white rose) = 1 (Tudor rose). Of course, to make that 1 work, other numbers were involved.

3 Wives and 2 Sides

Henry Tudor traced his claim to the throne to the same source as everyone else since 1460: John of Gaunt. Gaunt married three times, and his wives and mistress (who later became his third wife) made for more than a messy personal life. The personal was definitely political in the medieval royal family, and Gaunt's descendants were involved in all the great battles of the Wars of the Roses. It turns out, to create enough chaos to plunge the country into years of civil war, all you needed is a wife, a mistress, and descendants who are willing to fight for a throne they didn't inherit. With all of this, you end up with the opposing Yorkist and Lancastrian factions.

As historian Helen Carr puts it, 'The Tudor dynasty was born out of John of Gaunt's adultery.'[4] First, Gaunt married Blanche of Lancaster in 1359. She had three children who survived: Philippa of Lancaster, Elizabeth of Lancaster, and Henry Bolingbroke. Blanche died in 1368. Gaunt then married Constance of Castile, who was claimant to the throne of Castile itself. They had a daughter Catherine who married the king of Castile. During his marriage to Constance, Gaunt began an affair with Katherine Swynford. That's where things got really interesting.

Gaunt and Swynford had four children who survived: John, Henry, Thomas, and Joan. Gaunt immediately acknowledged them all as his children and took responsibility for them. They weren't eligible for the name Lancaster, so he gave them the name Beaufort. The name Beaufort was inspired by a former French possession of John of Gaunt, a chateau based in the Champagne region of north-east France. Gaunt had inherited the lordship of Beaufort, and even though he lost it to the French in 1369, the name remained.[5] The Beaufort family became the source of one of the most famous dynasties in English history.

After Constance of Castile died in 1394, everyone thought Gaunt would make another politically advantageous marriage. But he didn't. He married his mistress on 13 January 1396,[6] making Katherine Swynford wife number three. Then he struck a deal with King Richard II and the pope in 1397 to declare the Beaufort children legally legitimate according to church and state law.[7] Now the Beauforts could inherit 'whatsoever honours, dignities, pre-eminencies, status, ranks, and offices, public and private, perpetual and temporal, feudal and noble there may be' as if they had been born in wedlock.[8] At the time, no one could have imagined that the notion of inheritance might ultimately have royal implications. As Henry IV's health was failing, he took steps to shore up the succession of his son and heir. In 1407, John Beaufort requested a confirmation of his legitimacy. At that time it was discovered the original Act had been amended to include the words *'excepta dignitate regali'* or 'except to the royal dignity'. In other words, the crown was off limits. It didn't seem significant at the time – Henry IV had four healthy sons and there was no reason to consider a Beaufort claim.[9] Even so, from the middle of the fifteenth-century until the beginning of the seventeenth, a Beaufort descendant ruled England. How did that happen?

Eldest son John Beaufort was made Earl of Somerset just a few days after being legitimised. He helped Richard II in his struggle with the Lords Appellant and was consequently inducted into the Order of the Garter. Next son Henry quickly sought an ecclesiastical appointment – so quickly, in fact, that he didn't get the king's permission. He was forgiven and went on to become a cardinal. Third son Thomas was appointed one of the king's knights. He eventually became the duke of Exeter. And daughter Joan married Ralph Neville, a member of the powerful Neville family.[10]

As time went on, some of the Beauforts were strongly supportive of Henry VI and the Lancastrian side of the family. John Beaufort's son Edmund, now duke of Somerset, battled Richard, Duke of York, for preeminence at court and in France during the 1440s. The ongoing struggle for power between Somerset and York was a driving factor in the rising tension that led eventually to war. Somerset was killed at the first Battle of St Albans in 1455, fighting to protect Henry VI's reign.[11]

Not all the Beaufort descendants supported Henry VI. Joan Beaufort and husband Ralph Neville had several children, many of whom were supporters of the Yorkist claim to the throne. Son Richard was the earl of Salisbury and became lord chancellor. His son Richard became the earl of Warwick. Both supported the duke of York's claim that he should be rightful king. When Salisbury and Richard of York were killed at the Battle of Wakefield in 1460, Warwick stepped in to support Edward, the new duke of York.[12] Warwick earned the title 'Kingmaker' when Edward became King Edward IV in 1461.[13] But Warwick became disaffected and turned against Edward IV and ultimately helped restore Henry VI to the throne in 1470. Warwick was killed when Edward IV retook the throne in 1471. There were plenty of betrayals and battles among family members who played both sides against the middle and changed sides when it suited them, hardly the clean narrative Henry Tudor and Shakespeare described.

14 Years Spent in Exile

This identification of Henry Tudor as the rightful Lancastrian heir was promoted by Margaret Beaufort, Henry's mother. A brilliant strategist, Margaret Beaufort had played prominent roles at the courts of both Henry VI (as his kinswoman, this was expected) and Edward IV (this was unexpected, as she had supported Henry VI publicly). She extended her influence into the reign of Richard III, carrying the robe of Queen Anne at her coronation. While she was active in Richard's court, she was also conspired with Elizabeth Woodville to promote the idea that Henry Tudor and Elizabeth of York marry and make a claim for the throne.[14]

When Henry VI and his son Prince Edward died, the Lancastrian claim was nearly gone. According to Polydore Vergil, an Italian historian, young Henry Tudor was the 'only imp now left of Henry VI's blood' and therefore a threat to the Yorkist throne. Only 14 years old, Henry had to leave the country. Along with Jasper, Henry Tudor fled England, heading for Lancastrian-friendly regions of France. The weather was against them, and storms blew them instead to the duchy of Brittany.[15] While Henry

Tudor was in exile, he was kept in a series of fortresses, a 'guest' of Francis, Duke of Brittany, unable to leave or move around at will. He developed a sense of having to live to on the defensive, unsure about whom to trust, always on his guard. In 1476, Francis planned to return Henry to England, but Henry managed to slip away at St Malo, escaping to sanctuary.[16] As he had before, he managed to keep himself safe by his wits.

It was not the typical or ideal upbringing for a future king of England, but it turned out to be just the training he needed. Henry Tudor made his first attempt to return to England as part of the Buckingham rebellion just months after Richard III was crowned. Buckingham's army was stranded by a severe storm and many deserted. By the time Henry and his forces reached English shores, he sensed trouble and turned around.[17] He was right – Buckingham had been captured, tried, and beheaded. Many of the rebels slipped away and eventually joined Henry in Brittany. The first attempt may have failed, but Henry wasn't finished.

In December 1483, Henry celebrated Christmas with a service at Reims Cathedral. That day he publicly pledged to marry Elizabeth of York and return to claim the throne of England.[18] He spent nearly two years gathering forces and preparing to invade the country. By early 1585, he was styling himself as King. A letter written to friends in England, undated but assumed to be mid-1485, is signed 'H.R.' as if he were already on the throne.[19] In August of 1485, fourteen years after he had fled the country, he returned with an invasion force to fight for the throne. He was practically unknown at the English court, more of a foreign invader than anything else, challenging a crowned, anointed king. The odds were against him. But he was about to change history.

21 Days and the Beginning of the Reign
Henry Tudor became king of England when he defeated Richard III and his forces at the Battle of Bosworth 22 August 1485. Right? Well, yes and no. Yes, that's what happened and what people experienced. Henry Tudor's forces defeated Richard's forces, and Henry Tudor became king. But once Henry's first parliament met, the story changed.

Henry VII issued a summons for his first parliament on 15 September 1485, less than a month after Bosworth. Parliament convened at Westminster on 7 November. Henry addressed the Commons two days later, asserting that he was king by inheritance, not because of the battle victory. Parliament passed a bill that stated the crown and the country were vested in Henry VII and the heirs of his body 'from the said 21 August'.[20] The Commons later reminded Henry of his promise to marry Elizabeth of York, and he agreed. Other business was conducted, and the session ended 4 March 1486.[21] Henry Tudor reimagined how he became king. He created a narrative that claimed he was already the rightful king of England before the Battle of Bosworth and Richard, the duke of Gloucester, was the traitor. Henry's reign was the true one; Richard's was designated as 'false.' All those who fought for Richard were, therefore, traitors.

It was a masterstroke. According to the official parliamentary records, Henry VII's reign began the day before Bosworth.[22] Does one day's difference matter? Yes. According to Henry's version the throne was his by right, not by battle. His power and authority did not depend upon military victory – something that had proven far too unreliable during the reigns of Henry VI, Edward IV, and Richard III, all of whom lost their crowns on the battlefield. Henry VII certainly didn't want to create the impression that fighting for the throne was an option during his reign. He positioned himself as the only heir and the true claimant to the throne. His rule was bigger than any single battle. He was the true king. By changing the date of his reign, Henry VII changed the narrative and forged ahead.

1 Wedding of Roses
Henry Tudor's narrative depended on marriage to Elizabeth of York. However, he had a few things to do first. He arranged for his coronation in Westminster Abbey on 30 October 1485. It was an opportunity to introduce himself to his people, and the king knew he had to make the most of it. Although it's Henry VIII who is usually associated with royal magnificence in dress, his father knew the value of dressing the part. He needed to prove himself worthy of the crown, dressing himself and his court in greatness.

By having his coronation before the wedding, Henry VII established the presumption that he was king in his own right and that his reign was supported by, not dependent on, marriage to the House of York. Henry VII and Elizabeth of York were married in Westminster Abbey 18 January 1486. The marriage represented the union of the houses of York and Lancaster.

It was essential that Henry marry Elizabeth of York. That was the core of the plan Margaret Beaufort and Elizabeth Woodville had devised during the reign of Richard III. Henry had gained followers for himself in exile when he promised to marry Elizabeth back in December of 1483. In the years since that declaration, he had relied on Yorkist supporters and on his commitment to joining the houses of York and Lancaster to gain the throne. As the daughter of Edward IV and the niece of Richard III, Elizabeth was the highest-ranking Yorkist. The future of Henry's reign depended on having Elizabeth at his side.

Edward Hall, a lawyer and historian born during the reign of Henry VII, was author of *The Union of the Two Noble and Illustre Families of Lancastre and Yorke*, more commonly known as 'Hall's Chronicle'. It was written during the final years of Henry VIII's reign and published 1548. The *Chronicle* describes the marriage of Henry and Elizabeth Hall, the effect of the marriage, and the hope of an heir:[23]

> By reason of which marriage peace was thought to descend out of heaven into England, considering that the lines of Lancaster and York, being both noble families equivalent in riches, fame, and honor, were now brought into one knot and connected together, of whose two bodies one heir might succeed, which after their time should peaceably rule and enjoy the whole monarchy and realm of England.

All of this was part of a carefully staged process of reinforcing Henry's reign. A draft of a speech intended for delivery to the pope includes a description of the marriage as having been made to 'put an end to civil war'.[24] Henry had staged the events to focus the right to the crown on himself and to present himself as actively ending the war. Neither outcome, according to this narrative, was accomplished on the battlefield; both outcomes were sanctified by the holy church at Westminster Abbey.

One marriage. One family. One rose. Lancaster and York were combined, and the union was physically displayed in the new red and white Tudor rose. It seems a natural conclusion. But that famous emblem, the Tudor rose, wasn't the natural outcome of two united families. It was a creation intended to reinforce a narrative that the new king was desperately trying to sell to his people.

Henry VII used his coronation to promote his own image and the image of his dynasty. The new king commissioned a Tudor tapestry of decorative hangings to adorn his court. This is one place we find the king creating the association of Lancaster and the red rose. There were red and gold roses embroidered in every possible location. Great amounts of money were spent on the red roses. Henry was deliberately and excessively associating himself with the red rose, even though past Lancastrian kings had used the emblem only occasionally.[25] The red rose was an essential part of the new dynasty's story, and Henry was doing everything he could to make it work.

The people of England were easily able to understand the message of a crowned and united red and white rose. This was a time when images and symbols were a primary means of communication. Henry VII went all in on his Tudor rose image. It carried through on his first progress to the north just a couple of months after the wedding. There were a few disturbances, a reminder that the work of establishing the new dynasty was far from over. Still, the journey was peaceful and celebratory overall. At York, the royal couple was greeted with a spectacle that must have pleased Henry: 'a mechanical devise displaying a gigantic red rose, which merged with a white rose before other bountiful flowers emerged'. When the royal couple visited York, the city put on a pageant with an elaborate display that reinforced Henry's message of the union of red and white. There was a very large red rose that combined with a white rose, and a mechanical device that placed a crown on top of the joined red and white rose. The Tudor rose had been crowned, a symbolic gesture that Henry's message was being received.[26]

Henry's narrative tied his reign to the future. Now the dynasty depended on the swift arrival of a male heir. With surprising speed, that hope was fulfilled: Prince Arthur was born 20 September 1486 – just eight months after the wedding. As the descendant of York and Lancaster, Arthur was the ultimate realisation of the Tudor rose. The birth of a son was the key to establishing a lasting dynasty.

A song, written to celebrate the birth of Prince Arthur, evokes the Tudor rose image:[27]

> I love the red rose and the white
> Is that your pure perfect appetite?
> To hear talk of them is my delight!
> > Joyed may we be,
> > Our prince to see
> > And roses three.

Just a little more than a year after Bosworth, Henry Tudor had been crowned and anointed King Henry VII. He married Elizabeth of York, Edward IV's daughter. He held an elaborate coronation ceremony for her on 27 November 1487. Lancaster and York, united and crowned. Together they produced a son, an embodiment of the Tudor rose narrative and the promise of the future of the dynasty. It's a stunning success story. But even that wasn't enough to mend the alternate claims to Henry's throne.

2 Pretenders

Henry VII worked hard to establish his new dynasty. He tapped into the story of the Arthurian legend by naming his son Arthur and arranging for him to be born at Winchester. It was a compelling narrative. But years of fighting for control of the throne had weakened the foundation of the monarchy. From the seizure of the throne by Henry Bolingbroke in 1399 through years of battles in the fifteenth century, many uneasy heads had worn the crown.

Henry Tudor's success in gaining the throne of England was an invitation for others to try to gain it for themselves. After all, Henry Tudor had appeared after fourteen years in exile, with no powerbase in England, and succeeded against a crowned and anointed king who was a famous warrior and had the royal army behind him. Henry VII did everything he could to preserve and strengthen his reign based on his contention that he was the one person who could reasonably claim the throne. But two key pretenders emerged that nearly toppled the Tudors: Lambert Simnel and Perkin Warbeck. Simnel and Warbeck both drew international backing, enjoying the support of France, Scotland, and Ireland.[28] Individually and together, they demonstrate the tenuous nature of the Tudor regime.

Lambert Simnel

In the first years of Henry VII's reign, rumours took hold about the location of the earl of Warwick, son of George, Duke of Clarence, and alternate claimant of the throne. Richard III had secured Warwick at Sheriff Hutton castle in North Yorkshire, but Henry VII decided he wanted the young earl kept more securely and put him in the Tower.[29] Rumors spread that Warwick had escaped. Henry VII and his council decided the solution was to remove Warwick from the Tower and have him make public appearances.[30] It was hoped this would put the rumours about Warwick living abroad to rest. The problem was there was an alternative Warwick making the rounds.

A young man calling himself Warwick turned up in Ireland and claimed to be the rightful king of England. The story took hold, and by March 1487, John de la Pole, the earl of Lincoln, abruptly left England and went to the court of Margaret of York, duchess of Burgundy. As sister of Edward IV and Richard III, Margaret was a loyal Yorkist who resented what she considered Henry Tudor's usurpation of her family's place on the English throne. Lincoln and Margaret supported Simnel's claim to be the earl of Warwick and the true king of England.

Happy to disrupt the reign of Henry VII, the Irish backed Simnel as well. Margaret of York and Lincoln arrived in Dublin in May of 1487. On 24 May, Lambert Simnel was crowned at Christ Church as King Edward VI.[31] Within two weeks, Simnel, Margaret of York, and Lincoln raised an army of mercenaries to join the Irish troops . They landed in Lancashire and began to march south. They were on the way to challenge Henry VII for the throne. Just twenty months after the Battle of Bosworth, the sitting king of England was about to be challenged on the battlefield once more.

The king was prepared. He gathered a force that was larger and better organised than that of the rebels. Henry VII was strategic, and his actions displayed the decisive, courageous behaviour of a king. He was able to gain dedication and loyalty of his troops as they met the rebels near East Stoke on 16 June 1487. The armies fought fiercely, and the battle lasted for about three hours. The king's forces outnumbered the rebel troops, being much better armed. When the rebels realised the game was lost and began to flee, the king's army turned furiously against them, and ultimately thousands were killed.

Simnel was captured at the battle, but instead of being imprisoned he became a member of the king's household. Henry VII decided that young Lambert Simnel, who was only about 10 years old, was too young to have been anything more than a pawn in the hands of rebellious adults. Writing during the reign of Henry VIII, Polydore Vergil claimed that Simnel worked in the kitchens for years and eventually became a trainer of the king's hawks.[32]

The Battle of Stoke is often referred to as the final battle of the Wars of the Roses. Henry VII had succeeded in 1487 where Richard III had failed two years earlier: he defended his crown in battle. But that victory would not be enough to make the Tudor throne and dynasty secure.

Perkin Warbeck

The second pretender was in many ways even more dangerous than the first. The mystery of what had happened to the two sons of Edward IV in 1483 has never been solved. When Edward IV died, the nation expected his son to become Edward V. The young king returned to London alongside his uncle, Richard, the duke of Gloucester. As was tradition, young Edward V was installed in the Tower of London. His brother Prince Richard soon joined him. But within a few weeks, instead of celebrating the coronation of Edward V, London celebrated the coronation of King Richard III. The marriage between Edward IV and Elizabeth Woodville had been declared invalid, and all their children had been declared illegitimate. As summer 1483 turned to autumn, rumours spread that the two boys were dead. In any case, they were never seen again. Now the ongoing question of what had really happened to the sons of Edward IV was about to rise again and create a potential disaster for Henry VII.

Apparently possessed of regal looks and bearing, Perkin Warbeck claimed to be Prince Richard, the younger of Edward IV's sons who had been imprisoned in the Tower. As there was no proof about what had happened to the two young boys, Warbeck was able to spread the rumor that his older brother Edward had been killed, he had escaped, and he was now emerging to claim his throne. Warbeck went to Ireland in 1491 and then to France in 1492. Bad relations with England persuaded the French King to welcome Warbeck and treat him as a royal.

Once again, Margaret of York supported a pretender to the Tudor throne. She actively promoted Warbeck's claim to be her nephew and the rightful king. She welcomed him in Burgundy as Prince Richard and publicly acknowledged him. Margaret even wrote to the pope asking for papal recognition of Warbeck's claims.[33] Margaret also asked Isabella of Spain to promote him. She was so active in supporting Warbeck that Henry VII complained to about 'the great malice that the Lady Margaret of Burgundy beareth continually against us.'[34]

The prospect of a marital alliance between England and Spain with suggested plans for Katherine of Aragon to marry Prince Arthur worried Scotland and France. The French-Scottish alliance worked in Warbeck's favour after an initial failed attempt to land in England and claim the throne in 1495. He was welcomed grandly in Scotland by James IV, who recognised him as Richard, Duke of York. The king of Scotland supported him financially.[35] Foreign support continued to spread. When the Holy Roman Emperor died, Warbeck attended his funeral alongside some of Europe's most powerful rulers, where he was recognised as king of England.

In response, Henry VII took decisive action. From a dynastic perspective, he clarified his position that Prince Richard had died in the Tower by creating his son Prince Henry as duke of York. There could be only one duke of York, so giving Prince Henry the title was a way of saying Prince Richard was dead. From a military and economic perspective, the king established military and economic alliances with powerful kingdoms, which enabled him to weaken foreign support of Warbeck. He strengthened his own army, adding a small royal yeomanry to serve the purposes of protecting the royal family and project royal supremacy.[36] Recognising military prowess would not be enough; he continued to rely on diplomacy to shore up his military power.

Henry VII also had to deal with Warbeck's supporters in England. Significantly, William Stanley, a man Henry had trusted and who had been instrumental in the victory at Bosworth, not to mention his stepfather's brother, was accused and found guilty of supporting Warbeck's claim. Stanley confessed to the crime, possibly because he was hoping for mercy. But Henry knew his actions had to demonstrate his power and authority, so he went forward with Stanley's execution.³⁷ Henry's decisive actions weakened English support for Warbeck and made him even more reliant on foreign support.

James IV and Warbeck attempted another invasion of England in September 1496, arriving in the North where they expected to benefit from a long history of Yorkist support. But the hoped-for support did not materialise, as people in England rallied for King Henry and fought back against what they saw as a Scottish invasion. James began to lose enthusiasm for Warbeck and his claim.³⁸ The king of Scotland retreated rather than face the better prepared English army, and Warbeck fled to Ireland. Henry VII and James IV soon signed their own agreement, which eliminated the chance that James would support Warbeck or other pretenders.

Now without Scottish or French support, Warbeck took advantage of the English Cornish rebellion in 1497. The possibility that this local trouble had sown widespread distrust of Henry VII, Warbeck decided to attempt another invasion. He landed in England and gathered support, and as his army marched south his ranks swelled to an estimated 6,000 men. His followers proclaimed Warbeck to be King Richard IV as they marched toward London. Warbeck and his army reached Exeter in September and attempted to break down the city gates. But the city was well defended in the king's name, and Warbeck's army lost an estimated 200 men.³⁹ They headed toward Taunton, but the commitment to Warbeck was waning. With the king's army approaching, Warbeck deserted his forces and fled with a few key supporters on 20 September 1497.

Warbeck went to Beaulieu Abbey and demanded sanctuary. The king's forces tracked him, and royal troops surrounded the abbey. Warbeck decided to surrender and beg for mercy. After all, the king had been merciful to Lambert Simnel before. Henry wanted him alive so he could get a public confession that he was an imposter.⁴⁰ Warbeck confessed, provided the name 'Perkin Warbeck' as his true identity, and relinquished his claim to the throne. He was sent to the Tower of London.

Two years later Warbeck and the earl of Warwick, who had been in the Tower since the beginning of Henry VII's reign, were accused of attempting to escape and put Warwick on the throne. There is some evidence Warwick and Warbeck were set up so the king could use the excuse to order their execution and demonstrate the power of the Tudor regime. The elimination of the two rebels cleared the way for Ferdinand and Isabella to send their daughter Katherine to England to marry Prince Arthur. It looked like the rebellions were at an end.

Numbers and the Tudor Rose

In a stroke of genius, Henry Tudor had his marriage to Elizabeth of York symbolise many things:

- The partnership of York and Lancaster, forever united
- The trustworthiness of Henry himself, as he had promised to marry Elizabeth and he was fulfilling that promise
- The confirmation of his right to rule, with marriage to the Yorkist princess as a stamp of approval
- The complete resolution of any question about who should be rightful King of England
- The promise of the future, as surely their union would provide a son with the strengths of both Lancaster and York.

The two most prominent Tudor monarchs, Henry VIII and Elizabeth I, consciously associated themselves with the Tudor rose.

Although Arthur was the one hailed as the Tudor rose at his birth, after Arthur's death, the future of the Tudor dynasty rested on young Prince Henry. When Henry VII died in 1509, the teenage Prince Henry, result of the union of York and Lancaster and embodiment of the Tudor rose, was proclaimed king. Henry VIII quickly married Katherine of Aragon and arranged a joint coronation. Thomas More created a suite of "Poems on the coronation of King Henry VIII of England and Queen Katherine of Aragon" that includes several images of the Tudor rose representing Henry and a pomegranate representing Katherine.[41]

Katherine's pomegranate symbol has a rich history. It goes back to Greek mythology, representing fertility and regeneration for Persephone, and carries into the bible where it is associated with God's commandments and Christ's resurrection. It was also important to Katherine's family. When she was a child, she was with her parents Ferdinand and Isabella when they conquered Granada in 1492. To celebrate the victory, the pomegranate (*granada*) became part of the Spanish royal arms.[42] It was part of Katherine's royal identity long before she became queen of England. Like Henry's Tudor rose, it was an important part of her family identity.

The Tudor rose and the pomegranate were consistent symbols throughout the coronation ceremonies of Henry and Katherine. Contemporary descriptions talk about the ceremony being full of roses and pomegranates.[43] This was echoed by a volume created by Stephen Hawes, 'A Joyful Meditation to All England (1509)', which included a woodcut. In the image, Henry VIII is represented under a large Tudor Rose. Hawes, who was seeking patronage, describes the couple in the poem:

> Two titles in one thou didst well unify
> When the red rose took the white in marriage
> Reigning together right high and noble
> From whose united titles and worth language
> Descended is by right excellent courage
> King Henry VIII for to reign doubtless.[44]

When she became queen in 1558, Elizabeth I also presented herself as the Tudor rose. She understood the need for spectacle and presentation of majesty as well as her father had. She participated actively and was an actor and patron in the drama of her coronation.[45] It was also important to Elizabeth and her government the events be recorded and remembered. Less than two weeks after the coronation, Richard Tottel received a license to publish his work, 'The Quene's Majestie's passage through the citie of London to Westminster the daye before her coronacion.' A copy was given to the queen and well as distributed with subsequent editions later in the year. There was a careful effort to preserve the memory and meaning of the occasion.[46] Elizabeth's procession was unique in Tudor coronations, representing an event in its own right, not simply a part of the coronation.[47]

There were several pageants performed along her coronation route to reinforce her magnificence and right to the throne. The first tableau was entitled the title was 'the uniting of the two houses of Lancaster and York'. There were three openings in the stage. On the top tier was the red rose of Lancaster, Henry VII, alongside the white rose of York, Elizabeth of York. These roses combined and reached down to the next level, where

Henry VIII was presented as the Tudor rose. He sat alongside Anne Boleyn. On the third level was a representation of Elizabeth herself, crowned with an imperial crown.[45] The red and white and combined Tudor roses reinforced Elizabeth's place as natural and true inheritor of the Tudor crown.

Elizabeth continued to use the Tudor rose symbol throughout her reign. For example, a crowned Tudor rose appears in the 'Pelican Portrait' by Nicholas Hilliard, painted around 1574 (and now owned by the Walker Art Gallery in Liverpool, England). It's also the image on a medalet commemorating the 'Hampshire', held at the National Maritime Museum in Greenwich. It's on a 1574 Elizabethan coin. And it's visible on Elizabeth's royal seals, some of which are held at the National Archives.[49]

The Tudor rose remained a defining and compelling symbol of the dynasty from start to finish.

Chapter Two

2 Crowned Queens

When Mary Tudor came to the throne in 1553, it was more than unusual – it was unimaginable, unnatural, even 'monstrous' according to John Knox. The reality of not one but two Tudor crowned regnant queens changed the monarchy forever.

The Queen is Dead, Long Live the Queen

In the fall of 1558, Queen Mary made a will that included these words 'Thinking myself to be with child in lawful marriage between my said dearly beloved husband and lord',[1] and leaving her crown to her expected heir, with husband Philip appointed as guardian and regent.[2] But as the weeks went by, she finally had to face the truth. She was not going to have a baby. She was dying.

As her health failed, parliament, her council, and even her husband urged her to name an heir. The only real choice to succeed the queen was the one person she didn't want: her half-sister, Elizabeth. Mary's reign had been dedicated to returning England to Catholicism. She did not trust Elizabeth to carry on that work. Mary had fought her entire life for her crown, had survived years of turmoil in her father's and her brother's reigns, and had staged a successful coup against the proclaimed reign of Lady Jane Grey. Edward had named his cousin his heir instead of his half-sister in hopes of maintaining his religious reform. But Mary Tudor had refused to go along with the plan. She had gathered supporters and taken the throne. Mary had her own ideas about religion and her divine destiny. She had married Philip of Spain and worked tirelessly to return her nation to the 'true faith'. She had hoped for a son to succeed her and carry on her work.

Mary had done everything she could to deny Elizabeth the crown. She raised suspicion about Elizabeth's paternity and even spoke about repealing the Succession Act of 1544 – the very act she had relied on to the take the throne herself. Philip strongly objected to this and encouraged Mary to name Elizabeth as her successor. Although he did not return to England himself, he sent his agent de Feria to ensure that Elizabeth would come to the throne.[3] Eventually, facing the reality of her lack of child and Philip's wishes, Mary wrote a codicil to her will. She stated that as God had not seen fit for her to have a child, she would be succeeded 'by my next heir and successor by the Laws and Statues of this realm'.[4] She could not bring herself to say Elizabeth's name,[5] but it didn't matter. Elizabeth would be next on the throne. Henry VIII had moved Heaven and Earth, changed the nation's religion, and married repeatedly to prevent his daughters from taking the crown. Even he couldn't stop it. The first crowned queen regnant of England would be succeeded by the second.

But how much did that really matter to the dynasty and the nation? Would the rule of a woman or even two women make a real and lasting difference?

Let's find out. Let's roll the numbers!

The Story of 2 Crowned Tudor Queens

The numbers let us know what a remarkable thing it was to have two crowned regnant queens in the Tudor dynasty. These women were not queens consort, married to kings. They were monarchs, rulers in their own right. They show us how these half-sisters and daughters of Henry VIII, changed the nature of the monarchy forever.

Mary and Elizabeth had been linked since Elizabeth was conceived. Anne Boleyn's pregnancy spurred Henry into action. He secretly married Anne, arranged to have his marriage to Katherine of Aragon declared invalid, his marriage to Anne officially sanctioned and planned Anne's coronation. Mary's life was upended forever because of her half-sister, even before Elizabeth was born. The two were declared illegitimate and removed from the succession in the Second Succession Act (1536) and returned to the succession in the Third Succession Act (1543). They were both excluded by Edward's 'Devise for the Succession' in preference for the Protestant Lady Jane Grey (more about Jane and her story in Chapter Five). In many ways it's fitting that the story of the first crowned regnant queen of England is the really the story of the first two. It might have been possible to dismiss one regnant queen as a blip in the tradition of male monarchy. Together, these two women reigned for fifty years. The reality of female rule couldn't be undone.

Several other numbers are important to this story.

0 Crowned Queens Before the Tudors were Men
Power in the Middle Ages was inherently male. The image of the Great Seal represented the two primary responsibilities of the king: one side showed the king administering justice, seated with his scepter; the other side showed him on his horse, sword raised, ready to defend his nation against all enemies. These images were echoed on coins and other symbols. A woman could not be a judge or a warrior. Therefore, a woman could not rule.[6]

Henry I had two legitimate children, his daughter Matilda and his son and heir, William Aetheling. In 1120, a tragedy rocked the family and the nation as the *White Ship* which was due to sail to England and included as passengers, the heir to the throne and other nobles, ran hard into the Quilleboeuf rock off the coast of France and eventually sank.[7] William Aetheling had been put on a small boat, but he had heard the cries of one of his half-sisters and ordered the boat to return to save her. In that attempt, the heir to the throne died.[8]

When Henry I died in 1135, his only legitimate child, Matilda, might have been an obvious choice as his only legitimate child. Henry's council had agreed to support her as heir. But she was a woman, which was clearly an obstacle. She was also unknown to the people and court. From 1110 to 1125, she had lived in Germany to become the wife of Heinrich V, the Holy Roman Emperor. Three years after the emperor's death, she went to Normandy to marry Geoffrey, the teenage count of Anjou. She was living there and pregnant when her father died. Stephen of Blois, her cousin, acted swiftly and claimed the English throne for himself. Many of the nobles who had pledged to support Matilda switched to Stephen's side. Matilda gathered support for her claim and appealed to Pope Innocent II to recognise her inheritance, and then, frustrated by his lack of support, took action herself.[9]

Matilda had considerable support. King David I of Scotland supported Matilda's claim and she raised an army of supporters in England. In the summer of 1141, her army – with her half-brother Robert of Gloucester at the head – defeated Stephen's army and captured the king at the Battle of Lincoln. Now in control, Matilda proceeded to Westminster to be crowned queen. But the expectations of a monarch didn't align with expectations of a woman. Chroniclers of her time were generally scornful of Matilda's demeanour after her victory. Pride and strong will are admirable in a king, but not acceptable in a woman. The anonymous author of *Gesta Stepani* complained that Matilda demonstrated was arrogant in her actions and had the audacity to call herself queen of England and enjoy it.[10] Modest and gentle were the behaviours expected of a woman, but not of a monarch attempting to claim her crown. Matilda didn't do what her male advisors told her to do; instead, she attempted to lead on her own terms. She was trying to emulate her father and create the persona of a monarch. But that contradicted with what was expected of her as a woman.[11] Matilda refused to accept the traditional female role expected of her.

In the end, Matilda was not crowned queen. But her influence did not disappear. When she ceded her claim to her son Henry (II) and left England, he sometimes used the name 'Henry FitzEmpress' (son of the Empress), referring to the fact his claim was through his mother.[12] Eventually, the Treaty of Winchester brought an end to the conflict in 1153. Henry recognised Stephen as king, and Stephen named Henry as his heir. Stephen died the next year and Henry, son of Matilda, ascended to the throne in October 1154.

That was as close as England came to having a regnant queen until 1553, nearly 400 years later. The specter of Matilda and civil war seemed to haunt Henry VIII, reinforcing his belief that women could not succeed to the throne. Henry made it the work of his life to prevent female rule. His daughters had other ideas.

3 Succession Acts of Henry VIII

Henry VIII wasn't great about admitting he'd made mistakes. When a marriage didn't work out, he simply pretended it hadn't really happened. And, since he wasn't really married, any child of that non-marriage wasn't a legitimate heir. Just in case anyone in the country wasn't following along with the royal wisdom, Henry had parliament pass three succession acts between 1534 and 1547. Henry VIII broke new royal ground when he gave parliament a role in the succession. The structure of Tudor government during the reign of Henry VIII allowed the king to use parliament to carry out his will and enact his succession acts. All three acts demanded obedience and included provisions and penalties for high treason.[13] In the final two acts, Henry is granted authority to designate further succession options in his will – something he does to a great extent.

The First Succession Act, formally 'Succession to the Crown Act 1533', specified that Elizabeth, daughter of Henry VIII and Anne Boleyn, was the heir to the throne. Mary, daughter of Henry VIII and Katherine of Aragon, was removed from the succession.[14] The bill ratified the king's marriage to Anne Boleyn and was intended 'to do away with all ambiguities regarding inheritance to the throne by nominating the children born of Queen Anne the first rightful heirs'.[15] It went on to declare it an act of treason for anyone to oppose the succession of those children. Henry's subjects were expected to swear an oath to obey this act.

Ironically, just two years later, the first succession act was undone by the second. Anne Boleyn fell dramatically and violently from favour, and her fall took Elizabeth's place in the succession down with her. All the efforts of the previous years had to be overhauled. On 1 June 1536, there was a different queen at the king's side, and both previous marriages had been declared invalid.

The Second 'Acte for the establishment of the succession of the Imperyall Crowne of this Realme' or more briefly Succession Act of 1536, pronounced the king's first two marriages to have been invalid.[16] It provides specific details regarding why the king's two daughters were excluded and barred from having any claim to their father's throne. That left the king without a legitimate heir – nearly thirty years into his reign. The Act addressed this. First, it identified as heirs the future children of Henry and his new wife, Jane Seymour. Then, just in case, it provided Henry the authority to name his own successor if he had no children to succeed him. This could be accomplished by letters patent or his will.[17]

Even after finally having a son in 1537, Henry VIII wasn't finished marrying or creating succession acts. The catalyst of the Third Succession Act seems to have been the king's embarking on a dangerous military campaign, when in 1544, Henry prepared for what would turn out to be his final attempt to invade and defeat France. It might have been helped along by Katherine Parr, who worked to provide a more settled family life and often had all three children at court. Some think she might have encouraged Henry to add his daughters to the succession. It was a good plan because, despite three other marriages in the seven years since Jane Seymour's death, Henry had produced no more children. Henry's own family history had taught him that sometimes one son was not enough. So, he decided to expand the succession.

Formally 'Succession to the Crown Act 35 Hen. 8 c.1', the Third Succession Act reinstated both Mary and Elizabeth as heirs of the king. The Act clarifies that only God could dictate whether Edward would eventually have heirs of his own, and even whether Henry would have children with his 'entirely beloved wife … that now is', or whether Henry might eventually have additional children with another wife.[18] Therefore, he set out his will. If Edward died without children, and if his future children died without children (or failed to arrive), the crown would pass to Mary and her heirs, provided she married with the consent of the council. Then, if Mary died without children, the crown would pass to Elizabeth. The Act also gave Henry the power to address the succession further by letters patent or in his will.[19] However, the two daughters were not made legitimate, something that would have ramifications for the rest of the dynasty.[20]

At this time, there was every reason to believe that Edward would grow and have children of his own, so the possibility of Mary or Elizabeth, let alone Mary and Elizabeth, coming to the throne was remote. Ironically, Henry's decision to involve parliament in the succession shaped the rest of the dynasty. The third Succession Act was the basis of Mary's refusal to acknowledge Edward VI's 'Devise for the Succession', which removed her and Elizabeth in favour of Lady Jane Grey. That same Act later ensured that Mary would be succeeded by Elizabeth.

2 Reimagined Coronations

The medieval tradition of coronation has been described as the time when 'the act of undergoing a coronation that made a man into a king, transformed him from a mere mortal to one appointed and approved by God to rule over his people'.[21] The male pronoun is not accidental or careless – it is an absolute part of the equation. Monarchy was male. What did this mean for Mary?

Faced with the dilemma of having a woman ruling over men some of the privy council suggested that parliament meet and declare Mary queen and then call for the coronation. However, Mary insisted that, according to tradition, her coronation must come before the first parliament of her reign. That order meant that the coronation sanctioned parliament, not the other way around.[22] A few days before her coronation, she called a meeting of her council and spoke about her coming to the throne. She told members of the council that she had entrusted her realm and her person to them and exhorted them to do their duties, making a special appeal to the lord high chancellor. She also stated her commitment to carrying out the task that God had given her 'to His greater glory and service, to the public good and her subjects' benefit.'[23] The humble stature of the queen, who remained on her knees throughout her address, brought tears to the eyes of her council, according to the ambassadors' report to the Emperor.[24]

The council moved forward to address the plan for a modified coronation. Mary needed a ceremony that followed the essential traditions that had shaped the monarchy for hundreds of years and had some unique elements and modifications to accommodate the crowning of a woman. For example, part of the coronation ceremony was the creation of the new Knights of the Bath. Traditionally, the man about to be crowned king would observe the ceremony of the bathing. Of course, this wasn't possible for a queen. Mary sent a male representative, the earl of Arundel, and the ceremony went on.[25] This is just one indication of how completely the ceremonies surrounding the coronation were based on the foundational belief the monarch would always be male.

The coronation ceremony itself was specifically designed for a king or a queen consort. Mary's coronation had to be reimagined to crown a queen who held all the power. Ultimately, Mary played both roles, and her coronation presented her as a queen and king – or as a queen with the power of a king. As parliament had not been called to change the religious laws, England remained a Protestant nation after Edward's death. Therefore, Mary was crowned in a Protestant ceremony, much to her dismay. One way Mary addressed this was to request that she be provided with Catholic oil, which was sent to her in secret and used with the knowledge of only Mary and a few others.[26] Contemporary descriptions of Mary's coronation are inconsistent. One manuscript describes her appearance as close to that of a queen consort, wearing a mantle and kirtle and with a circlet of gold adoring her head with her hair long and flowing.[27] Another describes her as dressed in traditional state robes of crimson velvet, similar to that associated with a male monarch.[28] Perhaps these discrepancies reflect people's confusion about how a woman could be the ruling sovereign.

The bishop of Winchester said these words: 'Sirs, here present is Mary, rightful and undoubted inheritrix by the laws of God and man to the crown and royal dignity of this realm of England, France, and Ireland, whereupon you shall understand that this day is appointed by all the Peers of this land for the consecration, inunction, and coronation of the said most excellent Princess Mary; will you serve at this time, and give your wills and assent to the same consecration, inunction, and coronation?' The people cried, 'Yea, yea, yea. God save Queen Mary.' A crown was placed on Mary's head three times. As was customary, she was crowned with St Edward's crown first and then with the imperial crown of the realm. Then Mary was crowned with a smaller crown specially made for her.[29] She was invested with the traditional regalia: ring, bracelets, scepter, and orb. The bishop of Winchester, fastened on the spurs and girt her with the sword, as he would have done with a king. Mary was crowned and anointed as a male monarch and a queen consort, and at the end of the ceremony Mary held two scepters: one of the king and one of the queen consort.[30]

Just five years later, the unimaginable happened again: the monarch was to be another woman. Elizabeth faced many of the same gender challenges Mary had faced. The unfortunate reality of a second woman on the throne was no more welcome than it had been the first time. All the perceived failures of Mary's role, from the loss of Calais and the bad harvests to the unpopular participation in her husband's war were blamed in large part on Mary's gender. Elizabeth was convinced she had survived a dangerous childhood, where she was out of favour and in danger of being married off into a faraway country in the reigns of her father, half-brother, and half-sister, because God desired her to take the throne. Several sources report that when she learned she would be queen, she responded by quoting scripture, 'This is the Lord's doing, and it is marvelous in our eyes.'[31] Because of this deep belief, 'Elizabeth was untroubled by feelings of inadequacy on account of her sex.'[32]

Even so, many in the country had serious reservations about the accession of another woman. Elizabeth took decisive steps to begin her reign in the right way. In some ways, Elizabeth stepped in her half-sister's footsteps. Like Mary, she moved ahead to her coronation before calling parliament. Nicholas Bacon advised Elizabeth to do so, reasoning, 'the English lawes have long since pronounced, That the Crowne once worne, quite taketh away all defects whatsoever'.[33] She wore her sister's coronation robes, which had been tailored to fit and flatter her figure.[34] Bishop Oglethorpe administered the customary oaths to Elizabeth that had been administered to Mary and to the kings before her: to keep the laws and customs of England, to keep peace to the church and the people, and to execute justice in mercy and truth. Elizabeth was anointed as queen and received the symbols of power associated with the monarchy. The scepter and orb came last. At that point, she was crowned in a similar mode to Mary: first with St Edward's crown, then with the imperial crown, and finally with a smaller third crown. Some scholars think this might have been the crown that had been made for her mother, Anne Boleyn.[35]

As Mary had, Elizabeth emerged from her coronation as both king and queen. But unlike Mary, she did not rush to assure her council and her country that she would quickly marry. Elizabeth's comments about marriage were ambivalent, sometimes indicating determination to marry, other times indicating determination to remain single. Instead of relying on marriage to secure her claim to the throne, throughout her reign, Elizabeth simply positioned herself as chosen by God to be the monarch and therefore not subject to the natural limitations of her gender. She used her coronation to reinforce her place on the throne as a fait accompli. Young and vibrant, she greeted the crowds and spoke with her people during her coronation procession, building on an existing enthusiasm about her reign. She was the Tudor rose, purely English in her descent (compared to the Spanish heritage of Mary), beloved by and devoted to her people.

Both Mary and Elizabeth were crowned as women in a ceremony designed for men. They were both crowned according to religious laws they did not accept – Mary was crowned as supreme head of the Church of England and Elizabeth was crowned in a Catholic ceremony (the final English monarch to be crowned as a Catholic). They both followed the tradition of being crowned before their first parliaments, not relying on parliamentary approval for their coronations. The impact of these coronations was also strengthened because a second woman was crowned immediately following the first. Mary's status as crowned regnant queen couldn't be dismissed as a one-off; it was the first in a series. True, two is a short series, but the repetition of queens regnant contributed to its sense of staying power.

42 Percent of the Tudor Dynasty Ruled by a Queen
When female rulers took the throne in the Tudor dynasty, they held on. Elizabeth I's was the longest reign of the dynasty. Between them, Mary and Elizabeth ruled for half a century, from 1553 to 1603. The length of female rule matters for several reasons. In all, 42 percent of the Tudor dynasty was under the rule of a woman.

Mary and Elizabeth extended the dynasty into the next century. When Edward VI died childless, women were the only option to succeed to the throne. The Tudor claim was narrow in scope. Margaret Beaufort was the only child of John Beaufort. Henry VII was her only son. By the time of Henry VII's death, he himself had only one son. That didn't mean there weren't other family members who might have claimed the throne. The response of Henry VII and his son to close male relatives was to eliminate them because they represented competition. Henry VII's execution of the earl of Warwick in 1499 and Henry VIII's execution of the duke of Buckingham in 1521 are just two examples of the Tudors trying to preserve their claims to the throne by eliminating possible rivals.

Securing the throne for the future meant the Tudors had to produce male heirs, something they struggled to do. Only Henry VII had two legitimate sons who survived early childhood. Henry VIII had one legitimate son who died before having children of his own. Henry VIII's elder sister Margaret had a son, King James V of Scotland, whose only living child was a daughter. Margaret's other child was a daughter, Margaret Douglas. Henry VIII's younger sister Mary had a son who died young and two daughters, Francis and Eleanor. Both of those daughters had daughters.

There were far more Tudor daughters than sons, which for a dynastic family created a problem in the minds of many at the time. Ultimately, it fell to the two daughters of Henry VIII to carry on the Tudor reign.

The significance of their reigns goes far beyond length. The reigns of Mary and Elizabeth demonstrated that female rule was not something that could be ignored. Mary enacted laws that preserved the notion of female rule by defining the power a female monarch would hold. The Queen Regent's Prerogative Act 1554, passed by parliament, enshrined the power of the regnant queen. It stated that the crown came to Mary as the 'true and undoubted Heir and Inheritrix thereof, and invested in her most Royal Person, according unto the Laws of this Realm'. As such, she was entitled to 'enjoy and use such like Royal Authority, Power, Preeminence, Prerogative and Jurisdiction … as the Kings of this Realm her most noble Progenitors have heretofore done, enjoyed, used, and exercised.'[36] By making this a law, Mary laid the foundation for any queen who would follow. Mary's approach to asserting her power led Bishop John Alymer to observe that having a woman ruler was not as dangerous in England, as men had thought it would be.[37]

Elizabeth's long reign allowed her religious settlement to take hold on the nation. Henry VIII's changing laws about religion, Edward VI's devoted efforts to move the country firmly into reform, and Mary I's equally devoted efforts to eliminate heresy and restore the nation to its Catholic heritage had shaken England for decades. Religion was the fabric of lives in early modern England, from the beliefs they lived by to the way they ate, the holidays they observed, and the way they cared for the poor and terminally ill. Repeated changes in the 'official' religion of the country disrupted people's everyday lives. In addition, prominent leaders of the 'other' faith were forced to leave the country or sometimes executed for their beliefs. When the next monarch came along and the belief system changed again, church leadership was often inconsistent, and people's sense of security was significantly compromised.

Elizabeth's reign saw its share of religious chaos, particularly after the arrival of Mary, Queen of Scots, in England in 1568 and the pope's excommunication of Elizabeth in 1570. But even as persecution against Jesuits increased in the later years of Elizabeth's reign, her longevity reinforced the spread of the Elizabethan church. By the end of her reign, the majority of her subjects had been born and baptised into her church. That did not mean there was no Catholic resistance, but the fact that she spent nearly fifty years on the throne helped permanently establish the Anglican church.

Elizabeth I was the only regnant queen in English or British history to remain single throughout her reign. This had the advantage of avoiding the dangers of childbirth or the problems of being drawn into the wars or crises of her husband's country. It also ensured the end of the Tudor dynasty. However, Elizabeth had cultivated a relationship with James VI of Scotland, who would be her heir. This ensured the continuation of the Church of England. In this and many ways, her legacy continued.

100 Percent of Dynasties after the Tudors had at Least One Regnant Queen
After the Tudors, all the subsequent dynasties had at least one regnant queen.

As they descended from Henry VII, the Stuarts could be considered the Tudors, part two. And like the Tudors, two women ruled in the final years of the dynasty. In fact, parliament actually decided a Protestant woman was a better option to take the throne than a Catholic male heir. When James II married Catholic Mary of Modena and they had a son, parliament invited Princess Mary and her husband, William of Orange, to invade England and take the throne. The pair reigned as joint monarchs from 1688. When William died in 1702, he was succeeded by Queen Anne, who reigned until 1714 and oversaw the Acts of Union, which united England and Scotland. It's quite easy to draw the conclusion that the female Stuarts were more successful rulers than their male counterparts, as half of the Stuart kings were forced off the throne by parliament (and one was beheaded for treason).

The crown then passed to the Hanoverians. This dynasty began with a series of German kings named George and then William IV, who passed the throne to his niece, Victoria. The young queen came to the throne to great rejoicing in 1819. As a single woman, one of her early decisions was choosing a consort. Thanks to the lessons of Mary I, the consort was a royal but not a king of another country. Prince Albert lived permanently in England and focused his efforts there. The royal couple were extraordinarily successful in producing children, marrying their nine children and numerous grandchildren into royal families throughout Europe and earning Queen Victoria the title of 'grandmother of Europe'. Victoria's reign lasted into the twentieth century, and she was the longest-reigning monarch of her time. Victoria and Albert's son Edward started the House of Saxe-Coburg-Gotha.

The Saxe-Coburg-Gotha dynasty took the name of Windsor during World War I to break its association with Germany. And the longest-reigning monarch of that dynasty, and in fact the British monarchy, was once again a queen: Her Majesty Queen Elizabeth II. On the throne from 1952 until 2022, the queen steered the country and the monarchy through various crises and into the modern era. She is the only queen much of the country has ever known and is the essential image of the British monarchy for much of the world. As the longest-reigning monarch in English or British history, the queen oversaw a constitutional change that will affect the monarchy in the future.

After the abdication of James II in 1688, when Mary and William were invited to take the throne, parliament established its role related to the succession. Going forward, the sovereign would rule through parliament, and the succession to the throne would be regulated by parliament. The regulations of the Act remained in place until the Success to the Crown Act (2013), which amended the provisions of the Bill of Rights and Act of Settlement passed in 1688. Specifically, the new Act eliminated the practice of primogeniture, through which a younger son would displace an older daughter in the line of succession. This Act was evident at the birth of Prince Louis of Cambridge in 2018. For the first time, the male brother did not replace his older sister – Princess Charlotte held her place in the line of succession.

Numbers and Queens

The rule of women led to several important changes. One thing that changed was the nature of royal marriage. Mary's marriage to Philip was different. He was not king of Spain when they were married, but he was the heir and became king a few years later. With the king of Spain married to the reigning queen of England, and their child destined to become king of both countries, the international stage was set more permanently. Mary might have resisted full involvement in Spain's wars early on, but ultimately England was involved. Despite Mary's adamant support for the pope, she fell afoul of him when Philip's Hapsburg family continued its battle with Rome. Philip's decisions for Spain determined England's foreign policy. After Mary's death, Elizabeth knew she faced the same danger if she married a foreign royal. That concern is likely one of the reasons she resisted pressure to marry her foreign suitors and ultimately refused to marry at all.

Elizabeth's determination to have 'one mistress and no master'[38] consolidated the power that Mary had Philip had shared into one. She was the monarch, and although she worked with her privy council and maintained good overall relationship with parliament, her power as monarch was considerable. After the years of Edward's lord protector and then council ruling while he was underage, and after Mary limiting the power Philip could control but taking his advice and council on government matters, Elizabeth was alone at the top of the power structure.

Monarchy changed with Mary and Elizabeth. It wasn't easy, and it wasn't pretty. Mary reimagined the coronation and the law to gain the same power as the men who ruled before her. She created the space for herself to rule. Elizabeth followed, proving Mary's reign was not a one-off. She did what no other woman has done: rule alone and unmarried for her entire reign. She managed her court and her diplomatic relationships with flirtations and coy behaviour, but she kept herself out of any relationship that would limit her power. She would have 'no master' indeed.

The assumptions about women not being able to rule at all was disproven by Mary's rule. Mary successfully took the throne in the face of a state-led attempt to displace her. She rallied her people, gathered support, convinced powerful men to come to her side, and bravely rode at the head of her troops. She refused to wait for parliamentary approval of her reign but went boldly ahead with her coronation. She directed parliament to enact laws that clarified her power. When challenged by a rebellion, she again rallied her people and put it down quickly. She put the country on the path to return to Catholicism, something many had been wanting for years.

Elizabeth disproved the assumption that a woman could not rule alone. She gathered an excellent council to advise her, specifically instructing William Cecil to tell her what she needed to hear not what she wanted to hear.[39] But she had the final say. In times of Catholic rebellions and attempts to put Mary, Queen of Scots, on her throne, Elizabeth continued to appear before her people and nurture their support. She spoke to her troops fighting the Spanish Armada, as any king would have. She outlasted her enemies and her friends, against all odds managing to die peacefully in her bed.

Women could rule. And they could rule on their own.

Since the death of Elizabeth I, women have been on the throne for a collective 150 years, or 32 percent of the time. The longest two reigns in British royal history are those of women. Women were on the throne during some of the most significant events of British history: the union of England and Scotland, the Industrial Revolution, and the extreme modernisation of life and technology that has followed the end of World War II. While the power of the monarch has consistently lessened over the years, the last queen represented a sense of history and continuity that no one else has. Her seventy-year reign is unlikely to be equaled.

And finally, 470 years after the Succession Act of 1543 that put Mary and Elizabeth back into the succession and on the path to becoming queen, the Succession Act of 2013 eliminated the male preference in primogeniture. A long-awaited acknowledgement that monarch does not equal male, as Mary and Elizabeth proved so long ago. When Mary Tudor came to the throne in 1553, many people were unsettled by the thought of a woman on the throne. The ruler must adhere to that image of power, sitting on a horse with his sword raised high, ready to defend his people at home and abroad. Mary and Elizabeth made female rule work. They were not perfect; each failed in some ways and succeeded in others. But their reigns changed the Tudors, changed England, and changed the world. We are still experiencing the effects of their reigns.

Chapter Three

We 3 Kings

The Yorkist and Lancastrian kings saw the crown change hands six times between 1461 and 1485, most often in battle. The three Tudor kings succeeded in ending this pattern, achieving peaceful transitions of power over a sixty-eight-year period. The Tudor kings faced down challenges and kept their thrones safe from foreign and domestic threats.

Birth of a Prince

On 15 October, 1537, some of the most important people in England gathered at Hampton Court Palace, which the king had been renovating and embellishing to represent his wealth and magnificence. The chapel royal, where the ceremony took place, had been freshly redecorated and now sparkled under a lavish blue hammer-beam ceiling dotted with stars and angels. The chapel was fitted with a large platform for the christening font because Henry VIII wanted all who attended to have a good view of the future of his dynasty: the christening of his son Edward.

According to contemporary reports, torch bearers led the procession from the queen's chambers to the chapel.[1] The leading nobles and figures of the land crowded in to celebrate the king's son, including the officers of the household; chaplains, abbots, and bishops; the king's councilors; Thomas Cromwell, the lord privy seal and lord chancellor; the duke of Norfolk and other nobles, and the archbishop of Canterbury, Thomas Cranmer. There were leading women as well. The child was carried by the Lady Marquis of Exeter, and there were nurses and the midwife. And, importantly, a young woman and a little girl who would prove to be some of the most important figures in Edward's life: his half-sister Mary, who was his godmother, and his half-sister Elizabeth.[2]

It was a pivotal moment for the king and the dynasty. Henry had taken the necessary step toward another peaceful transition of power. The success of the dynasty depended on this. The Yorkist and Lancastrian kings had experienced trouble maintaining control. How long could the Tudors maintain the throne?

Let's find out. Let's roll the numbers!

The Story of 3 Tudor Kings

The three Tudor kings all had one big job: secure the dynasty for the future. The numbers tell the tale of three kings and their efforts to ensure the survival and success of the Tudor dynasty. They came to the throne in different ways, and they ruled differently. Ultimately, the supply of kings ran out and the dynasty went to the women. But for sixty-eight years, the three Tudor kings held onto power and their crowns and established a lasting dynasty.

1 Traditional Royal Succession

In theory, the Tudors assumed they would more or less follow medieval plan for royal succession, which was pretty straightforward. 'The king is dead. Long live the king.' A succession plan based on the necessity of an adult son ready to take over proved inadequate during much of the fifteenth to seventeenth centuries. In 1413, Henry of Monmouth became King Henry V upon the death of his father, Henry IV. That transfer of power demonstrated precisely what the royal succession should look like. The problem was it would not happen again for nearly 100 years. Not until the death of Henry VII in 1509 did a crown peacefully pass from father to adult (or nearly adult) son. Prince Henry was crowned King of England just four days before his eighteenth birthday. So, the medieval tradition of primogeniture and the king's two bodies worked in 1413 and then again in 1509. And that transition of power from Henry VII to Henry VIII was the only time it would happen in the Tudor dynasty. After Henry VIII's accession, the crown would not pass from father to adult son again until the death of James I and accession of Charles I in 1625. In other words, a traditional succession happened only three times in a 200-year period.

The Tudors demonstrate the tenuous nature of the succession. Henry VII came to the throne by way of the battlefield. Edward VI came to the throne as a child and never ruled as an adult. It doesn't sound like the makings of a lasting dynasty. However, in contrast to their recent Plantagenet predecessors, no Tudor was forced from the throne.

In the fifteenth century, winning the crown had proven much easier than wearing it and especially keeping it. In the nearly 100 years before the start of the Tudor dynasty, one king had been deposed (Richard II in 1399); four kings had lost their crowns in battle (Henry VI in 1461, Edward IV in 1470, Henry VI for a second time in 1471, and Richard III in 1485); and one king had been imprisoned in the Tower and someone else crowned in his stead (Edward V in 1483). That makes it all the more surprising that none of the Tudor kings lost his crown in the council chamber, on the battlefield, or in the Tower. Once the Tudors were on the throne, they all maintained control until they died in their beds.

Henry VII experienced serious challengers to his throne, but he was able to defeat them and maintain control. Even in the face of these challengers, foreign powerhouses France and Spain did not attempt to invade England. After Henry VII, the throne of Tudor kings was even more secure. Henry VIII and Edward experienced rebellions, but there were no significant challenges to their place on the throne.

3 Religions for 3 Kings

Sixteenth century Europe saw religious change, chaos, and often violence across the Continent. The church was the centre of everyday life for people across Tudor England. People of the time lived according to the beliefs they were taught in Sunday services, which everyone in the village attended. The church was responsible for the major events in people's lives: baptising babies, conducting marriages, hearing confession, and offering last rites and support in burying the dead. From 'cradle to grave', life revolved around the church, and the church was the most important institution in medieval life.[3] The stories of the Bible, both Old and New Testament tales, were known to the people through church teachings and through poetic adaptations.[4]

The shift in religion from early in the reign of Henry VII to the end of the reign of Edward VI is remarkable. The Reformation came to England during the reign of Henry VIII, bringing extraordinary change. Even so, and despite conflicts and prosecution of different believers at different times, the Tudors managed to avoid the civil war and huge massacres of other nations. The Tudor kings used religion to shape their reigns and manage their power and authority. Each made the most of his relationship with church leaders and practices to reinforce his control.

Henry VII

Henry began his reign with a procession from Bosworth to London where he went to St Paul's to give thanks and leave his banners.[5] Two of the people at the heart of Henry's inner circle were devout in the church: his mother, Margaret Beaufort, who acted as queen dowager, and John Morton, who became chancellor and archbishop of Canterbury.[6] Henry VII was able to secure the pope's support of his new dynasty. This was important: without other obvious supporters, the pope's validation of the Tudor claim to the throne was essential. Henry made the most of his relationship with the church and with Rome, especially early in his reign.[7]

- **4 Popes**: Innocent VIII was Henry VII's first pope. He declared the new king and his heirs to be legitimate rulers after Bosworth and supported Henry VII during the rebellion of Lambert Simnel in 1487. In 1492, he was succeeded by Pope Alexander VI who took Henry's side against Perkin Warbeck. Alexander died in 1503 and was succeeded by Pope Pius III for a few weeks, then by Pope Julius II who issued the dispensation allowing Katherine of Aragon to marry the brother of her late husband. At the time, it seemed a straightforward request that would promote good relations between England and Spain.
- **8,000 Churches**: There were 8,000 or more churches throughout England during Henry VII's reign. Often, the monasteries had the best libraries and latest technology available in villages. Bishops had secular responsibilities as well as religious ones – they were able to raise an army from parishioners if necessary to support the king. Some also sat in the House of Lords.
- **100 religious houses in London**: London was filled with soaring churches and religious buildings, including St Paul's Cathedral and Westminster. The king required that bishops provide service to the state as well as to

the church. Henry VII objected to the 'privilege of sanctuary' for those accused of treason because someone who would betray the country was an enemy to the Christian faith.

- **4 Archbishops of Canterbury**: Cardinal Thomas Bourchier crowned Edward IV in 1461, Elizabeth Woodville in 1465, and Richard III and Anne Neville in 1483 before crowning Henry VII in 1485. John Morton became archbishop of Canterbury and then lord chancellor in 1487. He held both positions until his death in 1500. Henry Deane served as archbishop from 1501 to 1503, and then Pope Julius II nominated William Warham archbishop of Canterbury. Two months later the king made him lord chancellor. Warham was a leader in government and religious affairs through the death of Henry VII and into the reign of his son. The dual role of leading the work of church and state was a habit of Tudors that carried into his son's relationship with Thomas Wolsey.

Henry VIII

The establishment of the Church of England was shaped by Henry VIII's personal affairs – his desire to remarry and especially his obsession with having a legitimate son to succeed him. After becoming supreme head of the church, Henry eagerly received the spoils of the dissolution of the monasteries and published the Bible in English. Still, he wasn't driven to wholescale reform or worship. Henry VIII remained essentially a Catholic in his faith and practice. He firmly believed he was God's appointed king, and during his reign that came to mean the king's will was God's will.

- **7 Sacraments**: On 11 October 1521, Pope Leo X rewarded the efforts of a young Henry VIII with a glorious religious title: 'Defender of the Faith' in appreciation for his book *Assertio Septem Sacramentorum* or *Defense of the Seven Sacraments*.[8] It was a positive but short-lived moment in Henry's long and complicated relationship with the papacy. It's possible Thomas More, a devout Catholic and at this point close friend of the king, helped Henry create the work.
- **2 Archbishops of Canterbury**: Henry VIII's first archbishop, William Warham, was a carry-over from the court of Henry VII. He resigned as lord chancellor to make way for Wolsey and hung on after Wolsey's fall. Warham was willing to recognise Henry as supreme head of the church

only 'so far as the law of Christ will allow', and had he not died in 1532, Warham might have had the same fate as Wolsey. Thomas Cranmer became Henry's second archbishop, thanks in part to the influence of the Boleyns. He served as archbishop for the rest of Henry's reign and was holding Henry's hand when the king died.[9]

- **1 Leader of 'the Church' in England (and it's not the pope)**: In 1534, parliament passed the Act of Supremacy, which ended the ecclesiastical leadership of the pope in Rome and declared the king to be supreme head of the Church of England. This reimagined England's relationship with the powerful nations of France and Spain, with the Hapsburg Empire, and all of Europe; restructured English society without the spiritual, practical, economic, and social scaffolding of the church; and led to the most significant rebellion of Henry's reign, the Pilgrimage of Grace. It made possible the official publication of the English Bible. Eventually, it led to years of religious chaos and periods of violence in every other Tudor reign, and far into the future.[10]

Edward VI

Although his father had initiated the English Reformation, it was left to the young Edward VI to carry it forward in terms of real religious (rather than political) reform. Henry VIII remained largely conservative in his beliefs and worship; his focus was being able to manage his marriages and later reap the financial rewards of the dissolution of the monasteries. Edward and his advisors, on the other hand, were interested in reforming worship and in encouraging (and, if necessary, forcing) people to change their beliefs.

- **1 Archbishop of Canterbury**: Cranmer was Edward's only archbishop of Canterbury and was at the heart of his religious life. From baptising the young Prince 15 October 1537, through the years of religious reform, Cranmer was a stalwart supporter of the young king.[11] He advised and guided the king's reformation efforts. During the coronation, Cranmer encouraged young Edward to take on the role of Josiah, the young king of ancient Judah, and commit to destroy the remaining vestiges of idolatry.[12]
- **2 Books of Common Prayer**: On 15 January 1549, the House of Lords passed the Act of Uniformity, legally abolishing the Mass and requiring

that the new Book of Common Prayer constitute religious services in England.[13] Thomas Cranmer drafted and supervised the creation of the book, which attempted a compromise between Catholic and Protestant positions – and neither side liked it. The revised prayer book was issued in 1552, which was intended to further reform.[14] Its use was short-lived, and it was not widely used, as Edward VI died 6 months after it was issued, and Mary quickly outlawed it.

- **6 1/2 Years of Reform**: Edward's reign lasted from 28 January 1547 until 6 July 1553. During that time, he succeeded in making significant progress in religious reform. But his serious illness in early 1553 threatened ongoing reform, and his presumed heir was his half-sister Mary, a devout Catholic. His final attempt to ensure reform by bypassing Mary in the succession would not succeed.

7 Consorts Among 3 Kings

The presence and character of the queen consort is an often overlooked factor in a dynasty's success. It's generally believed that Henry VI's return to power was much more about the dedication and determination of his wife Marguerite of Anjou than about the king's own desire to retake his throne. In the case of the first two Tudor kings, a very different approach to marriage and family life demonstrates the differences in the characters of Henry VII and his son. Even so, both men used their wives and families to strengthen their hold on the throne and increase their power and authority.

Henry VII

Henry VII married once. His wife was a political choice, not one he made himself. According to Vergil, Margaret Beaufort saw the controversies of Richard III's reign as an opportunity to promote Henry Tudor's claim to the throne. But it was not strong enough on its own; it needed a boost. That boost would come in the person of the assumed Yorkist heir, Elizabeth of York. Margaret Beaufort told her physician, Dr Lewis to communicate a message to Elizabeth Woodville, Elizabeth of York's mother, when he next saw her. Elizabeth Woodville had retreated into sanctuary when Richard III ordered the arrest of her brother and son shortly after the death of her husband Edward IV. Wary of Richard's subsequent actions, Elizabeth Woodville remained in sanctuary, so Margaret Beaufort couldn't contact her in person. The message was that 'the time was now coom when as king Edwardes eldest dowghter might be geaven in maryage to hir son Henry'. According to the record, Elizabeth Woodville was 'so well pleasyd with this devyse' that she not only agreed, she offered to do all she could to procure the support of Edward IV's friends.[15] When she got word that the former queen agreed, Margaret Beaufort secured the help of Reginald Bray to begin recruiting more support for Henry Tudor.[16]

In 1483, Henry Tudor publicly promised to marry Elizabeth of York at a Christmas service.[17] This helped him secure the support of Yorkists who were disenchanted with the politics of Richard III and preferred Edward IV's daughter. But although Henry was committed to the marriage and made the promise in a church before witnesses, he did not wish his reign to be based on his marriage or the Yorkist claim. He claimed the throne on his own and was crowned on his own. Only after parliament reversed the illegitimacy of Edward IV's children did King Henry VII, as he was by then, marry her 18 January 1486 and make her his queen consort.

The marriage was an immediate dynastic success, as Elizabeth quickly became pregnant. Henry was convinced the child would be a son and used the occasion to tap into the legend of King Arthur. Both sides of the York/Lancaster wars claimed to descend from Arthur, so the baby would be further evidence of the union of the two families. Merlin had described the original King Arthur as the heir of a red king and white queen. Now Henry and Elizabeth would produce the same. Henry VII turned out to be right about the gender and Prince Arthur was born in Winchester Castle – legendary seat of Camelot. The minstrels celebrated with songs about the baby Tudor who was the result of the union of red and white roses.[18]

Elizabeth had proven an ideal wife with the birth of Arthur. She bore the king six more children: Margaret (born 1489), Henry (born 1591), Elizabeth (born 1491 and died 1495), Mary (born 1496), Edmund (1499 and died 1500), and Catherine (born and died 1503). Over the years, their relationship developed from a political alliance to a real relationship, as evidenced by their comforting each other when they learned of Arthur's death.[19] When Elizabeth died in 1503 after the death of Princess Catherine, the king became increasingly paranoid about the future of the dynasty. Henry VII made some inquiries about marrying again, but he did not remarry. He commissioned an elaborate chapel in Westminster Abbey for his descendants and an elaborate memorial for Elizabeth. When he died six years later, he was buried by her side. It was the most successful marriage of the Tudor monarchs.

Henry VIII

The story of Henry VIII and his marital record is the stuff of legend. He was married more often than any English monarch in history. In an age when monarchs married for politics, Henry VIII preferred to marry for love.

Katherine of Aragon originally came to England to marry Prince Arthur, an international coup for the Tudors as it secured an alliance with the well-respected and powerful Ferdinand and Isabella of Spain. Katherine and Arthur had an elaborate public wedding 14 November 1501 to reinforce the alliance. Arthur died just six months later, creating a significant problem for Henry VII and Ferdinand. The two kings debated and disagreed about Katherine's dowry and her future after Arthur's death. She was betrothed to Prince Henry, but that agreement was cancelled.[20] When Prince Henry became King Henry and chose to marry Katherine, he selected a bride he knew and admired.

The choice of Anna of Cleves as Henry VIII's fourth wife was the most traditional in terms of royal marriage. She represented not a personal but a political selection. That was probably at the heart of what was wrong – Henry preferred to make his own decisions. Things went wrong when Anna did not recognise Henry when he burst upon her disguised as a messenger in January 1540.[21] She didn't understand the English society or the English king. But their relationship got better after the marriage was annulled, and Anna remained in England as the 'King's sister'. They had a friendly relationship until Henry's death in 1547.

The remainder of Henry's wives were Englishwomen. They were all, in fact, ladies-in-waiting before they married the king. Trolling his wife's court for a new wife was a habit of Henry VIII's. Anne Boleyn served in the household of Katherine of Aragon before replacing her; Jane Seymour served in the household of Anne Boleyn before replacing her; and Catherine Howard served in the household of Anna of Cleves before replacing her. Henry found his final wife, Katherine Parr, in the household of his daughter Mary.

Henry's first three wives fulfilled their dynastic duties by providing the king with one child each. Jane Seymour was the most successful, as she provided Henry with his much-wanted son. Katherine of Aragon and Anne Boleyn both had daughters. Ultimately, Henry was a surprising success in providing heirs – all three of his children took the throne, and they reigned a combined fifty six years.

Both Henry VII and Henry VIII relied on their wives (in Henry VIII's case, some more than others) to forge alliances, strengthen relationships with foreign governments and with powerful nobles at home, and express their will. Henry VII made a political marriage for his daughter Margaret as well, underscoring his efforts to establish the dynasty abroad.

68 Years of Tudor Kings
The Tudor dynasty is one of the most famous and important in history. Its monarchs are among the most famous historical characters, with Henry VIII making an appearance at the first Major League baseball game in London and Elizabeth I appearing in blockbuster movies and television shows. Even if they don't know the full history, most people have at least heard of the Tudors and can tell you Henry VIII had a bunch of wives. They were destined for the throne. Right?

Wrong. The beginning of the Tudor dynasty depended on an unknown figure cobbling together a group of mercenaries and discontented nobles, landing in a country that had forced him into exile, and defeating a strong, more well-trained, and better prepared royal army. That alone was astonishing. Then he had to quickly move to take and solidify power, despite having spent half his life abroad and not a single night at court. The country had been devastated by years of civil war, and the monarchy had been the centre of the upheaval: nearly all the previous kings for more than a century had either seized the throne through power and politics. The exceptions were Henry V and Henry VI, who inherited the throne, but Henry VI did so as an infant and relied on competing factions to rule his court until he was ultimately defeated on the battlefield and his throne seized – twice. In other words, stable monarchy was not something people had experienced much in England of late. Why should the Tudors be any different? An unknown man at the head with a dubious claim to power facing down a history of power grabs for the throne.

Seen that way, it's stunning the dynasty took hold at all. But it did. The Tudor kings maintained a family dynasty with succession of father to son for nearly seventy years. Their shared vision of the dynasty drove their actions and the ways they are remembered.

- Henry VII: The first Tudor king tends to remain on the sidelines of history. He is easily overlooked in the shadow of his son, Henry VIII. But it's on the first Henry Tudor's shoulders that the task of creating the story of the Tudor dynasty lay. His efforts created a foundation for the more outgoing members of his family to perform their roles to perfection.
- Henry VIII: The life of Henry VIII is full of contradictions. He was a second son but still came to the throne. He was married more often than any monarch in history. He defended the Catholic faith and was praised for his devotion, and then set himself up as the supreme head of the Church of England. He is the only monarch who was succeeded by all three of his children. He spent a fortune on establishing the image of his dynasty and built up royal defenses and residences. After his thirty-eight-year reign, the Tudors had been on the throne for sixty-two years – slightly longer than the Lancastrians and more than twice as long as the Yorkists. He also beheaded two wives and various ministers and is typically credited with executing more people than any other Tudor monarch. So, mixed.
- Edward VI: King Edward VI was always a boy king – he died just four months shy of his sixteenth birthday after a reign of nearly seven years. He ruled with a council but never ruled on his own – the only monarch about whom this can be said. But although his reign was much shorter than his two predecessors, in one way he was more well-suited for the crown than either of them: Edward was born the heir to the throne and spent his entire life preparing to be king of England.

The Tudor dynasty was founded by a man who was a stranger to court and courtiers, who had spent fourteen years in political exile, and who had limited connections with the powerful nobility. His wife had a better claim to the throne as the daughter of Edward IV. Without a family connection among the nobility, Henry relied on a collection of supporters who had helped him gain the throne and developed relationships with powerful courtiers through Margaret Beaufort's connections. Ultimately, Henry VII limited the power of the nobility and established a strong financial foundation to maintain the dynasty. He managed to stay alive long enough for his son to inherit the throne and be crowned within days of his eighteenth birthday.

Henry VIII's desperation to have a houseful of sons to succeed him led him to take the extraordinary step of breaking with Rome and declaring himself supreme head of the Church of England. This resulted in a dramatic upheaval not only of court life, but of life for people throughout the country. When Henry VIII decided to break with Rome so he could marry Anne Boleyn, he opened the floodgates to religious confusion, chaos, and violence that would grip the country for years. The whiplash of changing laws about religion, both during and after Henry VIII's reign, continued to upend life and require that people actually altered what they believed, the way they worshipped, and how they lived their lives. Thousands died for their beliefs during the Tudor dynasty, and they died being told their beliefs were wrong.

Edward VI's short changed England's religious history and created the foundation for the future of the Anglican church. Edward's two versions of the Book of Common Prayer created the form and structure of Anglican worship and provided the model for future versions. Edward's vision of religious reform was a substantial shift in the way religion was practiced in England, and his efforts caused ongoing reverberations through the Tudor period and beyond.

The lack of religious security was echoed by political and international insecurity. England had been weakened during the Wars of the Roses; Henry VII spent his reign trying to reestablish the nation's standing abroad and refill the royal treasury. But Henry VIII squandered much of his father's efforts, setting England adrift from Catholic Europe and spending freely to create his reality of magnificence in royal palaces, royal trappings, and the royal wardrobe. He also spent heavily on efforts to conquer France, a matter of vanity more than anything else. Edward's efforts to push religious reform isolated England further and created a succession crisis when religion became his criteria for naming an heir.

Each of the three Tudor kings had a vision of the dynasty and how it would progress. Each succeeded and failed in his own way.

In terms of notoriety, Henry VIII overshadows his father and his son. How could he not? He physically towered above them both physically, surpassing his father's height and stature even as a teenager. His selection of Hans Holbein the Younger as court painter means that we have extraordinary views of Henry as king. I've heard people say Henry VIII is not only one of the most recognised and recognisable monarchs in English history, but he's also the only one who can be recognised from an outline. Hands on hips, legs apart, staring right at the viewer – Henry VIII perfected the Superman pose centuries before Superman.

In addition, Henry VIII reigned longer than his father and son combined. He had nearly forty years to leave his stamp on his country. Here's the breakdown:

- Henry VII: 23 years, 242 days
- Henry VIII: 37 years, 281 days
- Edward VI: 6 years, 159 days

Henry VIII's personality made him larger than life. He was always the centre of attention. Particularly early in his reign, he was surrounded by men who seemed to be his friends, and he pursued enjoyment and fun. He was a vigorous competitor as an athlete, excelling in sports such as jousting and real tennis. As disappointments and frustrations stacked up, his temper became shorter. His physical health deteriorated over the years, with the injury on his leg, headaches, and other ailments contributing to his bad temper. Not to mention the attention-grabbing six marriages, along with the outcomes: annulling three marriages and beheading two wives. It was an unprecedented track record that has, fortunately, never been replicated. But despite all the drama, Henry VIII was probably not be the most important or significant Tudor King.

From a religious perspective, if you ask which Tudor king had the most lasting impact on the Church of England, that position would go to Edward VI. Edward's reign shaped the early 'Protestant' church, and even though the use of that term in his reign doesn't mean the same thing it means today, the foundation of the Anglican church was built during Edward's reign. His Book of Common Prayer, first printed in 1549 and revised in 1552, was the first prayer book to include the complete forms of service for daily and Sunday worship published in English. Today Anglican congregations throughout the world use a variation of the Book of Common Prayer. Other prayer books, including Methodist and Presbyterian books, borrow from it. And language from the rites and passages have found their way into common language.

And from a dynastic perspective, it was Henry VII who started the dynasty and made sure it had all the elements it needed to succeed. Henry VII created the image and identity of the Tudors with his marriage to Elizabeth of York and his widespread use of the Tudor rose and the accompanying narrative. He provided an heir and a spare. He negotiated a marriage alliance with one of the most powerful families in Europe, Ferdinand and Isabella. He then created another with the Scottish. He fought off serious challenges to his throne. He filled the treasury. And then he managed to hang on until his second son was old enough to take the throne as an adult. Henry VII built the foundation of the Tudor dynasty and of the bridge from medieval England to early modern England.

Of course, it turned out that the greatest challenge the Tudor dynasty faced was not dangers from abroad or even from rebels and rebellions at home. It was from lack of sons. The Tudors were notoriously bad at having sons. It turned out that Henry VIII provided the daughters necessary to carry on the Tudor dynasty for another fifty years.

Numbers and Kings

The story of the Tudors is so familiar to us that we usually think it was inevitable. In most cultural representations, most movies and television shows, we jump in part way through the reign of Henry VIII and focus on the soap opera quality of his marital misadventures.

But the story of the three Tudor kings and the numbers that tell that story reveal the astonishing vulnerability of the Tudor dynasty. The crown passed in the traditional way – royal father to adult son – only once over the dynasty. The dynasty started with a battle and ended with a foreign king coming down from Scotland to take over. The Tudor kings were gone long before that final event: for the first time in history, women took the throne and ruled England.

From the three Tudor kings we are reminded that the people shouting the loudest don't always have the most to say. And for all the image of male magnificence, it would fall to women to extend the Tudor dynasty through the end of the sixteenth and into the seventeenth century. A woman would eventually become the longest-reigning Tudor monarch and give an age her name.

Chapter Four

4 Cornerstones of Elizabeth I's Success

Most people consider Elizabeth I's reign as the pinnacle of the Tudor dynasty, a Golden Age with Gloriana at the helm. It feels like an inevitable and wonderful end to the dynasty. But the reality was more complicated: an insecure queen who spent her reign fighting to hold onto her throne.

Heart and Stomach of a King

The second half of 1588 was a time of war and worry for Queen Elizabeth and her people. Philip of Spain was flexing his considerable strength and had declared a holy war against England. He presented his quest as a religious one, to invade England, replace the excommunicated usurper queen with a Catholic ruler, and return England to the true church. For years, Catholic priests had come to Rome to be trained and then had returned to England in disguise and been hidden around the country, spreading the word of God, and preparing for the overthrow of Elizabeth.

Facing the threat, Robert Dudley was stationed at Tilbury in charge of the land army. As the Royal Navy and the English weather battled and battered the Spanish Armada, fear of invasion remained high. Even after the initial danger waned, the Spanish posed a risk. Dudley invited Elizabeth to join him at Tilbury and be presented to the troops. She delivered a rousing speech, a contemporary copy of which is held by the British Library and available on their website. Elizabeth's speech is well known, particularly the bit about her use of the tradition of the king's two bodies: her physical body might be that of a woman, but her body politic was that of a king of England.

> I know I have the body of a weak and feeble woman; but I have the heart and stomach of a king, and of a king of England too, and think

foul scorn that Parma or Spain, or any prince of Europe, should dare to invade the borders of my real: to which rather than any dishonor shall grow by me, I myself will take up arms, I myself will be your general, judge, and rewarder of every one of your virtues in the field.[1]

We know this moment, thanks to the frequent depictions in movies and television programs. Elizabeth is presented as the warrior queen. Cate Blanchet's character in *Elizabeth: The Golden Age* wears male armor and sits astride her horse, her long red hair blowing around her. A fascinating image that decorates a handwriting book for children shows the queen in her royal gown and armor, with her large ruff and flowing skirt adorned by pieces of armor. Most portraits show the queen in her regal and expected gowns, adorned with pearl, ruffs, and a steely manner.

It's easy to assume from this that English victory was certain from the start, that the Spanish and the overall Catholic threat was doomed to fail, and that Elizabeth turning into the Gloriana of the Armada portrait was a long-expected outcome of her reign. The success of the Tudor dynasty now feels inevitable. But its two most important figures, the first and last Tudor monarch, were some of the least likely rulers in history. Elizabeth was declared illegitimate by law, removed from the succession by her father and her brother, and the wrong gender and religion. How did the least likely Tudor monarch become the dynasty's most successful ruler?

Let's find out. Let's roll the numbers!

The numbers tell us the story of an unlikely ruler, a woman haunted by her past who faced repeated challenges to her throne. The numbers tell us that Elizabeth's ultimate success rests on four cornerstones of her reign.

A Foundation of 4 Cornerstones

The life of Elizabeth I doesn't feel like a mystery. She's the subject of numerous books, television programs, and movies. She even makes a huge splash on the Black Adder series, brilliantly played by Miranda Richardson as 'Queenie'. She's frequently at or near the top of 'best monarch' or 'best queen' polls. The big facts are well-known and fairly juicy: daughter of Anne Boleyn who was supposedly a whore and Henry VIII who had six wives, follower and half-sister of 'Bloody Mary', wearer of huge dresses and ropes of pearls, foil to the prettier and more pious Mary, Queen of Scots, eventually really old and buried under thick white makeup and gigantic ruffs. She never got married and died of old age, having lived a long life. She ended the Tudor dynasty on a high note.

Pretty straightforward, right? But the real story is far more complicated. She was declared illegitimate by her father before she was three years old, then again by her half-brother and half-sister. Many Catholics considered her a usurper and the pope encouraged her people to get her off the throne, exonerating them from any sinful act necessary to do so.[2] The king of Spain launched an attempted invasion of England, and he had plenty of supporters. She was the subject of several assassination attempts, and Mary, Queen of Scots, claimed her throne from day one. She was definitely the least likely of Henry VIII's children to inherit the throne and the least likely to be able to hold onto it. But she was also savvy, strategic, pragmatic, and determined.

45 Years with a Cecil at the Heart of Government

One of Elizabeth's first actions as queen would turn out to be one of her most important: the appointment of William Cecil as her principal secretary. When Elizabeth came to the throne, England was facing significant international challenges. In France, King Henri II had encouraged his son and daughter-in-law to claim the throne of England as their own. With Mary, Queen of Scots, claiming the English throne, France appeared poised to invade and secure their interests through control of England and Scotland. King Philip II of Spain had been king of England during his marriage to Mary I and was preparing to take that job again through his offer to marry England's new queen. In that way, Philip could continue to lead England further into the arms of Catholicism in general and the Hapsburg Empire in particular. Under the rule of its second regnant queen, England appeared isolated and weak, utterly vulnerable to the more powerful nations in Europe.

Nearly forty-five years later, when Elizabeth died peacefully in her bed and the crown passed without controversy to James I, England had proven itself against France and Spain and continued to grow as an independent nation. Yes, there were challenges – war with Spain continued, problems with France threatened. But England remained independent, and

Elizabeth withstood rebellions, the direct threat of Catholics, and even the assassination attempts associated with Mary, Queen of Scots, to evolve into Gloriana and give her name to the age. She had survived and thrived over the longest reign of all the Tudors, and she had done so with one man at her side for nearly her entire reign. It was not a husband, it was her secretary, supporter, and champion, William Cecil. And by the time Cecil died toward the end of Elizabeth's reign, he had trained his son Robert to take his place.

It seems impossible to think of Elizabeth's reign without the support, intelligence, hard work, and ruthlessness of the Cecils, father and son, who were literally at the centre of everything. William Cecil went to St John's College in Cambridge, where he met Roger Ascham and John Cheke, some of the most well-known scholars of the time. He married Cheke's sister Mary and had one son, Thomas. Mary died in 1543, and Cecil married for a second time to Mildred Cooke, who was considered one of the most learned women of the time. Mildred was well connected at court; her sister Anne was the wife of courtier Sir Nicholas Bacon.

Cecil moved to London where he watched religious politics that continued to ebb and flow. Although he was committed to reform and what became known as the Protestant faith, he spent his life carefully navigating the relationship between religion and politics. Cecil was drawn to court and government, and 'his mind, like his pen, was a precision instrument of his service to the Tudor monarchs'.[3] He served Edward VI and was among the twenty-four councilors who signed the agreement implementing Edward's 'Devise' to make Jane Grey the queen.[4] Cecil managed to survive the fallout and was chosen to bring Cardinal Reginald Pole back to England in 1554. As the years went on, Cecil enjoyed ongoing favour at court and had numerous well-placed contacts there. He had remained close to Cardinal Pole despite their differences in religion. Cecil had a sense of change as 1558 dawned. Elizabeth came to London on 25 February with a large retinue[5] and Cecil met with her there.[6] That meeting would signal a change for both of them, the start of a partnership that would shape their lives and the future of England.

By the time she became queen, Elizabeth had already known Cecil for many years. He had been served at court and become surveyor of her lands in 1550, which provided him an opportunity to be in contact with her and provide support to her through Edward's and Mary's reigns.

Elizabeth appointed Cecil as her Secretary on 20 November 1558. Her first recorded speech as Queen was the one to him:

> I give you this charge, that you shall be of my Privy council and content yourself to take pains for me and my realm. This judgment I have of you: that you will not be corrupted with any manner of gift, and that you will be faithful to the state, and that without respect of my private will, you will give me that counsel that you think best, and if you shall know anything necessary to be declared to me of secrecy, you shall show it to myself only. And assure yourself I will not fail to keep taciturnity therein, and therefore herewith I charge you.[7]

Cecil went to work immediately. One early task was making sure European powers immediately knew of Mary's death and Elizabeth's accession. Internally, the transition from one queen to another needed to be addressed. Cecil appointed the marquess of Northampton, the marquess of Winchester, Sir Thomas Mildmay, and some of Mary's officers to manage her funeral. Cecil also began assembling the men he felt best suited to form the queen's government. His notes include Archbishop Heath of York, the marquess of Winchester, the earl of Shrewsbury, the earl of Derby, Sir Thomas Cheyney, and Sir William Petre – recommendations that Elizabeth fully supported. Cecil wanted offices in the privy council to be filled with members of the royal household. In Cecil's plan, the offices of lord chamberlain, vice chamberlain, comptroller, and secretary would be the key members of the household. That meant he would attend council meetings. In Cecil's government, there would be no second secretary – he would fill the duties alone, using his powers to the full.[8]

Elizabeth's first parliament was held in January 1559, and it was the first public test of Cecil's leadership. Cecil was determined that the country quickly return to the reform movements that Mary's reign had interrupted. The legislation was complicated and resistance to recognising Elizabeth as supreme head of the Church of England was one sticking point in the House of Lords. After an adjournment for Easter, parliament returned and passed a bill identifying the queen as supreme governor of the church. It also repealed Mary's heresy laws, providing Protestants the right to worship, and shaped Elizabeth's powers. The Act of Uniformity specified the second prayer book of Edward's reign as the doctrine of the Church of England. With Cecil's guidance and supported by his colleagues, parliament had quickly overturned Mary's years of return to Catholicism.

The Acts of Supremacy and Uniformity enacted by Elizabeth's first parliament decisively set England apart from Catholic Europe. It was nothing short of revolutionary.[9] Cecil was the guiding force of these Acts and the other business of Elizabeth's government. He worked tirelessly to review everything that was done in the queen's name. But the relationship was not always easy. In late 1559 or early 1560, Cecil wrote a resignation letter:

> It may please your most Excellent Majesty,—With a sorrowful heart and water eyes, I your poor servant and most loyal subject, an unworthy Secretary, beseech your Majesty to pardon this my lowly suit, that considering the proceeding in this matter for removing of the French out of Scotland doth not content your Majesty, and that I cannot with my conscience give any contrary advice, I may, with your Majesty's favour and clemency, be spared to entermeddle therein … [10]

Ultimately, Cecil did not resign, and the queen did take the advice he and her council had offered. Cecil remained faithful to Elizabeth's request that he tell her what she needed to hear, not what she wanted to hear. He was steady throughout the crisis of Mary, Queen of Scots, working alongside Walsingham and implementing the execution warrant in a way that allowed Elizabeth to claim she hadn't wanted it carried out. He was key to English preparation for the Spanish Armada. It was after that when Cecil faced personal losses and failing health. He also saw the emergence of the earl of Essex, a rival at court for Cecil's son and chosen successor Robert. Cecil continued his crushing work schedule as long as he could, asking the queen in 1591 if he could retire. She begged him to stay, pleading that she couldn't succeed without him. At this point, he began turning over more work to Robert, although he continued to work from home.

By 1598, Cecil's health was seriously failing. He requested and received permission to miss the Order of the Garter ceremony. It's said the queen visited him at his home and even fed him herself. He died on 4 August 1598. The extraordinary service he offered Elizabeth was key in maintaining the consistency of her reign. He summed up his life in a final letter to his son, Robert: 'Serve God by serving the queen, for all other service is indeed bondage to the devil.'[11]

25 Progresses: The Queen on the Road

Elizabeth I knew the success of her rule depended on the support of her people. She took that seriously. Her coronation progression was slowed by her insistence on stopping along the way to speak with and offer thanks to the throngs who had come out to greet her. Elizabeth knew most of her people would never come to London and be able to see her, so she used royal progresses in the way her father and grandfather had: to take royal court to the people. Progresses represented a sort of stage production where Elizabeth, her subjects, her hosts, and her government took measured, rehearsed steps in order to achieve a planned and hoped for result: personal and political benefits all around.

Most years during her reign, Elizabeth went on a summer progress. This resumed the practice of the first two Tudor monarchs: Henry VII and Henry VIII went on several progresses, using them to generate support for the monarchy and discourage or put down rebellions. Elizabeth focused on the first goal for her progresses: she wanted to show herself to her people, meet with them, provide a sense of monarchial magnificence. She tended to travel shorter distances than her father and grandfather, and she stuck to areas that were already supportive rather than visiting regions of rebellion. Even so, Elizabeth's progresses were an extraordinary series of events that contributed to her reputation and success.

Progresses enabled Elizabeth her to accomplish several goals: see the people, project majesty to those who would not otherwise have the opportunity to see her, avoid or at least procrastinate meeting with some ministers from England and abroad, delay decisions she didn't want to make, and take favoured foreign ministers with her to show off her people and her popularity.

The queen's progress in 1561 lasted seventy-six days and took her into Essex and Suffolk. Thomas Weldom, Elizabeth's cofferer, kept a detailed record of the queen's expenses at each place she stayed during her trip. The cost per day varied from £83 (or £41,200 today) to £146 (£72,500) for an astonishing total of £8,540 (£4,239,000).[12] Not surprisingly, the sums attracted the attention of William Cecil, who was eager to save funds for other endeavors.[13]

Why did Elizabeth, typically a frugal monarch, spend so extravagantly on her progresses? For one thing, in 1561 the queen was facing controversies and growing concerns over her marriage and the succession. The previous fall, Dudley's wife Amy Robsart had died suddenly in circumstances many found suspicious. Dudley had been cleared and the death declared an accident, but rumours that Dudley or even the queen herself had been involved swirled through England and Europe. Elizabeth's decision to continue her dalliance with Dudley rather than marry a suitable foreign suitor was a source of great frustration for Cecil. On the day Elizabeth left London for her progress, Cecil wrote to Sir Nicholas Throckmorton that the queen was not likely to marry the king of Sweden and that he would probably end his consideration of coming to England. Cecil went on so express his desperate desire for Elizabeth to marry and have a son: 'God send our Mistress a husband and by him a son that we may hope our posterity shall have a masculine succession.'[14] Being away from court offered Elizabeth a temporary respite from facing her troubles and dealing with Cecil's frequent reminders about her need to marry.

Still, she wasn't always able to completely evade questions about marriage and the succession when she was on the road. Queen Elizabeth made two progresses to universities in the first decade of her reign: to Cambridge in 1564 and to Oxford in 1566. Her visits there are thought to have had several intentions. She visited to honour and support the men who oversaw them: William Cecil was chancellor of Cambridge in 1564,[15] and Robert Dudley was chancellor of Oxford in 1566.[16] She put her power on display in recognised seats of learning. She also took the opportunity to review the learning of the day and to make recommendations on the training of the politicians and churchmen of the future.[17] At the same time, the universities saw the royal visits as an opportunity to win the queen's favour and, through their entertainments and activities, to offer counsel to their monarch[18] Both universities took this opportunity to provide Elizabeth with input on two of the matters most at issue early in her reign: religion and the succession (including the question of the queen's marriage).

Although her progresses had many of the same goals as those of her father and grandfather, Queen Elizabeth's were distinct in one obvious way: the places she stayed. Elizabeth, unlike Henry VII and Henry VIII, frequently stayed with her subjects. This allowed her to spend more time with a variety of people. She selected hosts as a way to publicly signal favour. She also determined who could afford her stay, estimated how much they could afford, and stayed for anywhere from a night or two to up to a week. She considered it a powerful recognition for her host, which of course it was. This choice also shifted the cost of her stay from the crown to the people. Naturally, Elizabeth's assumptions about what her officials could (or should be able to) afford did not always reflect the reality for her hosts.

In a letter to Christopher Hatton written 10 August 1579, William Cecil compliments Hatton on his extraordinary home: 'I found a great magnificence in the front or front pieces of the house, and so every part answerable to other, to allure liking.' Understanding and in fact sharing Hatton's experience of having spent considerable funds to expand and embellish their homes, Cecil went on to say, 'God send us both long to enjoy Her, for whom we both meant to exceed our purses in these.'[19] The cost of hosting and entertaining Elizabeth and her court could be crushing. Late in the reign, Sir Thomas Egerton provided feasts for the queen that included 24 lobsters and 624 chickens, cooked in new ovens that required 48,000 bricks. That cost alone came to more than £2,000.[20]

Wherever the queen was became into the royal court, and that court was intended to impress. It was also intended to be more accessible than was customary in the rest of Europe. In France, for example, the monarchy used pageantry and ceremony to reinforce the superiority of royals to common people, and to emphasise the distance between the king and his subjects. Queen Elizabeth, by contrast, recognised the value of creating a bond with her people. From the beginning of her reign, Elizabeth relied on a personal monarchy; she continued this through her progresses. She used personal visits to encourage loyalty and unity among her subjects.

Elizabeth's progresses put people in the centre of court, near enough to the queen to see her closely and even address and petition her – people who would not otherwise have that experience. They represented a series of extended negations through which queen, counsellors, hosts, town leaders, and people expressed themselves, requested attention and actions, and attempted to create a better path in the future. Everyone had a part to play. In a visit to Worcester in 1575, 'the people, being innumerable, in the streets and Churchyard, crying to her Majesty, "God save your Majesty! Gove save your Grace!" Unto whom she, rising, shewed herself at both sides of her coach unto them, and oftentimes said, "I thank you, I thank you all."'[21]

0 Masters: The Marriage Game

Elizabeth had plenty of reasons not to get married. For one thing, the experiences of her immediate family did not offer a sense of happily ever after. Elizabeth was considered a prize in the international marriage market, where unions were made for political power, not love. The laws of the time made the husband supreme in a marital union. Still, everyone expected Elizabeth to marry so she could take two very important steps to ensure the safety of the nation: 1) pass along the duties of ruling to a man who would be inherently better able to carry them out, and 2) have a son to inherit the throne and lead the dynasty into the future. Elizabeth played the marriage game, receiving offers from foreign princes and English nobles. The Spanish ambassador, Count de Feria, had a ringside seat to events in England. On 21 November, just a week after Elizabeth accession to the throne, he wrote to Philip 'The more I think about this business, the more certain I am that everything depends upon the husband this woman may take.'[22] The question was never if she would marry but whom.

One of Elizabeth's earliest suitors might seem the most ironic. Elizabeth's claim to her throne was based on her father's determination that it had been wrong to marry his dead brother's wife. Doing so had meant his first marriage invalid and had opened the way for him to marry Elizabeth's mother Anne Boleyn. Now the husband of Elizabeth's dead sister wanted her to marry him. Awkward! Still, Philip considered it beneficial to find a way to make an alliance with Elizabeth. Philip instructed de Feria to make an offer to Elizabeth. De Feria planned to appeal to Elizabeth's vanity by reminding her that her half-sister married a prince and future king, suggesting Elizabeth herself would wish no less grand a marriage. Philip and de Feria thought it was an offer Elizabeth couldn't refuse.

Elizabeth said she was considering Philip's proposal while her ministers were working on the peace treaty with France. When the treaty was enacted, Elizabeth refused Philip's proposal. On 19 March, de Feria wrote that Elizabeth had said she could not marry Philip because of religion. Philip replied a few days later that he was sorry but desired continued friendship with the queen. It was diplomacy at its best – a political offer of marriage, a face-saving consideration, a political delay in response, a respectful decline, and a gallant acceptance of the refusal with the age-old expression 'we can still be friends'. It lasted for a while, but by the 1570s and 80s the relationship had gone devastatingly wrong.[23]

Other suitors in the early years were plentiful. There were seven key contenders early in Elizabeth's reign:

- **Henry Fitzlan,** the 12th earl of Arundel, who had served in the courts of Henry VIII, Edward VI, and Mary I. He seemed to have been more convinced of his chances than anyone else, especially Elizabeth.
- **Sir William Pickering,** a Protestant and apparent rival for the earl of Arundel's suit. He's reported to have told the ambassadors he was not a suitor and knew that the queen 'meant to die a maid'.
- **James Hamilton, Earl of Arran,** whose marriage to Elizabeth was supported by John Knox. He had also been considered a possible husband for the widowed Mary, Queen of Scots.
- **Duke Adolphus of Holstein,** who was son of King Frederick of Denmark and half-brother of Christian III of Denmark. He was a Protestant, a key factor but not enough to sway Elizabeth.
- **Christopher Hatton,** who joined the queen's service shortly after she took the throne and reportedly impressed her with his dancing. He was a strong voice for Elizabeth in the House of Commons, eventually becoming lord chamberlain in 1587. He died in 1591, shortly after a visit from Elizabeth.
- **Prince (and later King) Eric of Sweden,** who started courting Elizabeth while he was a prince and continued after he took the throne. He felt an alliance with England would serve Protestant Sweden well. Elizabeth didn't return his feelings.
- **Archduke Charles of Austria,** who was a favourite option for Spain and the Holy Roman Empire (after Elizabeth turned down Philip). Religion was an unsurprising sticking point; Charles would not give up his Catholic faith and Elizabeth would not give up hers.

Despite all the other men who offered international support or domestic stability, the one man Elizabeth probably really loved and wanted to marry was Robert Dudley. Elizabeth's relationship with Dudley spanned five decades and was one of the defining relationships of her life and her reign. They were close in age and had known each other for years. According to Dudley, he had known Elizabeth since she was 8 years old. That would date their friendship from 1541, the year that Elizabeth's stepmother Katherine Howard fell dramatically from favour. Dudley reported that, after Katherine's execution in 1542, Elizabeth had told him she would never marry.[24] Dudley was publicly acknowledged as a favourite of Elizabeth, and he spent considerable time with her at Hatfield. He was there when Elizabeth received the Great Seal on 18 November 1558. She appointed him her Master of the Horse in the first days of her reign. He accompanied the queen when she left Hatfield on 23 November and headed to London.[25]

The problem was his wife. Amy Robsart was a barrier while she was alive, and the scandalous nature of her sudden death in 1560 created an even bigger barrier. After Dudley was cleared of any wrongdoing, he returned to court and enjoyed the queen's favour. But despite his repeated attempts to woo and win her, Elizabeth was unmovable. Dudley staged a dramatic public proposal at Kenilworth in 1575, pulling out all the stops to win over the queen and convince her to marry him. She refused again, and they both seemed to realise their marriage simply wasn't possible. Dudley pursued other women and eventually married Lettice Knollys. Elizabeth was furious and never forgave Lettice, but Dudley was allowed to return to Elizabeth's presence and continued to support her through the rest of his life. He wrote to her shortly before his death in 1588, and she kept that letter near her bed, inscribed with the words 'his last letter'.[25]

As Elizabeth's reign went on, she embodied the idea of the 'Virgin Queen' more and more. But there was one last courtship. The final negotiations for the marriage between Elizabeth I and Francois, Duke of Anjou, took place between 1578 and 1582 and represented the final real possibility of her marriage. At this time, a significant focus of Elizabeth's ministers was the diplomatic impact of the marriage on foreign relations, particularly with ongoing tensions in the Low Countries and Spain. The age difference was a concern, as Anjou was 23 and Elizabeth was 45. The privy council was concerned about the danger of childbirth at Elizabeth's age and had doubts about the political benefits. Even so, Anjou pressed on and became the only suitor to court Elizabeth in person, arriving at Greenwich in August of 1579. Elizabeth, who had ruled alone for twenty years, was charmed by him.

The English people were less charmed than their queen. In the face of resistance of her people and government, Elizabeth could not commit. The possibility of marriage continued, and Anjou returned to England in late 1581. In November, Elizabeth said she was ready to marry him, but members of the council and the ladies of the bedchamber railed against the idea. Elizabeth felt trapped by having to make a decision that would disappoint and possibly anger Anjou and the French or her own council and people. She had to choose between affection and happiness for herself or security for her kingdom. Sensing her resistance, Anjou tried even harder to win her over.[27] Eventually, Elizabeth chose the security of her reign. She told Anjou she could not marry him but would be as attached to him as a friend as if he were her husband.[28] She realised the days of being courted were at an end, and she expressed her sadness in a poem, 'On Monsieur's Departure', which includes this heart-felt passage:[29]

> Some gentler passion slide into my mind,
> For I am soft, and made of melting snow;
> Or be more cruel, Love, and so be kind.
> Let me float of sink, be high or low;
> > Or let me live with some more sweet content,
> > Or die, and so forget what lover e'er meant.

Ultimately, Elizabeth was remembered the way she had once expressed: as a queen who having reigned from 1558 to 1603, lived and died a virgin.

2 Queens, 1 Crown: The Queen of Scots
When Mary I died, Elizabeth was not the only one to claim the throne of England. Supported by her father-in-law King Henri II of France, Mary, Queen of Scots, and her husband the dauphin claimed to be king and queen of England. Catholics believed that Henry VIII was never legally married to Anne Boleyn, so their daughter was illegitimate. That meant the descendant of Henry VIII's sister Margaret Tudor, Mary, Queen of

Scots, was the rightful heir to the English throne. Francois and Mary created a coat of arms that quartered the arms of England with their own. Sir Nicholas Throckmorton, who was England's ambassador to Scotland in 1558, sent a drawing of the coat of arms to William Cecil, Elizabeth's new secretary.[30] It was a visible manifestation of the claim Mary would make for the rest of her life.

After a short time as queen consort of France, Mary returned to Scotland as a young widow and married Henry, Lord Darnley, against the wishes of Elizabeth and her own lords of the congregation. She quickly became pregnant, and the marriage quickly fell apart. Darnley was arrogant and unkind, demanding more power and authority than Mary was willing to offer. On 9 March 1566, Darnley and other lords stormed Mary's castle, murdered her friend Rizzio, and captured her. She was at the mercy of Darnley and the lords. She managed to get Darnley back on her side, and with the help of her supporter Lord Bothwell, she and Darnley escaped the lords and regained power.[31] The reconciliation with Darnley didn't last, and the night of 9 February, Kirk O'Field, where Darnley was staying, blew up. Darnley had escaped from the house, but he was found dead in the garden. In the drawing of the event created for Cecil, baby Prince James is shown crying 'Judge and revenge my cause O Lord.'[32]

After a likely forced marriage to Bothwell, Mary's popularity collapsed, and she was forced to abdicate. Elizabeth initially supported her right to the Scottish throne, writing 'We do not think it consonant in nature that the head should be subject to the foot.'[33] But when Mary fled to England, Elizabeth realised Mary had become a figurehead for Catholic rebellion. The pope himself encouraged English Catholics to take steps to remove the 'usurper' from the throne.[34] Mary's presence in England set off a series of Catholic rebellions, which continued through the 1570s and 80s. With Mary as an alternative monarch, there was significant concern about plots to assassinate Elizabeth, free Mary and install her on the throne, and restore the Catholic faith to England. The rebellions had the support of France, Spain, Parma, and some Catholics in England. With Mary as the ready-made alternative, there was a Catholic invasion of ideas, complete with clandestine priests, priest holes, and unrest. Elizabeth may have lamented that she and Mary weren't two milk maids with pails on their arms, and they both may have stressed their family relationship. But there was only one crown, and they both wanted it.

When Catholic zealot Anthony Babington hatched a plot to kill Elizabeth and put Mary on the throne, Elizabeth's spymaster, Francis Walsingham, knew all about it. He convinced one of Mary's supporters, Gilbert Gifford, to come over to his side. Walsingham was intercepting the letters between Mary and the conspirators, employing the use of Thomas Phelippes as a cipher- and codebreaker. He bribed the brewer who delivered beer barrels to Mary – the same brewer Mary was bribing to hide her letters was actually turning them over to the government. When Babington wrote about a plot to kill Elizabeth, all Walsingham had to do was wait for Mary to reply. If she agreed, she would be guilty of treason.

Mary did agree. Phelippes deciphered the letter and sent it to Walsingham and Cecil. They moved against Mary, Babington, and the others. Mary was arrested 11 August 1586. When her apartments were searched, agents found copies of additional ciphers. Mary protested her innocence and accused Walsingham of entrapping her. In a way, he had: he made it possible for her to communicate with the rebels and to agree to their plans. Ultimately, Mary was tried in October and declared guilty on 25 October. She was sentenced to death.

It took Elizabeth several weeks to sign the death warrant. When parliament petitioned her 12 November to act, she insisted 'To your petition I must pause and take respite before I take answer.' She went on to explain:

> Princes, you know, stand upon stages so that their actions are viewed and beheld of all men ... And we must look to persons abroad as well as at home. But this be you assured of: I will be most careful to consider and do that which shall be best for the safety of my people and most for the good of the realm.[35]

Eventually, Elizabeth was convinced to sign the warrant. She later explained that after affixing her signature on 1 February 1587, she intended that it be kept safe and not carried out. She gave it to Willian Davison, who quickly contacted his friend Christopher Hatton. In his dual role as political councillor and personal favourite of the queen, Hatton was committed to her safety and to the death of Mary, Queen of Scots. Hatton and Davison passed the signed warrant to Cecil who called an immediate meeting of the council without the queen's knowledge.[36] The privy council sent a letter to Henry Grey, Earl of Ken, instructing the execution be carried out immediately. A copy of the letter is held at Lambeth Palace Library, and the signatures of Leicester, Burghley, Knollys, Walsingham, Hatton, and other ministers are a compelling reminder of the efforts they had taken to keep Elizabeth safe.[37] Within a week of Elizabeth signing the death warrant, Mary, Queen of Scots, was beheaded. She styled herself as a religious victim, dressing herself and her death in the colours of Catholic martyr.

Mary's presence in England had generated enthusiasm for Catholic zealots to rise up and put Mary on the throne. The battle between the two queens shaped Elizabeth's reign for nearly twenty years. Elizabeth was forced to take a more firm stand on religion that she had in the first ten years of her reign, giving in to the pressure of Cecil and Walsingham and others on her council. She was always the last to believe Mary really wished her deadly harm, resisting the call for her execution. Elizabeth knew she and Mary were both vulnerable as female monarchs, both susceptible to the changing love and devotion of their people. With her own story of a mother who was beheaded as queen, Elizabeth was personally horrified at the thought of sending Mary to her death. The guilt of Mary's execution remained with Elizabeth for the rest of her life, causing her grief and pain in the days before her death.[38]

Elizabeth and Mary had been linked since Mary's birth, when Henry VIII began negotiating to bring her to England as Edward VI's future wife. That would have made her Elizabeth's sister and England's queen consort. Henry's plan did not happen, but the idea lives of Elizabeth and Mary were linked from that moment on. In a world of men, these two women ruled as monarchs, as rivals, and as cousins. Their lives and deaths changed history.

Numbers and Elizabeth's Reign

In many ways, Elizabeth's reign was the crowning achievement of the Tudor dynasty. It was also a reign of terror, poverty, danger of foreign invasion and domestic uprising, and religious chaos and violence. For Elizabeth, the victories did not come easily – from her path to the crown to the tortuous journey of her time on the throne.

The reign of Elizabeth proved that women could wear the crown. She managed to do it with the help of consistent councilors instead of a husband. She used her status as a single woman to play foreign politics and to engage her council in an extended game of courtly love to keep herself at the middle of the action while the men around her did her bidding. She used her progresses to develop a steady relationship with her people, bringing her court and her glory to them. Her complicated with Mary Queen of Scots was a real danger for Elizabeth, but she came out the victor once more.

We learn the power of the creative female ruler from the way Elizabeth built a successful reign.

Chapter 5

5 Tudor Monarchs (Or is that 6?)

How is power transferred from one monarch to the next? According to medieval tradition, when one king died, his successor immediately succeeded: 'The king is dead, long live the king.' But did it happen immediately? Did being selected as heir by the king qualify someone to take the throne, or did laws govern the succession? Who determined the next monarch: king, parliament, or the people? These questions came into sharp focus when Edward VI created his 'Devise for the Succession' and surprised most of his kingdom by making Jane Grey his heir.

The Search for 'Heires Males'

King Edward VI had been a healthy baby, child, and youth. But in the early spring of 1553, he became quite ill. When his half-sister Mary visited him in February, she had to wait three days to see him because he was so sick. When she was eventually was escorted to see him, and they had a positive conversation. Mary's supporters had been pleased that she had been 'received and entertained with greater magnificence' than at any previous time during Edward's reign.[1] The king's health improved over the next few weeks. His better health and positive interaction with Mary promoted confidence at court.

However, this illness seems to have made him start thinking more seriously about the succession. Even a nice conversation with Mary had not changed Edward's feeling that leaving his throne to a Catholic would prove disastrous for the realm. As he had not married and had a child, Mary was the heir. And the king's health declined, the earl of Northumberland became extremely concerned as well.[2] Henry VIII had remade the future of the crown according to his wishes three times. As president of the council, Northumberland encouraged Edward to do the same.

A copy of the 'Devise for the Succession' in Edward VI's own hand still exists.[3] In it, Edward details his wishes for the future of the monarchy. He agreed with his father that the descendants of Margaret Tudor should be excluded. But he made a significant change when he decided to exclude his two half-sisters as well. Edward specifically anticipated and favoured any male heir over living females, specifying in his early draft that his crown go to the 'heires males' of Frances Brandon and then the 'heires males' of her daughters. However, as his illness worsened, Edward modified the 'Devise' to exclude Frances Brandon and leave the crown to 'Lady Jane and her heires males'.

The lawyers convened on 12 June.[4] After a few days to review and discuss the matter, Chief Justice Lord Montagu declared that carrying out the devise after the king's death would be treason, and that even creating it was treasonous. When Northumberland heard their answer, he was furious and called Montagu a traitor. On 15 June, the king himself met with them and with 'sharp words and angry countenance' demanded they obey him. He said he would have everything ratified by parliament. The chief justice asked for a general pardon if Mary were to eventually come to the throne, and the king agreed. The 'book in parchment', as Edward called it, received the Great Seal on 21 June and was signed by most of the major figures in the government.[5]

In taking this step, Edward had the least to lose. If he recovered, he could have asked parliament to ratify the agreement. If he died, it would be his council, particularly Northumberland, who would be left with the task of implementing the plan. If it failed, they would pay the price. It was an audacious move that could have had an impact similar to his father's break with Rome or his grandfather's seizing the crown at Bosworth. It was his chance to 'make sense of his short reign' and assert himself against his father's will.[6] Edward felt he had preserved the reform movement he was so devoted to by rearranging the succession according to his wishes. His council and lawyers signed the Devise. Northumberland was prepared to implement it. Would it be enough?

Let's find out. Let's roll the numbers!

Were There 5 or 6 Tudor Monarchs?

The numbers tell us that Edward's Devise ended up revealing the role of three important groups in determining the successful transfer of power at this moment in Tudor history: the king, the council, and the people. The numbers also reveal the volatile nature of power as people competed for it.

There were three recognised monarchs in July 1553: Edward VI, Jane, and Mary I. Both Jane Grey and Mary Tudor were proclaimed queen in the days after Edward died. The two-week period after Edward's death reveals the complications about how power was transferred from one monarch to the next and highlights how Henry VIII's repeated attempts to shape the future had unintended consequences for the rest of the dynasty.

2 Previous Tudor Transitions

Although it had been clear who would inherit the throne when Henry VII and Henry VIII died, there was action behind the scenes setting up the transition to the next reign. Henry VII's death on 21 April 1509 was not announced for two days. The fourteen men who were with Henry VII when he died kept the news a secret, carrying on with the feast of the Order of the Garter on 23 April as if the king were still alive in his rooms. Prince Henry was likely told during evensong, and the king's death was finally announced after supper.

Just weeks from his eighteenth birthday, Henry VIII came to the throne as a minor and had not been well prepared for his new role. Henry VII's two counsellors, Empson and Dudley, made a play for power, but their reputations and associations with the king's most unpopular policies persuaded others to exclude them. A tight knit group of councilors, with Lady Margaret Beaufort, Archbishop Warham, Richard Fox, John Fisher, Thomas Howard, and Lord Herbert guided the new king.[7] Henry turned 18 on 28 June and took full control.

When Henry VIII died on 28 January 1547, he had recently revised his will and established a council to carry out the business of government in the name of his young son. As the king was breathing his last, two of his closest advisors were busily plotting how they would depart from the king's wishes and shape the new regime in their own way. Edward Seymour, Earl of Hertford, and Sir William Paget saw an opportunity to gain power in Edward's reign, and they managed to take it.[8] It was a poorly kept secret that the two men were seeking to have control of Edward's reign. When Chapuys reported about the possibility of the king's death, he believed that Hertford and Paget would end up in charge.[9] The two men worked quickly when the king died. On 29 January, Hertford brought Edward to Enfield, where Elizabeth was staying, and he told them of Henry's death. Wriothesley, the lord chancellor, announced Henry VIII's death to parliament on 31 January, and Edward was proclaimed king later that day.[10]

These transitions had been managed, but they proceeded according to expectations, tradition, and the law. What Edward had in mind for the next transfer of power would challenge all those things.

2 Versions of the 'Devise for the Succession'
The series of succession acts in Henry VIII's reign were necessary as he changed his mind about the validity of his marriages and therefore legitimacy of his daughters. The actions reinforced an idea that the crown could be awarded according to the wishes of the sovereign. Years later, the historian Rapin countered that those laws had been enacted in 'compliance with the arbitrary dictation of a monarch to whom it was dangerous to refuse anything'.[11] Henry's actions may have convinced Edward he now had the right to do the same. After all, his father had disregarded the first Succession Act when he created the second and had disregarded the second when he created the third. Why shouldn't his son disregard the third and come up with his own plan?

Henry VIII had already anticipated the possibility of Edward's line ending a decade earlier. The Succession to the Crown Act 1543, specified that after the death of Edward and any children he had, the crown would pass to Mary and her issue, then to Elizabeth and her issue. This Act was reinforced by Edward's own parliament, which passed the Treason Act 1547. That Act created three new kinds of high treason: stating that the king was not supreme head of the church, attempting to deprive the king or his heirs of his title, and interrupting the succession to the throne. Edward's 'Devise' attempted to bypass both the Succession to the Crown Act 1543 and the Treason Act 1547 by creating letters patent that named a different heir than the one established by parliament.

The 'Devise' version 1: This initial draft of Edward's 'Devise for the Succession' assumed Edward would live long enough for Jane and Guildford Dudley to have a child, which would hopefully be a son. Northumberland envisioned himself having a large role in that regime, essentially ruling on behalf of his son and daughter-in-law and then their son. However,

Edward's illness progressed so quickly it became clear he couldn't wait for that son to appear. He had to make a change.

The 'Devise' version 2: In this version, Edward added two important words: 'and her'. Rather than the crown passing from Edward to the 'heires males' of Jane Grey it would pass to Jane 'and her heires males'. Frances Brandon, who should have been ahead of her daughter in the succession, was bypassed completely. Jane was turned into a sort of place keeper until she had a son, and he grew up. The king and council assumed that Jane would make Guildford a king and turn the government over to Northumberland.

Both versions of the Devise reveal Edward's goal for the next monarch: Protestant and male. He couldn't accomplish both immediately, but he believed he and the council had set things up to get to that desired end. They underestimated both Jane and Mary, who were not willing to go along with what the men around them were planning.

13 Days: Who Was Queen?
The monarchy's survival depended on continuity of succession. That's why Henry VIII worked so hard to specify exactly what should happen in the future. The power to rule passed immediately upon the king's death to the next king. So, what happened after the death of Edward VI? Jane Grey was proclaimed queen 10 July, and Mary Tudor was proclaimed queen 19 July. There is a gap between Edward's death and Jane's proclamation. Some deny that Jane was ever queen. Who ruled England for the thirteen days after Edward's death? Let's take a look at the days following Edward's death.

6 July: Edward VI died at Greenwich Palace.
Edward VI's condition had been deteriorating for several weeks. There were reports that a woman was administering something to the king that was hoped to restore him to health, and other reports that Northumberland was poisoning him. To ward off the rumour that he was already dead, Edward appeared at a window at Greenwich, but his appearance was 'so thin and wasted' that it was assumed he would not live long.

Edward died on 6 July and is reported to have said a prayer that included, 'Lord God, deliver me out of this miserable and wretched life, and take me among thy chosen.' After speaking briefly with Doctor Owen, he spoke his last words, 'I am faint; Lord have mercy upon me, and take my spirit', and died.[12] His death was kept secret for four days so the final plans for the succession of Jane Grey could be put in place.

7 July: Spanish representatives write to the Emperor that they were told of Edward's death.

Jehan Scheyfve and Simon Renard, two of Charles V's ambassadors to England, along with two other colleagues, travelled to London and on 7 July were preparing to 'demand audience of the king'. They were informed the king had died the night before and went to court to see if they could discover if it was true. They also tried to 'ascertain how matters stand with regard to the designs of the duke of Northumberland'. They had already reported rumours that Northumberland was attempting to change the succession. They reported that they had heard Edward had appointed the daughter of the duke of Suffolk to the crown, saying in error that the claim to the throne came though her father.[13] Jane's claim came from her mother, Frances Brandon, who was Henry VIII's niece.

The ambassadors also reported that Northumberland had seized the treasury and appointed men to reinforce the watch at the Tower of London. They expressed concern about rumours that Northumberland was attempting to capture Mary. They believed Mary was in real danger and 'her promotion to the Crown so difficult as to be well-nigh impossible'. Mary had told her advisers that she planned to proclaim herself queen by letter. She was determined to call on friends and supporters to help her prevail against Northumberland's plans. The ambassadors describe Mary's resolve: 'My Lady has firmly made up her mind that she must act in this manner, and that otherwise she will fall into still greater danger and lose all hope of coming to the throne.'[14] They go on to say they don't fully understand Mary's resolve given the strength of Northumberland's position. Interestingly, they assumed the people of England would not support Mary in her quest for the crown: 'The actual possession of power was a matter of great importance, especially among barbarians like the English. Were the question to be settled according to right, there was no doubt as to where the right lay, but if arms and a popular rising were to decide it, the result must be very uncertain.'[15]

At the end of the letter, the ambassadors reported that the lord admiral of England and the earl of Shrewsbury had taken control of the Tower, which they believed confirmed the king's death. They also reported there were warships on the Thames, indicating that Northumberland was prepared to use the military to install Jane Grey on the throne. The Spanish ambassadors clearly doubted that Mary has any chance of prevailing against Northumberland.

8 July: Mary summons Sir George Somerset, Sir William Waldegrave, and Clement Heigham.

Facing the strength of Northumberland and Jane Grey's supporters, Mary acted swiftly and decisively. She established herself at Kenninghall, one of the properties her father had given her. From here, she summoned supporters including Somerset, Waldegrave, and Heigham.[16] She was informed of Edward's death while at Kenninghall. She gathered her supporters and household, told them of the king's death, and assured them that by the laws of God and the land she was the rightful Queen. She was very popular in the area, and her supporters recognised her as Queen. Mary's decision to go to Kenninghall instead of London was the right one. She was surrounded by supporters and positioned to build a strong base to challenge Jane Grey and Northumberland.

9 July: Jane Grey went to Syon House, where the duke of Northumberland told her about Edward's death.

On 9 July, Mary Sidney visited Jane at Chelsea and accompanied her to Syon House to meet Northumberland. Mary said Jane would receive 'that which had been ordered by the king'.[17] (It seems Mary did not yet realise Edward was dead.) Northumberland, Northampton, Arundel, Huntingdon, and Pembroke met with Jane. They called in Jane's mother, the duchess of Northumberland, and the marchioness of Northampton. At this point, Northumberland broke the news that Edward was dead and that Jane had been named as his successor. The councilors all knelt before Jane and pledged their oath to her.[18] Jane later described her unhappiness at the news and unwillingness to take the crown.

10 July: Jane Grey was proclaimed Queen of England.

On 10 July, Jane processed to the Tower of London in great style, with her mother carrying her robes.

That evening, she was proclaimed queen of England. The proclamation was lengthy because it had to introduce Jane as queen and explain her accession. It specified that Henry VIII's marriages to Katherine of Aragon and Anne Boleyn were both null and void, making both Mary and Elizabeth illegitimate and ineligible to inherit the throne.[19] Therefore, Jane was the rightful queen. Northumberland had instructed the heralds and members of the king's bodyguard to make the proclamation in four different areas of London.[20] The people of London were stunned by the news. They had been expecting Mary to succeed Edward.

The same day, Mary Tudor sent a letter to the privy council stating that according to the terms of the Act of Succession of 1554, she was now queen of England. Mary's claim rested on the fact that the Act had never been legally repealed. She demanded the obedience and loyalty of the council.[21] The letter from Mary was delivered by her servant Thomas Hungate to the council. Hungate was not favourably received. Northumberland told him 'he should have had more sense' and ordered Hungate thrown into a dungeon. Mary made clear she knew what the council was doing and how they were working to disrupt her legal claim to the throne. Still, she said she was willing to pardon them. The council replied that Jane was queen by right of ancient laws and Mary was disqualified by her parents' divorce. They told Mary to be 'quiet and obedient'.[22] Mary would not be deterred.

11 July: Mary Tudor headed to her land in East Anglia

Supporters continued to flock to join Mary at Kenninghall. She decided to move to Framlingham Castle, a larger and more secure location. As she travelled, locals, gentry, and justices joined her forces. Mary displayed her standard at Framlingham, proving her determination to fight for her crown. Aware that she would need to increase support, Mary asked her supporters to advocate for her. Thomas Poley went into Ipswich and declared for Mary, despite many leaders there publicly supporting Jane because they assumed Jane's access to the military would ensure her success. After seeing how many people were sympathetic for Mary's cause, Sir Thomas Cornwallis, the sheriff of Norfolk and Suffolk, shifted to Mary's side. Jane supporters had drastically underestimated popular support for Mary.

12 July: Popular support shifted dramatically to Mary

Town authorities in Norwich shifted from Jane to Mary on 12 July and sent men and arms to support her. The shift to her side was increasing at an encouraging rate for Mary. Five of Edward VI's ships had been forced into harbour, and their crews mutinied against their leaders and put themselves under the command of Sir Henry Jerningham, one of Mary's most ardent supporters. Horsemen and soldiers under the command of Henry Radcliffe and more under John Bourchier came to join Mary's cause.[23] Mary's gains among the military and nobility was helping even more people believe in her chance of success.

13 July: Ambassadors of Charles V meet with Jane's leaders.

The Lord Privy Seal, Arundel, Shrewsbury, Pembroke, Cobham, Mason, and Petre agreed to meet with the ambassadors of Charles V. At this point, the ambassadors were not demanding that Mary be named queen, but they were insisting that her safety be guaranteed. They also offered the support of Charles V for Jane's reign.[24]

14 July: Duke of Northumberland leaves London to pursue Mary Tudor.

The ambassadors reported to Charles they believed Northumberland, who had left that day to pursue Mary, would capture her within a few days. The ambassadors didn't believe Mary would be able to raise supporters without the Emperor's support, which Mary requested.[25]

Northumberland had been forced to go after Mary himself because his son Robert and others had failed to find and secure her. Some of Jane's supporters suggested she send her father to pursue Mary, but Jane wanted her father with her in London.[26] Northumberland realised council dedication might weaken without him there to keep an eye on things. In an attempt to maintain Jane's power, he assembled a large force in the Tower and urged the council to remain loyal to their oath to support Queen Jane. Then he left to capture Mary before she gained any more traction.

To strengthen and reinforce her image as queen, Jane asked for jewels to be presented to her so she could select the ones she most wanted to wear.

Perhaps more than any monarch since Henry VII, Jane would need the trappings of magnificence to convince her subjects of her right to rule. The royal jewels belonged to the crown, so as the proclaimed queen, Jane had every right to wear them.[27] The image of the monarch was a powerful tool in promoting authority, and Jane realised how much she needed it.

15 July: Mary gathered more support at Framlingham Castle.
Thomas, Lord Wentworth, was a respected nobleman in eastern Suffolk whose support Mary needed. She sent her servants to request his assistance. On 15 July, Wentworth arrived at Framlingham to support Mary. This was a significant advantage for her, and he came with a large army of gentlemen and tenants.[28] Wentworth's army reflects how widespread Mary's support was becoming, involving different levels of society. Her support was spreading into different parts of the country as well.

16 July: Mary and Elizabeth were declared 'base born.'
On 16 July, Nicholas Ridley, Bishop of London, went to Paul's Cross and preached a sermon that declared that the two daughters of Henry VIII, Mary and Elizabeth, were 'base born'. As they were born of incestuous relationships, they were not natural daughters of King Henry VIII. He concluded that civil law did not allow such children to inherit their father's title or property.[29] The sermon did not go over well, and the people murmured against Ridley. Overall, the citizens of London had been on Mary's side, and the common people were making their allegiance more well known. As a result of people speaking out for Mary, Jane's council strengthened the guard at the Tower.[30]

Jane issued another warrant to ask for support, asserting Edward's wishes that she be queen and emphasising the legitimacy of her reign. She boldly signed that and other proclamations 'Jane the Quene'.[31]

17 July: Northumberland arrived at Bury St Edmunds with a large force.
Northumberland approached the town of Bury St Edmunds on 17 July. The location was significant: it is the resting place of Mary Tudor, queen of France – Henry VIII's sister, Jane's grandmother, and the woman who was the source of Jane's claim to the English throne. Northumberland was planning to hold a general muster of his large and well-armed forces

the next day.³² But the large army would not be enough to save Jane Grey's reign.

Jane's council was concerned about Mary's growing support in London and throughout the country, and about the murmuring against Jane. They were beginning to realise their cause was lost. One by one, despite the efforts Jane had taken to keep her council locked in the Tower, members began to sneak out.³³ Without Northumberland's leadership, the council was deserting Jane's cause.

<u>18 July: Final full day of Jane Grey's reign.</u>

Jane's support had initially been considered insurmountable, particularly as she was established in the stronghold of the Tower of London. But that very building shifted from its role as palace of power to prison.

By the evening of 18 July, Jane's supporters had dwindled to her immediate family: her parents, her husband, and her mother-in-law, as well as some of her ladies.³⁴ She was still officially queen of England, but she must have realised things were changing at terrifying speed.

<u>19 July: Mary Tudor becomes Queen of England</u>

Privy council members Bedford, Pembroke, Arundel, Shrewsbury, Worcester, Paget, Darcy, and Cobham met at Baynard Castle. Earl Arundel was the first to suggest taking definite action. Even though he was Jane's uncle, Arundel was a Catholic and now believed supporting Jane had been a mistake. He begged the rest of the council to agree with him. Pembroke was the first to agree, followed by the majority of the others.³⁵ Jane's reign could not be saved. Now it was time for the council to save themselves. They proclaimed Mary the queen of England.³⁶

The earl of Shrewsbury and Sir John Mason visited the Spanish ambassadors and said only three or four of the council had willingly given their support to Edward's 'Devise.' The rest had been threatened and forced to agree. Shrewsbury stated that he, Mason, Pembroke, Arundel, Paget, and the three secretaries believed Mary to be the rightful queen. The ambassadors reported to Charles V that Jane's supporters had been swayed by the popular rising for Mary, the increase of her army, and the fact that seven of the best warships had pledged to support her. The ambassadors also reported that previous supporters of Jane were now ready to arrest Northumberland on Mary's behalf.[37]

Within hours, heralds and trumpeters appeared in the crowded streets of London and proclaimed Mary as queen. The people rejoiced, and the air was full of cries 'God save Queen Mary.' It was over. Arundel and Paget headed to Framlingham to pledge their loyalty to Mary and ask her to pardon the council.

Where was Jane Grey in all of this? She had been queen of England when she woke up that morning. She must have realised her hold on power was quickly fading away despite her attempts to shore up support. The council, which had agreed to support Edward's Devise and Northumberland's attempt to put Jane on the throne, abandoned her in the Tower. Not only that, they didn't even inform her what was happening. Their loyalty had never been to her as a person, it had been to a larger plan in which she was only a chess piece to be moved about at their will. As Nicola Tallis put it, 'Now the tide had turned, and the council had turned with it.'[38]

The council brought the duke of Suffolk, Jane's father, out of the Tower and informed him that Jane was no longer Queen. Suffolk went into Jane's royal apartments where she sat beneath the canopy of state. He took down the cloth of state and told her she was no longer queen. Her relief was evident. She had not desired the crown. She had done her best to protect it, win the hearts of the English people, and promote the religion she loved. But to succeed she had to rely on men's support, and that proved too weak to sustain her reign. Even her own council betrayed her. Mary had won the crown, and Jane was glad to see it go.[39]

Jane Grey had come to the Tower as queen, and now she would remain there as prisoner.

2 Proclamations, 2 Queens

Jane's proclamation as queen had been long and complicated. It was accompanied by as much ceremony as possible. Machyn describes the trumpet blowing and the herald proclaiming that 'my lady Mary was unlawfully begotten' and thus went through the city 'proclaiming Queen Jane'.[40] It emphasised that Jane's accession 'by the Grace of God',[41] attributing the act to God instead of the men on earth working frantically to make it happen. The proclamation was also printed and disseminated throughout London. Despite all the assurances that Jane was the rightful queen, contemporaries describe a less than enthusiastic response to the proclamations that were read and distributed in London.

When Mary was proclaimed queen on 19 July, everything was different. Mary's proclamation was considerably shorter than Jane's because it had an easier job. Mary was the expected heir to Edward VI, and she was well-known to her people. Her place in the succession had been a matter of law since the Third Act of Succession in 1543. Accordingly, Mary's proclamation was only about a ninth as lengthy as Jane's had been.[42]

Machyn notes that when Mary was proclaimed queen of England, the response was joyful and celebratory. When the proclamation was read at the cross, 'There was Te Deum, with song, and the organs playing, and all the bells ringing through London, and bonfires, and tables in every street, and wine and beer and ale, and every street full of bonfires.'[43]

9 Women Who Could Have Been Heirs to the Throne

Edward VI did his best to provide for a Protestant succession. He had hoped to leave his throne to a male as well as a Protestant, but that wasn't possible. It's ironic that after the lengths Henry VIII went to throughout his life and marriages to prevent a woman coming to the throne of England, when Edward approached death, there were nine women who had a legal claim to the throne.

Listed in the traditional order (and ignoring Henry VIII's decision to exclude the descendants of Margaret Tudor), those women were:

1. Mary Tudor, daughter of Henry VIII
2. Elizabeth Tudor, daughter of Henry VIII
3. Mary, Queen of Scots, granddaughter of Margaret Tudor
4. Margaret Douglas, granddaughter of Margaret Tudor
5. Frances Brandon Grey, daughter of Mary Tudor
6. Jane Grey, daughter of Frances Brandon, granddaughter of Mary Tudor
7. Katherine Grey, daughter of Frances Brandon, granddaughter of Mary Tudor
8. Mary Grey, daughter of Frances Brandon, granddaughter of Mary Tudor
9. Margaret Clifford, daughter of Eleanor Brandon Grey, granddaughter of Mary Tudor

Ultimately, the only option Edward had was to leave the throne to a woman and hope she quickly had a son. Instead, it would be women, specifically the two half-sisters he had tried to disinherit, who would rule for the next fifty years.

The preponderance of females as possible heirs lasted through the rest of the Tudor dynasty. During Mary's reign, her focus was having a son with her husband Philip. But while she waited for that to happen, she had cousins at her court: Margaret Douglas, Katherine Grey, and Mary Grey. Mary seems to have carried no grudge against the Grey sister; in fact, she had been content to keep Jane in prison and not execute her until the Wyatt rebellion forced her hand. Some think Mary was eager to explore naming Margaret Douglas as her heir instead of Elizabeth. Philip convinced Mary to maintain Elizabeth as her heir.

When Elizabeth came to the throne, she was especially resistant to speak about her possible heirs. She did not have good relationships with the Grey sisters and, when they married without her permission, she reacted strongly and imprisoned them both. Another woman, Arbella Stuart, was also considered as an heir in Elizabeth's reign. Arbella was the daughter of Charles Stuart and granddaughter of Margaret Douglas. After her parents died when she was 7 years old, Arbella became the ward of her grandmother, Bess of Hardwick, an ambitious and prominent figure in Elizabeth's court. Court politics shifted in the 1590s, and James VI of Scotland eventually became the heir. But for years, it looked like Elizabeth's successor might be another woman.

Numbers and Monarchs

Who had been queen after Edward died?

The heart of the question was who held the power of determining the succession: parliament or the king. Had parliament helped Henry VIII define and determine the right of succession or simply acknowledged and accepted the king's will? Parliament had passed a law naming Mary as Edward's successor. The final Act of Succession had not been repealed. Until parliament met and ratified Edward's letters patent, did Mary remain the heir?

In Tudor England, however, the extraordinary events of July 1553 didn't centre on the legality of Edward's claim. It was a succession crisis and possible civil war. Edward VI had intervened in the established succession plan. The question was the power of the monarch, especially as a minor, to select his successor contrary to established law.

For any part of the plan to succeed, Edward and Dudley needed the support of the privy council. Sovereignty of England did not reside solely in the monarch during the Tudor dynasty. Parliament was involved in matters of war, regency, or the succession. The crown of Henry VII 'rested on a parliamentary Act'.[44] Henry VIII used parliament to change the succession. During the reigns of Mary and Elizabeth, parliament was recognised as a tool for carrying on the work of the nation. Jane was established as queen and in control of the council and the government, as well as having the military power to enforce her rule, almost everyone believed she would keep her throne.

One important person said no: Mary Tudor.

Whatever the legal underpinnings of the Succession Acts and Edward's Devise, Mary had believed in her right to inherit the throne for her entire life. Her mother had instilled in her an absolute faith in her religion and her legitimacy. Mary never wavered. And outside of the chambers of power in London, the people sided with Mary. She was Henry VIII's daughter. She had been popular from the time of her birth. People probably would have preferred a younger brother and king to Mary, but they did not prefer Jane Grey. Mary asked for support, and she got it. Edward and his government, then Jane and her government somehow overlooked the level of popularity Mary and Elizabeth enjoyed. They also overlooked the power of the people.

People across the country rallied to Mary's side. She enjoyed support of Catholics and Protestants and of multiple levels of society. However important the king and parliament were, this episode revealed how important the wishes of the English people were in the success of the reign. It was a lesson Elizabeth Tudor never forgot.

King Henry VII, unknown artist, 1505, England, UK, Europe. (*Alamy*)

Hans Holbein the Younger (1497–1543), Portrait of King Henry VIII (1491–1547), 1540. (*Alamy*)

Portrait of Anne Boleyn. (*Alamy*)

Queen Katherine of Aragon (1485–1536), first wife of King Henry VIII (1491–1547). Painting by Michael Sittow. (*Shutterstock*)

Queen Anne of Cleves (1515–1557), fourth wife of Henry VIII. Portrait by Hans Holbein the Younger, 1539. (*Shutterstock*)

Portrait of Katherine Parr after John Master – oil on panel, circa 1545. (*Alamy*)

Edward VI (1537–1553) as Prince of Wales in 1546. (*Alamy*)

Queen Mary I. Mary Tudor, Queen of England by Anthonis Mor, oil on panel, 1554. (*Alamy*)

Lady Jane Grey, vintage engraved illustration. Colorful History of England, 1837. (*Shutterstock*)

Tower of London. (*Shutterstock*)

The Rainbow Portrait of Queen Elizabeth I. between circa 1600 and circ 1602. (*Alamy*)

Tudor Rose in Sepia, Architecture Details of old building in Somerset England, sepia tone horizont photography. (*Shutterstock*)

Queen Elizabeth I, (1533–1603), Queen of England 1558–1603, being carried by her courtiers. (*Shutterstock*)

October 10, 2014, Hampton Court Palace, London, England. (*Shutterstock*)

Queen Elizabeth I by Nicholas Hilliard c 1573. (*Alamy*)

Mary Stuart Queen of Scots, Vintage engraving. From Popular France, 1869. (*Shutterstock*)

Chapter 6

6 Very Different Wives

Henry VIII married and got rid of more wives than any monarch in English history. With so many wives and stories, it's easy to think of the king being on a marital merry-go-round, treating marriage casually throughout his reign. In reality, Henry believed deeply in marriage. Especially early on, he wanted nothing more than a deep and lasting relationship with a woman he loved. The problem was, he also needed a son.

The Marrying Game

In medieval and early modern times, securing the succession meant providing at least 'an heir and a spare'. And both of those terms meant 'boy'. Henry VII had succeeded in this task quickly: Prince Arthur, Duke of Cornwall, was born less than a year after his father's coronation. Henry VIII had a momentary success early in his reign: on 1 January 1511, Katherine of Aragon delivered a son. Baby Henry was the first living child of the couple, and initially everything seemed to be going well. The baby was christened 5 January in a lavish ceremony. The jousts held in celebration were some of the largest and most elaborate of the reign. The celebration is detailed in the Westminster Tournament Roll, held at the College of Arms. It seemed that Henry VIII and Katherine of Aragon had provided for the future of the kingdom.

Celebrations came to an abrupt end 22 February when Prince Henry died. Even though both parents were devastated, there was every reason to believe that Henry and Katherine would be able to have more sons. After all, Katherine had become pregnant quickly after their wedding. They were both young. Surely more sons would follow. The couple was still committed to each other and their future.[1]

It turned out those seven weeks of Prince Henry's life were among the happiest for Henry and Katherine. Although Katherine gave birth to a healthy daughter, Princess Mary, in 1516, no more living sons would follow. After her pregnancy in 1518 ended in a stillbirth, Katherine would have no more pregnancies. By the mid 1520s, Henry had one illegitimate son, Henry Fitzroy, but he had no legitimate son to follow him on the throne. After nearly twenty years on the throne, he had failed in his great dynastic duty. That could not be God's will. Something must have gone wrong.

Having convinced himself that he must have erred in marrying the widow of his brother, Henry embarked on a dedicated quest to have a son. Over the years, he changed from the 'loyal heart' title he gave himself to a man who was able to dispense with wife after wife. He moved through his marital merry-go-round with ruthless efficiency. Or did he?

Let's find out. Let's roll the numbers!

How the Six Wives Shaped Henry VIII's Reign

The numbers tell us that Henry's approach to wives and marriage changed over the years of his life. Although each of the women he married had her own story and deserves to be recognised, not all of Henry's marriages were created equal. The numbers reveal that the king tried, especially early on, to have lasting marriages. Things just didn't work out the way he planned.

70 Percent of the Reign with Katherine and Anne

Prince Arthur's death in 1502 left Katherine of Aragon stranded in England. The two families considered a marriage between Katherine and Prince Henry. Ferdinand instructed the duke de Estrada to tell Henry VII, 'we know that it is a good thing for both parties'.[2] But money proved a sticking point. After the death of Isabella of Castile, the marriage was less appealing to Henry VII and he instructed his son to repudiate the agreement that he and Katherine marry.[3] Katherine remained in England, and her financial situation became desperate. She sold her gold and silver plate to pay her expenses, and she could not pay her servants.[4] Katherine wrote to her father in March 1509 saying that she could no longer endure the unkindness of Henry VII or no longer sustain herself. She ended the letter with a request that he resolve the matter before her life was 'sacrificed' by all that she must endure.[5]

And then everything changed. It must have seemed like a miracle to Katherine when Henry VII died on 21 April 1509 – almost exactly seven years after Arthur's death. Six weeks later, on 11 June, she married Henry VIII at the church near Greenwich Palace.[6] Katherine likely felt this was fulfillment of her destiny. Thomas More, who waxed eloquent about the virtues of young King Henry VIII, was equally taken with Katherine of Aragon. He praised her as a consort for the king, pointing to her own descent from great kings and prophesying that she would 'give you a male heir in a short while, a protection in unbroken line who shall be supported on every side'.[7]

Henry fell in love with Katherine easily; he had a 'happy capacity for falling in love' that lasted throughout his life.[8] He had known Katherine for years, and over that time she had demonstrated a strong character and made herself into an ideal partner for the young king. She was older and could guide the young King who had been so devastated at the loss of his mother, offering a steady support as he energetically explored his new royal role.

Katherine loved Henry in a way none of his other wives did because she knew him as no other wife did. She lived with him when everything was possible, when he had the potential to become a moral, political, military leader in the finest tradition. Katherine was happy to be at Henry's side. Her love for her new husband was a powerful force that he depended on.

The problem was that she was expected to give the king sons. For Henry, having sons was more than a dynastic necessity. It was a way to prove his manhood, to outdo his father, and to compete with his European rivals Francis I and Charles V. Katherine was frequently pregnant, but the short life of their baby boy was becoming a distant memory. After years of marriage, there was one child, Mary. For Katherine, it was enough. Mary could be queen of England, as Isabella had been queen of Castile. She could unite with a great king and bring the kingdoms together for the greater glory of God, as her parents had done. Katherine was committed to the plan.

Henry disagreed. He may have respected and loved Katherine, but he was determined to have a son. That meant ending the marriage. Strangely, even after knowing her so well, Henry assumed she would go along with his plan to annul their marriage. True to herself, Katherine refused. She had fought for her marriage at the beginning, and she would fight to maintain it until the very end. She was iron-willed, something Henry had appreciated in the past, but he came to resent her when she stood in the way of his getting what he wanted. Despite Katherine's relationship to the Emperor Charles and her strong support throughout England and Europe, Henry succeeded in marrying again. There were many who considered Katherine of Aragon the true queen of England until the day she died in January 1536, but Henry had already moved on.

Thanks to the success of her courtier father Thomas, Anne Boleyn grew up in two of the most glamourous and glittering places of Europe: the household of Margaret of Austria and the royal court of Francis I of France. She was consistently described as bright, intelligent, and proficient in French. She may have begun a friendship with Marguerite of Angoulême, the sister of Francis I who became a patron of religious reform.[9]

Anne returned to England in 1522 and took part in the Chateau Vert pageant, [10] historically associated with the character of Perseverance.[11] Contemporary impressions of Anne's looks are not especially flattering. John Barlow describes her as less attractive than Elizabeth Blount.[12] The Venetian diplomat Sanuto described her as 'not one of the handsomest women in the world', mentioning in particular her dark complexion and small breasts. He did admit she had 'black and beautiful' eyes.[13]

Even if she wasn't a classic beauty, around 1526 Anne had caught the king's eye and quickly captured his heart. Anne was experienced at playing the game of courtly love, which she had mastered at the court of Margaret of Austria.[14] Henry's court was full of young men who were full of desire, and games of courtly love centred on the queen and her household, providing a sort of safety valve for letting off sexual pressure.[15] Anne had used courtly love to navigate her way through the French and then the English court, and she would use it to navigate a relationship with Henry VIII that would change England and Europe forever.

Henry and Anne began with courtly love, as evidenced by the seventeen love letters he wrote to her. The letters give us a tantalising but incomplete glimpse into the relationship. For one thing, we don't have any of Anne's replies. In addition, the letters are undated, so we don't know exactly when they were written. However, they seem to fall into categories that give a bit of context. There is a group that are classic examples of expressions of courtly love. These letters are mostly written in French and contain amorous and suggestive word play. Henry positions himself in the role of Anne's 'humble servant' again displaying the tradition of courtly love.[16]

There seems to be a shift when Henry stresses his question about 'your whole mind concerning the love between us two'.[17] Henry describes himself as being struck with the dart of love above a year, and he seems to be getting tired of waiting for a response. Henry asks Anne to 'give yourself up, body and soul, to me'. He's going beyond the bounds of courtly love, here, as the game adheres to strict rules that do not result in sex. Henry wants more. He wants Anne to be his mistress. Eventually, he offers to 'take you for my only mistress'.[18]

It's here where Anne takes a gamble. Perhaps she was willing to lose the king and to retreat into a quieter life. Perhaps she was determined not to end up discarded as her sister had been. Perhaps she was so secure in the king's love for her that she felt she was playing the game with the cards she needed. In any case, she declined the 'only mistress' offer.

At some point in 1527, Anne sent Henry a gift he described in a letter he sent to thank her: a 'ship in which a solitary damsel is tossed about' and accompanied by a fair diamond. This is seen by many as a sign of an agreement: Henry and Anne are in for keeps. By mid-1527, Henry was seeking a divorce from Katherine of Aragon.[19] He was committed to marrying Anne and making her his queen. For her part, she promised him love, the fulfillment of his desires, and a son.

After seven long years of failed attempts to convince the pope to see things his way, Henry took matters into his own hands. He broke with Rome and set himself up as supreme head of the Church of England. He created Anne Boleyn as marquess of Pembroke in September of 1532.[20] He took Anne of a royal visit to Francis I in France as if she were his wife. And sometime along the way, they finally started sleeping together.

It's possible there may have been some type of commitment ceremony before witnesses in November of 1532.[21] There was almost certainly some kind of secret marriage on or around 25 January 1533.[22] Whatever the case, by April 1533 Anne was being recognised as queen. Her pregnancy was known at court, from her own hints and the king's. On 15 April Chapuys wrote to Charles V that Henry had implied Anne was pregnant, and he went on to describe Anne attending mass for Easter Eve in full royal estate and treated as queen.[23] With Cranmer as archbishop of Canterbury, everything was in place for Anne to become queen at last.

Anne Boleyn was crowned queen of England on 1 June 1533. It was the first state ceremony following Henry's assertion of independence from the pope's jurisdiction and establishment of himself as supreme head of the Church of England. The legitimacy of the coronation itself relied on the reconfiguration of religious authority.[24] Thomas Cranmer had sworn an oath to the pope, but he promised he would do nothing contrary to the laws of God or the laws of England. He identified the king as his authority.[25] Significantly, Anne was crowned with St Edward's crown, which had previously been reserved for the crowning of monarchs not consorts.[26] This crown was the heart of the coronation regalia. It brought all the mystique and history of royal coronations right to Anne and the child she was carrying. Songs and verses were written in celebration,[27] and the ceremonies lasted four days.

Three months later, the child was born. Despite the hopes of the king and new queen and the assurances of doctors and nearly everyone else, the baby was a girl. She was healthy, and once again there was every reason to hope that healthy sons would follow. Henry and Anne's relationship had been tumultuous from the start, and she had displayed spirit and self-assurance that entranced the king and kept him focused during the lengthy path to their marriage. That same spirit started to shift after Elizabeth was born. Anne had to go on the defensive, and her independence and outspokenness were far less appealing as a queen than they had been as a mistress. Despite at least two more pregnancies, no healthy sons followed.

When Katherine of Aragon died in January 1536, Anne finally was the only wife and only queen. Henry and Anne are described as celebrating the death.[28] But the celebratory spirit was short-lived as Anne had a miscarriage on 29 January, the day of Katherine's funeral. Chapuys reported the miscarriage to Charles V, mentioning that the king seemed to be turning away from Anne and giving gifts to Miss Seymour.[29] Chapuys also reported a conversation where the king visited Anne after the miscarriage and said, 'I see that God will not give me male children.'[30] Despite this apparent breach in the relationship, the king continued his pressure on

Charles V to recognise Anne as his wife, indicating he had not yet decided he would end the marriage.[31]

Anne herself made a huge mistake when she overplayed the game of courtly love with Henry Norris, a close friend of the king. On April 30, Anne accused Norris of neglecting his courtship of Margaret Shelton because of his feelings for the queen herself. Perhaps angry at Henry's public courtship of Jane Seymour and wanting to feel the object at the centre of court attention, Anne said, 'You look for dead men's shoes; for if aught came to the king but good you would look to have me.'[32] Norris was rightly horrified at the statement: speaking of or even imagining the king's death was treason. Worse for Anne, others had heard her. She tried to make amends, begging her almoner to make a statement she was a good woman. She also pled directly with the king, as relayed years later by Alexander Ales to Elizabeth I. He described Anne holding the young Elizabeth and speaking with the king, who was clearly angry.[33]

Henry might have been angry, and Anne may have realised something was very wrong. There seemed to be a moment of calm when the royal couple appeared together on 1 May at the jousting celebration, but Henry left abruptly before the event was over. Anne never saw her husband again. She was arrested 2 May, and by 19 May she had been tried, convicted, and executed. The ten-year relationship that began with promises of endless love, with a king drawing hearts around her initials in a series of love-struck-schoolboy-like letters, with a break with the pope and Catholic Europe ended quickly and violently.

Between them, Katherine of Aragon and Anne Boleyn had been in a relationship with Henry VIII for twenty-seven years. The two women were, of course, rivals. But they were also joined in many ways. Thanks to the remarkable research of Kate McCaffrey, we know that Anne Boleyn and Katherine of Aragon owned the same printing of a Book of Hours.[34] They might have even read these books together, along with the rest of Katherine's household. They shared a deep commitment to their faith. The two women shared other things as well. They were strong, intelligent women. They gave birth to baby girls who grew up to be strong, intelligent women. They made strong impressions on their daughters, who would become the first two crowned regnant queens of England.

They also shared lengthy relationships with Henry VIII in the beginning and prime years of his life and reign. They were pivotal figures in shaping the king's reign, in setting up his ongoing search for the perfect wife. They shared some of his greatest moments and achievements and some of his bitterest defeats. They saw him turn against them and their love for him. After spending 70 percent of his reign with these two women, Henry VIII would never be the same.

And Baby Makes 3

It had taken Henry VIII about seven years to unravel is marriage to Katherine of Aragon. It took just nineteen days to destroy his marriage to Anne Boleyn. It was a terrifying time for those caught up in events, and in the end, six of the most influential people at court, including the queen of England, were dead – all at the king's command. Henry VIII had disinherited both daughters and now had no heir to succeed him. He had been on the throne nearly thirty years, and he was 45 years old. He needed a new wife.

Some royal courts might have expected Henry VIII to return to the typical practice of marrying a foreign princess now that his first two wives were dead. He might even take the opportunity to renew his ties with Catholic Europe now that Anne Boleyn was gone.[35] Before Anne's death, Charles V suggested that Chapuys offer the infanta of Portugal or possibly the duchess dowager of Milan and a wife for Henry.[36] But in fact Henry had already chosen the woman who would be his next bride.

Jane Seymour was an experienced member of the Tudor court. She had been in Katherine of Aragon's household [37] from at least 1529 onwards.[38] From her commitment to the cause of Katherine's daughter Princess Mary, it's easy and reasonable to draw the conclusion that she was a supporter of Katherine and not Anne Boleyn. She did serve in Anne Boleyn's household, and it was while serving there she began her relationship with Henry. She had a front row seat to Anne Boleyn's final months, and she knew the stakes of the game she was playing.

Jane came from a family with several sons, which may well have been part of her attraction to Henry. She also provided Henry what was likely a welcome change from the volatile and outspoken nature of his previous wife. Jane was a calming force in Henry's life. She did make her wishes known, petitioning for Mary to be allowed to return to court,[38] but only after Mary had reluctantly agreed to accept her father's position as head of the Church of England. Mary wasn't the child Henry was seeking. As quickly as he had moved to marry Jane, his patience was tested: it took her much longer to become pregnant than it had taken Katherine or Anne.

Henry had political worries as well as his subjects rebelled against him in October 1536. The revolt began in Yorkshire and spread under the leadership of Robert Aske. It was the most serious rebellion of Henry's rule, and it targeted the break with the Catholic Church and dissolution of the monasteries. Economic hardships caused by poor harvest and high food prices also contributed to the spirit of rebellion against the crown. Henry reacted decisively, and the rebellion was put down. The earl of Derby described an incident between Henry and Jane that gives us a glimpse of the relationship when Jane attempted to speak up for something she wanted. Known to be supportive of Katherine of Aragon and now a champion of Princess Mary, Jane seems to have been sympathetic to the concerns of the rebels. Derby describes her as kneeling before the king and begging him to restore the abbeys. Henry told his wife to get up and not to meddle in his affairs, reminding her of what had happened to her predecessor.[40]

But the tension melted away to happiness when Jane announced she was pregnant the following February. The Seymour family, with Jane's brothers Edward and Tom rising in influence at court, rejoiced, as did Jane and the king. When the queen retired to her chamber in September, anticipation grew as the nation looked forward to the birth of what surely would be a prince this time. This time, all the prophecies of a son were true: Prince Edward was born 12 October 1537. It had taken twenty-eight long years, but Henry VIII finally had a legitimate male heir who would live to succeed him. An elaborate christening was held three days later, with the prince's two half-sisters participating. According to some records, Edward was proclaimed prince of Wales, duke of Cornwall, and earl of Chester days after his birth.[41] Edward himself disputed this in his journal, where he wrote that he was about to be invested as prince of Wales when his father died.[42] But whether officially prince of Wales or not, Henry had a son and heir. His joy was complete. As it turned out, tragedy would soon follow.

Jane Seymour died only days after her moment of glory. Her death has been attributed to everything from a botched C-section operation performed in a desperate attempt to save the baby at the cost of the mother (there is no evidence of this) to the common occurrence of childbirth fever and catching a chill to food poisoning.[43] Whatever the cause, Henry was devastated. He had finally found a wife who could give him a son, and he had lost her. He wrote to Francis I, 'Divine Providence has mingled my joy with the bitterness of the death of her who brought me this happiness.'[44]

We don't know exactly when Henry's relationship with Jane started. We see clear evidence of it in early 1536 when Anne Boleyn is reported to have blamed her miscarriage in part on her grief at the king's dalliance with Jane. It might have started a few months before, but it's unlikely that Henry's serious relationship with Jane lasted more than about two years, and their marriage lasted just fifteen months. Despite the short relationship, Jane had succeeded where Katherine and Anne had failed. She had given Henry the next Tudor king. Unlike her predecessors, Jane was mourned and buried as a queen, and when Henry died ten years later, he wanted to be buried by her side in St George's Chapel at Windsor.

2 Weddings, An Annulment, and a Child Bride

Katherine of Aragon and Anna of Cleves shared something important: the middle name 'of'. That meant each was a political bride with a country or a duchy behind her. These were both international marriages, arranged for dynastic purposes. It didn't feel that way to Henry with Katherine of Aragon. When he married her, she had been in England for seven years. He knew her well. She understood the customs of the English court. She fit in with his family and got along with his sisters and with members of the court. In fact, except for that 'she didn't give me a son' business, Katherine of Aragon was in many ways the ideal consort. She even looked English, with fair skin and auburn hair.

Anna of Cleves was likewise a political bride, and the marriage between Anne and Henry was made for dynastic purposes. Anna was daughter and sister of a duke. But she didn't have the opportunity of spending seven years acclimating herself to the English court and getting to know Henry before their marriage. She was plunged into a strange environment with little preparation. We often hear how she seemed foreign to Henry, how her attire and scent was strange to him. Think about it from her perspective. She was born in Dusseldorf and grew up in the Schloss Burg castle in

6 Very Different Wives   91

Solingen. Her father was associated with moderate reform movements, and her mother was Catholic. An early betrothal to the duke of Lorraine was canceled in 1535.[45] Four years later, her family was in negotiation for her to marry the king of England. Anna was about 25 years old when she made what turned out to be a difficult journey to her new home.

Henry VIII was 50 years old and given his health problems he probably seemed older. His personality had become increasingly tyrannical over the years. He knew he needed another son, and he knew time was not on his side. When his new bride arrived in England, he hurried to Rochester Abbey on 1 January 1540 to meet her. Their first meeting was not a rousing success. Probably tired from her journey, Anna was watching bull baiting out her window when strange men came into her chamber dressed in cloaks, looking like messengers. Anna greeted them briefly, but she didn't pay particular attention. When one of the men said he had a token from the king for a New Year's gift, she thanked him. When he went so far as to embrace her, she is described as being 'abashed, not knowing who it was'. How could she have known the 50-year-old king of England was dressed as a courier? She was expected to see through the disguise and recognise her husband. Instead, she 'regarded him little' and went back to looking out the window.[46]

Henry was not impressed. He had dressed up in the past, bursting in on Katherine of Aragon and even Thomas Wolsey in disguise. Those in his court knew the king's love of games and masques; they knew how to play the game. Anna of Cleves, so recently arrived from a foreign court, did not. When Henry realised she had seen him without the trappings of kingship and had not been impressed, he withdrew and returned in his royal apparel. At this point, Anna recognised him and did him reverence, as did the members of her household. The two of them are described as speaking together.[47] Other accounts differ somewhat. According to one report, he was not able to speak twenty words with her.[48] The king declared himself 'not well handled' and told Cromwell he would not go forward with the marriage except for the great preparations already made and his fear it would cause 'a ruffle in the world'.[49]

Henry's wedding to Anna was spectacular, ironically his most public and grand. The marriage was short and, according to reports, disappointing. After spending a couple of nights with Anna, Henry told Cromwell he left her as good a maid as he found her. He went on to express his concern that if he had to remain in the marriage there would be no more children 'for the comfort of the realm'.[50] By spring, there was another reason the king was dissatisfied with his marriage. The queen's household was restored, opening opportunities for young women to come to court. One of them was Catherine Howard.

Anna of Cleves had spent the months since her marriage learning English and the ways of the court. She was becoming popular with the English people. But Henry was not happy. He revisited the question of Anna's previous precontract with the duke of Lorraine, stating the concern over that had rendered him unable to consummate the marriage. He wished the marriage to be reviewed. Parliament, with the king's allowance and 'the queen's consent too'[51] brought the matter before the Convocation, which met 6 July 1540.[52] At the same time, the lord chancellor met with Queen Anna and her interpreter and told the king that they believed she would agree to his virtuous desire to set aside the marriage.[53]

Anne was sent to Richmond, where she met with the king's commissioners. She must have felt frightened and alone. After all, the stories of Katherine of Aragon and Anne Boleyn, the wives who had displeased Henry, were well known. The commissioners told her the king wished for her consent in annulling the marriage. Perhaps because she had lived with Henry long enough to see his determination to get what he wanted, Anna agreed to his terms. She would give up her designation as queen and provide Henry with the easy way out. She even signed her name 'Anna daughter of Cleves' in recognition of her willingness to give up the title of queen.[55] By the end of July, the marriage was over.

Anna's new life as the king's adopted sister came with status: she had precedent over all the women in the kingdom except the king's wife and his daughters. She received a generous income and estates. In return, she agreed to remain in England. As requested, she wrote to her brother and told him Henry had adopted her as a sister. She appeared various times at court through the rest of Henry's reign.[55] Even though he was married to her for just six months, Henry's relationship with Anna of Cleves lasted more than seven years. She is the only wife to have a positive relationship with him after the marriage ended, although to be fair, that wasn't usually an option.

If the first meeting between Henry VIII and Anna of Cleves had forced him to face his own mortality when his future bride couldn't see his royal splendor shining through, Henry VIII solved that problem by choosing a wife who was sure to be dazzled by him. Catherine may have been a Howard, niece of the duke of Norfolk, and cousin of Anne Boleyn, but her she had grown up far from court. Catherine was raised in the chaotic environment of her father's stepmother, the dowager duchess of Norfolk, whose household was notoriously unsupervised. Katherine's first sexual relationship was with her music teacher, Henry Mannox, when she was only about 12 or 13 years old.[56] A few years later, she had an extended sexual relationship with Francis Dereham.[57] The pair entered into some kind of agreement, calling each other husband and wife. When the dowager duchess found out about the Dereham relationship, she packed Catherine off to court.

In many ways, Catherine was the perfect solution to the king's troubles. She was vivacious and pretty, according to contemporary reports.[58] She was also so inexperienced that the king seemed almost a god-like figure, dazzling in his fine clothes and sparkling jewels. Her family taught her how to behave to best attract and hold the king's attention and desire.[59] The king showered her with gifts, even during his marriage to Anna of Cleves. When the marriage to Anne was annulled, Henry moved quickly. He married Catherine on 28 July 1540. It was his second marriage that year, and he was very enthusiastic about this one.

Henry is described as smitten by his young wife, unable to keep his hands off her even in public.[60] His behaviour was remarked upon by courtiers who were probably entertained by the image of the ageing king and his young wife, the second queen he'd had that year. The French ambassador remarked upon Catherine's beauty and short stature and said the king showed her more affection than he had the others. And speaking of others, the ambassador goes on to say that Anna of Cleves was as cheerful as ever.[61] So, Henry at this moment was happy and it seems two of his wives were happy as well.

Given the difference in age, background, and experience, it's probably not all that surprising that this marriage didn't last. When Henry began referring to Catherine as his rose without a thorn he was imagining a version of her that didn't match reality. His newfound vitality, associated with a fitness routine he began in the early months of this marriage, didn't prevent a serious illness in early 1541. He became incapacitated and depressed.[62] Around the same time, Katherine's past was beginning to catch up with her. Joan Bulmer wrote to Catherine in July 1540, before she married the king, asking for a place at court and adding she is sure the queen of England would not forget her secretary, hinting at their shared past at the Dowager Duchess's.[63] It wasn't just the past that proved a problem – although it's not clear the exact nature of the relationship, Catherine started some kind of relationship with Thomas Culpepper. Culpepper was close to the king, which meant he travelled with Henry and Catherine. And in addition to Culpepper accompanying Catherine and the king on progress, Dereham returned to court and boasted that if the king died, he was certain Katherine would marry him.[64]

When the Northern Progress arrived at Hampton Court in November 1541, Henry held a special Thanksgiving service 1 November for the happiness his new queen had brought him.[65] But the rumours that were swirling were about to become catastrophic for the royal marriage. John Lascelles, whose sister Mary Hall had known Katherine in the duchess's household, told Cranmer about Katherine's youthful indiscretions. Cranmer slipped the king a note sharing the accusations on 2 November, just a day after the Thanksgiving service.

The king reacted with disbelief and self-pity. Desperate to maintain his version of Catherine as 'without a thorn', he ordered an inquiry to prove her innocence. When instead it validated the accusations, the king was so angry he called for a sword so he could kill the queen himself. Then someone in Catherine's household said the looks between Catherine and Culpepper indicated there was love between them.[66] Catherine and her ladies were confined to their chambers. Dereham firmly implicated Culpepper, telling his interrogators that Culpepper had succeeded him in the queen's affections.[67] The king had heard enough. He left Hampton Court, never to see Catherine again.

Catherine was deprived of her title as queen and imprisoned at Syon Abbey on 23 November. When she was found guilty by an act of attainder and transferred to the Tower in February, she would have seen the heads of Culpepper and Dereham on Tower Bridge. On 13 February 1542, about two years after she came to court to join Anna of Cleves' household,

Catherine was beheaded at the Tower of London and buried near her cousin Anne Boleyn.

After Catherine Howard's death, Henry found himself without a wife and without a replacement already in view for the second time in his reign.

3½ Years of Bachelor Life

Early in his reign, Henry VIII had no problem finding a new wife to replace the one he was getting rid of. He married Anne Boleyn while still legally married to Katherine of Aragon. He married Jane Seymour eleven days after executing Anne Boleyn. But twice in the reign, Henry spent some time as a bachelor: after the death of Jane Seymour and after the execution of Katherine Howard.

Henry described himself as devastated after Jane Seymour's death. After all, she had just provided him with a son who would succeed him. The king and his family wore mourning clothes. Henry kept Jane's clothes at Whitehall, and hers was the only portrait that hung in the royal collection by the time of his death.[68] Still, Henry is reported as being 'in good health and as merry as a widower may be' just a few days before Jane's funeral.[69]

It seems Henry was willing to be a little less impetuous in marrying again after Jane's death. He was also finding it a bit more difficult to find a willing bride. The king was now 46 years old and far from the athletic and energetic man who had married Katherine of Aragon and courted Anne Boleyn. His injured leg was getting worse. Even though he recovered, his health continued to deteriorate. Maybe it's not surprising that Christina of Milan famously declined Henry's offer of marriage, replying that if she had two heads she would be willing to give one to him.[70]

In 1540, Henry got back in the marriage game, eventually marrying two women in 1540. But after Catherine Howard's execution he became a bachelor once more. His reaction to his fifth wife's execution was very different from his reaction to Anne Boleyn's. After Catherine's death, Chapuys described Henry as showing greater sorrow for her loss than for the previous wives. He went on to say that the greater sorrow might be because he had no one else in view, no 'plan or female friend to fall back upon'.[71] There had been no question that Henry would marry again after Jane Seymour's death despite his deep mourning for her. In the case of Catherine Howard, the court seemed less sure the king would marry again.

There was another reason people weren't working actively to help the king find a new wife. In the Acts that included the attainder of Katherine Howard, parliament specified that 'an unchaste woman marrying the king shall be guilty of high treason'.[72] In addition, anyone who knew the woman was being deceitful and didn't reveal it would be guilty of treason as well.[73] This dampened the enthusiasm of families to line up one of their relatives to be the king's next wife.

In 1543, the king found someone who was clearly not a virgin but for whom that wasn't a problem, the twice-widowed Katherine Parr. She was at court during the illness of her second husband, Lord Latimer, when she caught the king's eye. He began showing her attention and giving her gifts in February, and in July the two were married. The king's final period of bachelorhood was at an end.

Once, Twice, 3 Times a (Married) Lady

Catherine Howard represented a chance for Henry VIII to believe in a version of himself that was powerful and manly enough to keep a young wife happy. The loss of that belief may have convinced the king to use war in the years following her death as his way of regaining his sense of himself.[74] Early reports about the possibility the king would marry again begin the midst of the battles with Scotland.

In January 1543, Chapuys wrote a detailed letter to Charles V about the ongoing trouble between Henry VIII and the Scots. The English king was trying to arrange for a marriage between the young Mary, Queen of Scots, and his son Edward. In the middle of this discussion is a description of a royal feast, attended by Princess Mary. Chapuys wrote that based on Henry's happier demeanor he was considering marrying again.[75] By early 1543, Henry was indeed courting Katherine Parr.

Katherine was twice married herself. The daughter of Maude Green and Thomas Parr, Katherine first married Edward Borough in 1529. After Borough died in 1532 Katherine married again in 1533, around the time of Anne Boleyn's coronation. Her second husband was John Neville, Baron Latimer. This seems to have been a happy marriage, and Katherine became close to her stepchildren. Latimer was older than his wife, and as his health declined Katherine secured at place in the household of Princess Mary.

Despite their religious differences, Katherine and Mary got along well. They were close in age, Katherine being only four years older. At that time, Katherine was in love with Thomas Seymour, uncle of Prince Edward. But she had attracted another admirer: the king himself. Realising Seymour was a rival, Henry sent him from court.[76] The king began sending gifts to Katherine in February.[77] Whatever her feelings for Seymour, Katherine was wise enough to understand court politics, and she and Henry were married on 12 July 1543. Henry's sixth wedding was a small celebration, as most of them had been. Both of the king's daughters attended the ceremony, which proved a foreshadowing of the positive relationship Katherine would have with both her stepdaughters through the rest of their father's life.

Although she's sometimes described as calm and quiet to the point of sounding drab, Katherine loved fine clothes, jewels, and shoes. She chose colours like crimson to best set off her skin and hair.[78] She wore royal purple for important occasions. She was particularly fond of jewels and shoes. She is described as wearing crosses, diamonds, and headdresses studded with jewels. She also spent freely on shoes, ordering nearly fifty pairs in one year, all of which were of fine colours and some of which were trimmed with gold.[79] In addition to clothing she commissioned for herself, Katherine Parr also inherited the splendid clothing and jewels of her predecessor, Catherine Howard.

In addition to looking the part of queen consort, Katherine behaved in ways that showed her understanding of the royal family. She was a warm and friendly stepmother to the king's three children, developing a relationship with Elizabeth in particular that would last for years. During the end of 1545, probably for the New Year's celebration, she ordered matching outfits for herself, Prince Edward, and Princesses Mary and Elizabeth, all made of cloth of silver.[80] She promoted family atmosphere at the king's court, and she is often credited with encouraging the king to return his daughters to the succession, which he did in 1544.

There was a potential disaster looming when Katherine spoke strongly to the king about religion. Henry's Catholic leaders tried to use this to displace her, attempting to convince Henry she was a danger to the reign because of her extreme reform beliefs. Somehow Katherine found out about the plan and modified her approach, explaining she was only trying to take Henry's mind off his painful leg and other troubles. She assured her husband she was ready to take his counsel. The king replied, 'Then, Kate, we are friends again', and embraced her.[81] The king was content, and the crisis passed. Katherine Parr would remain the queen and Henry's final wife until his death 28 January 1547.

Numbers and Wives

With half a dozen marriages, it's tempting to think of Henry moving through a series of interchangeable wives with similar experiences. But the numbers remind us that was not the case. Yes, the king was married six times. Six wives, six queens, six very different experiences.

Chapter 7

7 Coronations

Although it's about pomp and circumstance and appearance today, the coronation ceremony was an essential part of demonstrating the power of the monarchy in Tudor times. The changes in religion and authority shifted over the reign and was reflected in the seven Tudor coronation ceremonies and the celebrations that surrounded them.

The Crown, Once Worn

It was tradition for a new monarch spent the night before the coronation procession at the Tower of London. For Elizabeth I, it was not her first night at the Tower. During her sister's reign, Elizabeth had been imprisoned for several weeks in the Tower, reportedly staying in the same apartment her mother had occupied before her execution. Elizabeth recognised the full terror of the Tower during her first visit. To delay her imprisonment there, she wrote a lengthy letter to Mary I, protesting her innocence and taking so long that she missed the tide.[1] The next day, when she arrived at the Tower, she initially refused to enter.

Although she might not have expected to leave the Tower alive in 1554, her two-month stay ended on 19 May – the date of her mother's execution. Anne Boleyn had first come to the Tower to be crowned queen and returned three years later to be tried and executed. Elizabeth had come as a prisoner and was on the eighteenth anniversary of her mother's death. In 1554, it must have seemed such a relief to leave the Tower of London alive. Did she think she would ever return?

When Elizabeth returned to the Tower nearly five years later, everything was different. Her sister was dead, and, against all odds, Elizabeth was about to be crowned queen of England. As she embarked on the ceremonies and celebrations that would culminate in the crown being placed on her head, she seemed to think of her mother, who had come to the Tower first as queen and later as prisoner. Elizabeth compared that journey to her own, coming first as prisoner and now as queen. Elizabeth realised the full importance of the journey she had made from prison to monarch.

The medieval coronation ceremony was a sacred rite, a transmission of God's grace to the monarch, represented by the holy oil with which the monarch was anointed. It was also a political event, a way to demonstrate the power and legitimacy of the monarchy. It established the requirement for godly duty and popular obedience. The monarch swore an oath to the country, and the country pledged its loyalty to the monarch.[2]

The coronation ceremony was a service consecrating the new king (until the middle of the Tudor dynasty, it was always a king) with certain fixed rites and binding him with certain promises. The ceremony remained largely the same from 1307 to 1685. The coronation events began with a procession from the Tower, where the monarch stayed after the accession. The procession from the Tower to Westminster was likely instituted in 1377 and lasted until James II's coronation in 1685. When a queen consort was crowned at the same time as the king, a chair of a similar design was placed a step or two lower than the king's.[3]

The Tudor dynasty is one of the most famous in all of royal history, but their actual claim to the throne was tenuous. How important was the coronation ceremony to the Tudors? Were all the monarchs and consorts crowned? And does it matter?

Let's find out. Let's roll the numbers!

The Story of Seven Tudor Coronations

The numbers tell us that the coronation ceremonies, including the events that surrounded them, were vitally important to the Tudors. There was never more than a three-month space between the death of one monarch and the crowning of the next. The numbers tell the stories of a crown won in battle, a crown worn by a child who never grew to rule, and a sovereign's crown worn (for the first time) by two women, both of whom were legally illegitimate and therefore possibly unworthy of it. The coronation numbers also tell the story of Tudor consorts, those who were crowned and those who were not.

The seven Tudor coronations were vital to the success of the dynasty.

7 Coronations

1 Joint Coronation

Despite the number of marriages and consorts in the Tudor dynasty, there was only one joint coronation, where a king and queen consort were crowned together. It happened in 1509 with Henry VIII and his first wife, Katherine of Aragon.

Katherine's life in England up to her wedding to Henry and their coronation had been far from a fairy tale. It's true that she had a grand wedding ceremony when she married Prince Arthur. The people of England were delighted with the young princess, who came from Spain but thanks to her English heritage looked very much like an English rose. Arthur wrote to his father-in-law about his wife in glowing terms, and it certainly seemed the marriage was off to a good start. But it ended quickly and tragically with Arthur's death. Katherine returned to London as Dowager Princess of Wales just a few months after the wedding and became a pawn in the battle for money and power between her father and her former father-in-law.

Katherine had known Prince Henry for years and being kept away from him was one of the things she complained about in letters to her father.[4] The death of Henry VII changed everything for Katherine. Henry VIII was more than ready to take the throne and move away from the unpopular policies and advisors of his father's reign. The new king claimed his father had wanted him to marry Katherine, and that doing so was fulfilling the old king's dying wish. This might have been a handy excuse, as there is no evidence Henry VII wanted his son to marry Katherine at this point. Whatever his reasons, Henry wanted Katherine. He decided to marry her quickly and quietly so they could be crowned together.

Henry and Katherine's marriage was a quiet affair, but their joint coronation was a grand celebration. The couple left the Tower after spending the traditional time there and processed through the city of London where the streets were hung with tapestries and cloth of gold. The next day, Henry and Katherine processed to Westminster Abbey under their royal canopies where they were crowned according to the sacred ceremony. The people were asked if they would have Henry as their king, and they shouted their approval. After the ceremony, the spiritual and temporal lords pledged their loyalty.[5]

The coronation of Henry VIII and Katherine of Aragon was a bright promise. It was celebrated with poetry and music The spectacular celebration was a way to demonstrate that a new era was about to begin, led by a young couple who represented the hope of the future. Stephen Hawes created a text celebrating the coronation and reign, which was printed with a woodcut that shows Henry and Katherine young and full of promise.[6] There was every reason to believe this beautiful young couple would soon have children who would secure the dynasty for generations to come.

2 Kings Crowned Alone
Henry VII: 1485

In contrast to his later reputation as a penny-pincher and miser, Henry VII spent heavily in the first years of his reign. He understood the need to present himself as supremely royal, particularly as he was largely unknown to his subjects. His coronation was the first public event where he had the opportunity to introduce himself to his people as their king.

Henry VII ordered hundreds of yards of scarlet and other fabric to decorate Westminster Abbey, Westminster Hall, and the Tower of London. There was gold and silk for the canopy that was held over the king while he was anointed. The king's chair is described as being covered with silk and gold. There are significant expenditures on saddles for the procession from the Tower to Westminster, including cloth of gold to cover the king's saddle.[7] Considering the importance of the appearance of magnificence and royal authority, Henry VII understood that the cost of such trappings was an essential part of a successful coronation.

Hall describes the procession of Henry VII into London and his coronation as a time of great rejoicing. According to his record, people lined the streets cheering. On 30 October 1485, with all traditional ceremonies, he was crowned king.[8] Henry was relying on the visual trappings of royalty and the tradition of the coronation to convince his people that he was the rightful king and that the time of battles over the throne was behind them.

Henry used several elements of the coronation ceremony to reinforce his monarchy and magnificence. There was the divine will, epitomised in the anointing and the sacred nature of the ceremony as well as the acclamation of the clergy. There was the assent and approval of the commons and the nobility. There was recognition of his personal achievement and worthiness.

There was the connection to the traditions of the past. Henry VII used the coronation to combine all these elements to legitimise his power.[9] Importantly, he stood alone in that ceremony, king in his own right. He was not there because of a marriage to the daughter and heir of Edward IV; he was there because he was the rightful king. After his coronation, he would call parliament, have Elizabeth of York's legitimacy clarified, and then proceed with the marriage. But for his coronation, he was crowned alone, demonstrating his singular right to the throne of England.

Edward VI: 1547

The next individual coronation of a king was more than sixty years later. It was a very different event. The nation had known Edward VI since his birth in 1537, and he was destined to be king from the start. He had not fought for his crown – his father had repeatedly married to get a son and heir. All Edward had to do was survive (although that was not necessarily an easy task in Tudor times). Edward was the only Tudor raised from birth to take the throne. He came to the throne as a child and is the only crowned child king in English history never to achieve adulthood and full power. Edward's coronation was significant in the Tudor dynasty because he was the only Tudor monarch to rule only through a council.

The history of child rulers had not been successful in the 100 years before Edward. Henry VI had become king as an infant, and even though he lived well into adulthood, he never became an effective ruler. Richard II likewise became king as a child, and as he took control, he became a tyrant. Both Richard II and Henry VI were challenged by family members who took their thrones. Then there was Edward V, who was proclaimed king and never crowned. He disappeared in the Tower of London, and his uncle Richard III became king. It was not a happy precedent.

Perhaps that was one of the reasons that so much care went into creating a coronation experience that set young Edward VI up for success as king of England, even though the country was a protectorate once more.

Edward's coronation was pivotal because he was the first English king crowned as supreme head of the Church of England. Edward was formally proclaimed king before his coronation, and the privy council revised the coronation oath and ceremony. Edward's coronation took on religious reform and imperialism.[10] It was highlighted by a sermon by Archbishop

Cranmer, who promised a royal focus on religious reform. Cranmer was also establishing himself as the representation of God's authority, making clear the separation of English religious leadership from Catholicism and emphasizing that Edward's coronation oath had nothing to do with the authority of the pope.[11] The connection between Edward and the biblical Josiah laid out a plan that would lead to the radical change in worship throughout the country.

Edward's coronation was in part a way to communicate a new form of monarchical power in a nation that was on the brink of real religious reform. Cranmer was determined to help Edward VI push reform forward immediately, even before he came of age. His coronation sermon was an address to Edward, calling on the new king to banish papal authority and wipe out the vestiges of Catholicism. Like the biblical Josiah, Edward VI was endowed with divine authority.[12]

All this was at odds with the reality that Edward himself did not have the power to carry out everything envisioned in his coronation. He was the crowned and anointed king, but as a minor he was not yet able to act with the authority his father had. Still, his coronation set the stage for a reign that represented a new age of reform.

2 Queens Consort Crowned Individually
Elizabeth of York: 1487
Although Henry VIII owed his crown in part to his union with Elizabeth of York, two years would pass between their coronations. Three important events occurred between he two ceremonies: 1) parliament reversed the *Titulus Regius* that had declared Edward IV's children illegitimate, making Elizabeth the heir to the Yorkist claim; 2) Henry and Elizabeth had married in January 1486; and 3) Prince Arthur had been born that September. In short, Elizabeth had more than held up her end of the bargain. Henry was aware there were rumblings about the delay in her coronation, so he moved forward in 1487 with the plans for an elaborate event.[13]

In the days before the coronation, Elizabeth and her women withdrew so she would be able to make a significant impression on the people of London. They left Greenwich by boat in a stream of barges decorated with banners, arms, and badges. She was accompanied by her mother-in-law, Margaret Beaufort, Countess of Richmond, along with other political and religious leaders. Music was played as they processed to the Tower of London, where Elizabeth was received by the king in great style.[14]

On 26 November, Elizabeth emerged dressed in 'a kirtle of white cloth of gold of damask, and a mantle of the same suit, furred with ermine', with her hair hanging down and wearing a circle of gold and stones on her head.[15] Her sister Cecily carried her train as they processed on litters through the City to Westminster. The women supporting Elizabeth included Katherine Woodville, Duchess of Bedford, the duchess of Suffolk, the duchess of Norfolk, the countess of Oxford, and all their gentlewomen.[16] It was an important demonstrate that the highest nobles of the land supported the Tudors.

27 November was coronation day. The queen wore a kirtle and mantle of purple velvet and a circle of gold and jewels in her hair. She processed to Westminster Hall under a canopy of state. The earl of Arundel bore the staff, the duke of Suffolk bore the sceptre, and the duke of Bedford bore the crown. the bishops of Winchester and Ely supported her.[17] Elizabeth participated in similar rituals to those her husband had nearly two years earlier, prostrating herself in front of the altar as the archbishop of Canterbury anointed her with holy oil, set the crown upon her head, and gave her the sceptre and rod.[18] An anonymous author described the culmination of the event: 'And then the queen departed with God's blessing, and to the rejoicing of many a true Englishman's heart.'[19]

It was a moment of glory for Elizabeth, a triumphant return to Westminster. She had taken sanctuary there twice. After the defeat of Edward IV by the troops of Henry VI in 1470, Elizabeth Woodville took her children there for safety. Young Elizabeth was just 4 years old at the time. Years later, after Edward IV's death in 1483, Elizabeth Woodville and her daughters, son Richard, and brother went into sanctuary again at Westminster when Richard III took control of the realm. They spent nearly a year there. For Elizabeth of York, having experienced Westminster in such frightening circumstances, it was a vindication to be there as newly crowned queen of England.

Elizabeth of York went from near prisoner to crowned queen consort at Westminster Abbey. The second individually crowned Tudor queen consort went through the opposite journey at the Tower of London: first being there preparing for her coronation in 1533 and returning three years later as a prisoner to await her trial and execution. That consort is Anne Boleyn.

Anne Boleyn: 1533

Henry VIII staged an extraordinary coronation for a queen consort, Anne Boleyn, in 1533. It was intended to prove the legitimacy not only of the marriage but also of the Tudor supremacy and the construction of imperial England.[20] The first day of celebration was the procession by river to the Tower. The queen left Greenwich in an elegant barge accompanied by other richly decorated vessels. Music played along the way. It was described as a marvelous sight, 'the banners and pennants of arms of the crafts, the which were beaten of fine gold, illustring (reflecting) so goodly against the sun'.[21] There was a canon salute as the procession approached the Tower, with a final crescendo as Anne and the lord mayor pulled in.[22] The party was greeted by Tower officers and heralds, officers of state, and finally by the king himself who embraced his wife, laying his hands on both her sides and 'kissing her with great reverence and a joyful countenance'.[23]

The royal couple spent two days in the Tower and on 31 May processed to Westminster. Anne was at the height of her glory, firm in the king's affection and celebrated as Queen after seven long years of waiting. The procession left the Tower and included servants of the French ambassador at the head, followed by the gentlemen of the royal households. Next were knights of the Bath, council members, magnates, and peers. In all, about 300 marched slowly through the city, demonstrating their support of the king and his new marriage. Next came Anne in her litter. She was dressed in white and wore a coronet of gold, her dark hair hanging loose.[24] All this is reminiscent of the appearance of Elizabeth of York as she processed to Westminster.

Of course, Anne's place next to her king was more controversial than Elizabeth of York's had been, and there were notable absences in Anne's procession. Most conspicuous were the king's sister the duchess of Suffolk and the duchess of Norfolk. There were also the reports that the assembled crowds did not cheer or take off their caps to honour the queen, and that Anne had complained to the king when he asked how she liked the decorations 'I liked the city well enough, but I saw a great many caps on heads and heard but few tongues.'[25] Those reports can be countered by others that describe the 'utmost order and tranquility, all the streets and the houses being crowded with persons of every condition, in number truly marvellous; and in many places there were triumphal arches, pageants, and other decorations'.[26]

The importance of the event to Henry VIII is underscored by the risk he was willing to take to put his very pregnant wife through such an ordeal. The year of Anne's birth is not definitively known, but it's most likely 1501, making her 32 years old at the time of her coronation and first pregnancy. In Tudor times, that was thought to be toward the end of a typical woman's ability to bear a healthy child. Katherine of Aragon had conceived her final child at that age, and the pregnancy had not been successful. Henry had staked everything on the birth of a healthy son and heir. For him to put Anne through days of physically draining activities demonstrates the way he viewed the coronation as a personal vindication for himself and his role as an imperial King. It was in that sense a second coronation for the king himself.

On Sunday 1 June, Anne was accompanied by the two archbishops of the realm and other church leaders into Westminster Abbey. She was dressed in coronation robes that included purple velvet with ermine trim and the same golden coronet she had worn previously. Archbishop Cranmer prayed over Anne as she prostrated herself before the altar, anointed her, placed the crown on her head, and gave her the sceptre and rod of ivory. Significantly, when Cranmer crowned Anne, he used St Edward's crown, the most revered object of the royal regalia and something previously reserved for monarchs (not consorts).[27] Following the *Te Deum*, St Edward's crown was replaced with a lighter one.[28] The use of St Edward's crown was possibly used as a visual reminder that the child Anne was visibly carrying would be the next wearer of that monarchial crown.

Anne's coronation took on the questions of legitimate Tudor succession, papal authority, and English imperialism.[29] It was a dramatic statement that Henry VIII was 100 percent committed to his new queen and their child, whatever Catholic Europe or many of his subjects and nobility might think. He managed to put on a glorious public show of support with Anne at the centre. It was the culmination of seven years of courting Anne, navigating with the pope, deciding to go out on his own, and above all doing whatever it took to get a male heir. At the moment of Anne's coronation, it looked like Anne and Henry were on the brink of achieving everything they wanted. Within three years, Anne would be back at the Tower in very different circumstances.

2 Successive Regnant Queens Crowned
Many of the Tudor coronations had their share of controversy. Henry VII did not inherit the throne; he seized it on the battlefield. He was largely unknown to his people. Edward VI was well-known but a child, which meant his coronation as King didn't mean he had the power to rule yet. But none of those coronations were as fraught with controversy as the final two of the Tudor reigns: the coronation of queens regnant Mary and Elizabeth.

Both Mary and Elizabeth were inherently controversial as monarchs. Both had been removed from the royal line of succession by their father and their brother. Both had been declared legally illegitimate by their father meaning they could be considered ineligible to inherit anything, let alone a throne. No woman had successfully ruled the country, despite the attempts of the Empress Matilda and Jane Grey. The reign of woman was deemed monstrous and unnatural.

The act of coronation was essential in establishing the authority of the monarch throughout Tudor times. Although the monarch was considered to have received authority at the death of the previous one (in other words, 'the king is dead, long live the king'), the coronation was a public demonstration of that. All Tudor monarchs were crowned quickly after their predecessor's deaths. The coronation and the ceremonies surrounding it mattered a great deal to Mary and Elizabeth, who were staking a claim as female monarchs.

Previous texts and traditions associated with the coronation, including the fourteenth-century *Liber Regalis* and Henry VI's 'Ryalle Book', made the assumption the monarch would always be male. When planning the coronations of Mary and Elizabeth, councilors and advisers had to address changing religious laws, royal supremacy, illegitimacy, and gender.[30] The specifics of the ceremony during Mary's coronation mattered enormously to Elizabeth's, and both ceremonies mattered to all the queens regnant who followed. Crowning a queen was an enormous undertaking that changed the perception and definition of the monarchy forever.

Before dealing with the complexities of her coronation, Mary had to secure the crown, which had been claimed by Lady Jane Grey. In what can be considered the only successful coup of the Tudor regime, Mary established herself as queen within two weeks of Edward VI's death, garnering enough support that no military action was necessary to convince Jane and her supporters to yield. Some of Mary's councilors suggested that it would be better to hold parliament before the coronation to resolve questions of her legitimacy and intentions regarding religion. However, the Spanish ambassadors counseled Mary to proceed with her coronation as planned and hold parliament afterwards, as was traditional.[31] It was essential that Mary be seen to hold the power and authority to call and preside over parliament, rather than having parliament dictate the terms of her authority.

So, as planned, Mary was crowned on 1 October 1553 in Westminster Abbey. Simon Renard, a loyal supporter and counsellor of Mary's, described her coronation for Spain's Prince Philip (Mary's future husband). On the eve of her coronation, she came from the Tower to Westminster Palace in an open litter covered in brocade, followed by the coach carrying Lady Elizabeth and Anna of Cleves. On the morning of the coronation, the queen processed to the abbey and mounted the scaffolding so the people could see her. The bishop of Winchester officiated and crowned her with three crowns, then anointed her with holy oil.[32] Mary was dressed in crimson robes, the colour traditionally worn by male monarchs and queen consorts. The robes would later become the parliamentary robes, worn on the first official outing of parliament, and symbolising the relationship between monarch, God, and parliament.[33]

Renard's description of the coronation being held according to the old custom is a bit complicated. As parliament had not yet met, the laws of the land remained Protestant, and Mary was crowned according to those laws. However, Mary made the coronation her own by secretly incorporating oil that had been blessed according to Catholic rites rather than using oil that had been 'corrupted' by Edward's religion. The bishop of Arras sent the oil, explaining 'I am sending you the three holy oils the queen asked for' and going on to request 'I beg you to ask the queen's pardon because the vessel is not more ornate.' He was in a hurry to get it there in time for the coronation.[34] Mary also made a change to her oath, which was to obey the existing laws of England, by adding the words 'just and licit.'[35] She and

Edward's council would likely have a very different definition of 'just and licit' laws.

The protocol and regalia used for Mary's coronation followed that of a male monarch. But reports of exactly what happened sometimes differ. The plans for the coronation indicate that Mary would be anointed in six places and crowned three times, exactly as Edward had been. But the ambassadors report that Mary was anointed twice, and the papal envoy reported that Mary was anointed on the shoulders, breast, forehead, and temples. The envoy goes on to describe Mary as holding two sceptres after the coronation: the sceptre of the king and the sceptre of the queen consort. This description doesn't match others, but it might be that it captured Mary as a female monarch who required a new and different representation.

Just five years later, the unthinkable happened – a second woman ascended to the throne. Mary was as dedicated as her father had been to trying to provide the kingdom an heir to succeed her, but she had not produced any children. Eventually, she was compelled to leave her crown to her half-sister, Elizabeth. And the crown wasn't the only thing of Mary's that Elizabeth wore. Elizabeth wore Mary's coronation gown after the mantle and kirtle of cloth of gold and silver tissue were refurbished and altered to fit her.[37]

Elizabeth arrived at the Tower 12 January 1559 to prepare for the coronation and emerged two days later. She processed triumphantly through the city and on to Westminster, wearing a mantle made from 23 yards of gold and silver tissue.[38] Elizabeth's coronation procession celebrated her claim to the throne in a way that distinguished her from her sister while at the same time celebrating the idea of queens.

Elizabeth's inspiration for her coronation came from a woman whose memory she cherished: her mother. Elizabeth studied the account of Anne Boleyn's coronation with care. She used her mother's symbols in her coronation and throughout her reign. Although she spoke openly of her father and not her mother, it's clear from the beginning of her reign that Elizabeth was proud of be Anne Boleyn's daughter. Elizabeth chose to incorporate the symbolism of the Virgin Queen and, like Anne Boleyn, ordered Latin verses sung as she processed to Westminster Abbey.[39]

The connection to Anne Boleyn was an attempt to make an ideological point through pageantry.[40] The opening oration offered the queen loyal hearts that were tied to Protestant themes. The tableau at Gracechurch Street featured a retelling of the origins of the Tudor rose theme, with child actors playing Henry VII and Elizabeth of York, then Henry VIII and Anne Boleyn, and finally Elizabeth herself.[41] The inclusion of Anne Boleyn at this point is interesting. She demonstrated Elizabeth's pure English claim to the throne, separating her from the worries of Mary I being too closely tied with Spain and Rome. Anne's presence in her daughter's coronation procession shows Elizabeth's commitment to her mother's memory. Furthermore, presenting Anne as Henry's true wife in the pageant reinforced Elizabeth's legitimacy. Elizabeth did not take the further step of having parliament reinstate her parents' marriage; she simply moved on as if the issue were already settled. Other pageants along the route likewise celebrated the English, Protestant queen.

Descriptions of the coronation ceremony reveal some of its controversies, including what happened during the mass. Like her sister before her, Elizabeth was crowned before parliament met, meaning she too faced the tension of being crowned according to religious ceremonies she did not adhere to. Eyewitness reports about specifics of the mass offer contradictory descriptions. It's not even clear who celebrated the mass, Bishop Oglethorpe or Dean Carew of the Chapel Royal. Given the nature of the reports, it's considered most likely that the consecrated host was probably not elevated, and Elizabeth was at this point hidden from view.[42]

In accordance with tradition, Elizabeth was proclaimed queen four times, and the assembled crowd cheered in approval. She took the oath to uphold the law, and then the bishop of Carlisle anointed her. To the sound of trumpets, the coronation ring was placed on her finger, and she was crowned. Following tradition, she was crowned first with St Edward's crown, the culmination of the event in 1533 when Anne Boleyn had been crowned with St Edward's crown while pregnant with her. Then she was crowned with the Imperial crown of England. Finally, that crown was replaced with a lighter crown, which may have been the one created for Anne Boleyn.[43] She then walked from the abbey to Westminster Hall, orb and sceptre in hand, with a smiling countenance for all.[44]

The coronations of Mary and Elizabeth sought to balance tradition and change in a way that created a new type of monarch: a reigning queen. The ritual was important to both of them, and each queen sought to balance political, religious, and royal expectations with personal views and beliefs. The two images we have of Mary and Elizabeth associated with their coronations are the page from Mary's first plea roll and the later portrait of Elizabeth (thought to be a copy of an earlier original). They are similar, dressed in cloth of gold with their hair flowing, asserting their authority and power.

Bonus: 1 Possible Battlefield Coronation

One of the most storied and fanciful coronations of the Tudor dynasty might not have happened at all. It's the legend of Henry VII being crowned king immediately after the Battle of Bosworth, right there on the battlefield. If true, that would make it the first, although unofficial, coronation of the Tudor regime.

The story goes that the crown Richard III had worn into battle had been knocked off in the fight. Thomas Stanley, who was married to Henry's mother Margaret Beaufort, took the crown and placed it on Henry's head. The troops and people rejoiced. Although this is simply legend, it does reinforce the significance of the coronation ceremony as making real the transfer of authority from one king to the next. It also associates the notion of popular election of the monarch, something that Henry VII needed since he was essentially unknown in the country he was about to rule.[45] In any case, Henry VII had his official coronation at Westminster weeks after the legendary one of the battlefield.

Numbers and Coronations

A coronation in Westminster Abbey was a tradition that strengthened the monarchy itself as well as the individual monarch. During the coronation, the monarch was anointed with holy oil, a sign that God had selected the individual to rule. In addition, the coronation of consorts tells us a great deal about their spouses. Henry VII did not marry Elizabeth of York until after his own coronation, and she was not crowned until after the birth of their son Arthur. Henry VIII, in contrast, quickly married Katherine of Aragon and she was crowned alongside him. He later staged an elaborate coronation ceremony for Anne Boleyn in defiance of the pope and many of his subjects, who disapproved of the marriage. Two regnant queens crowned back-to-back is one of the many things that set the Tudor dynasty apart from history and from the future.

The coronation celebrations, including the traditions and events that surrounded them, were a vital experience of power and authority throughout the Tudor dynasty. A coronation did not guarantee a monarch would be safe on the throne: Richard II, Henry VI, and Richard III were recent (to the Tudors) examples of crowned kings losing their thrones. Mary, Queen of Scots, was forced to abdicate during Elizabeth's reign. Still, the coronation set the Tudor monarchs more firmly on their thrones and made manifest their claim to diving, political, and popular support.

Chapter 8

8 Royal Road Trips

Most people in sixteenth-century England would never visit London, never be welcomed at court, and certainly never have the chance to have an official audience with the monarch. Even so, public perception of the monarch and the royal court was essential in inspiring loyalty from the people. The Tudors used progresses through the country to demonstrate their magnificence, their authority, and their power to the public.

The Court on the Move

In the summer of 1578, Elizabeth went on progress into East Anglia, travelling for about a week into Norwich. This was an area the queen had not visited extensively before and would not visit again. There were concerns – Thomas Howard, the greatest magnate of East Anglia, had become involved in the plots surrounded Mary, Queen of Scots, and was executed just six years previously. The religious debate continued to rage, as did plots surrounding the Scots queen. Would Elizabeth be well received in the area?

Elizabeth was eager to counter such concerns by showing herself as a magnificent queen, fully in control of her realm, to as many people as possible. This and other progresses offered Elizabeth the chance to interact personally with her people, something she had done with great success since the time of her coronation. She never doubted her people's love, but at the same time she knew the necessity of nurturing it. Her regal presence, publicly displayed as she travelled in open carriages or on horseback, was one way of doing so. She spends time at numerous places, meeting with subjects and carrying out her work in full view of her people, which allowed her to display the magic of her touch. Whenever she travelled, Elizabeth was the 'centrepiece of a magnificent procession, with her household officers, ladies-in-waiting' and others.[1] It was a travelling pageant with the queen as star.

The longest-reigning Tudor, Elizabeth used progresses to shape the relationship between herself and her people. She made herself visible and available, travelling slowly and stopping to hear pageants and accept gifts along the way. In the cities where she stopped, she attended and participated in pageants and speeches, hearing the requests of individuals and the town leaders. Rulers before and after the Tudors travelled through the country as well, but Tudor progresses went well beyond the average – just like everything else about the dynasty.

Progresses were expensive and took extraordinary effort to pull off successfully. The entire royal court had to be transported, fed, clothed, and entertained for weeks in various locations. The logistics were a nightmare. For such a public relations exercise and the political benefit of strengthening public support, the Tudors were willing to pay the price. But was it worth it?

Let's find out. Let's roll the numbers!

8 Royal Road Trips that Shaped the Dynasty

The numbers tell us that the royal progresses had a significant impact on the perception of Tudor rulers outside of London. But they also reveal the crushing expense and controversial politics attempted by the monarch and court as well as the hosts. It was a public display of a complicated relationship.

The Tudor court was always on the move. Basic hygiene required that the court remain in a palace for just a few weeks at a time. During the spring and summer, those moves went beyond London into other parts of the country. This was for practical reasons in some ways – plague and other illnesses often came during these months, and London was crowded and therefore dangerous. Getting out of the city made good sense to avoid contagion and crowds.

But beyond the need for cleaning and the advantage of avoiding disease, the most important motive for spring and summer progresses was to see and be seen. It was important for the monarch to visit worrisome areas of the country. That way, the highest figures in the government could identify areas where trouble was brewing and make a preemptive strike to settle things down. In addition, the physical presence of majesty could be enough to convince would-be rebels to think twice about causing trouble. The size of the household and presence of guards and knights was a visual reminder of the power of the monarch.

Tudor progresses give us insight into the potential power of the royal presence.

1 Progress to Kick Things Off
Henry VII recognised that despite his success at Bosworth and magnificent coronation, there were places in the country that did not support him. For example, when royal emissary Sir Roger Cotam went to proclaim Henry VII's reign in York, he received city officials privately in his inn because he was worried about his safety if he made the proclamation in public.[2] York had been loyal to Richard III, as had other northern cities. Richard's supporters were numerous and potentially dangerous. Therefore, Henry thought it wise to head north on his first royal progress.[3]

Throughout his reign, Henry VII used progresses to visit important areas of the country, particularly those who were causing him trouble, and show off his power and authority. The progress provided an invitation for the people to demonstrate their loyalty and an opportunity for the king to demonstrate concern for his people and reward them for being on side. Tudor progresses were a two-way conversation with people outside of London, communicating loyalty and interest and support both ways. Henry VII chose to use that tool with special care in areas where loyalty was questionable.

Henry VII's first progress was to York, Worcester, Hereford, Gloucester, and Bristol in 1486. The king and queen left in spring 1486, less than five months after Henry's coronation and two months after his marriage to Elizabeth of York. The trip included stops in Waltham Holy Cross, Cambridge, Huntingdon, and Stamford before arriving in Lincoln for Easter celebrations. The king and queen were accompanied by 200 bowmen in an attempt to demonstrate his power to the north of England and discourage any rebellions or other claims to the throne. Civic authorities created elaborate pageants to incorporate history and myth to prove their loyalty to the king.[4]

Henry VII drew attention to his piety by celebrating Easter in Lincoln. On Holy Thursday, he washed the feet of twenty-nine poor men, the number representing each year of his age. He also distributed alms to them and other poor members of the city. He worshipped with the community, participating in each morning's High Mass and in evensong. He visited religious houses in several of the cities along the progress route. By celebrating Easter at Lincoln, the king tied his royal power to his piety, showing himself at High Mass and Evensong.[5] He maintained the dual focus on politics and religion through the progress, hearing services in Doncaster, Worcester, Gloucester, and Bristol.[6]

After Easter, Henry VII went on to Nottingham, then north to Doncaster, Pontefract, and Tadcaster before arriving in York. He spent about a week in the stronghold of his predecessor and recently vanquished enemy, Richard III. As he came closer to York his retinue swelled in number and glory, with many bishops, earls, lords, knights, esquires, gentlemen, and yeomen joining the progress to show military strength. The king personally took on greater glory at York, dressing in ermine robes and cloth of gold. It was a deliberate show of regal presence, as the king knew there were some in the area who hoped to raise insurrections.[7]

Henry's presence in York was especially important in the early moments of his reign, but the progress did not eliminate challenges or rebellions. Even while York was flattering the king with grand pageants and celebrations, uprisings were being planned. The Tudor king knew the importance of projecting an image of royalty and gaining the support of the local people to prevent a rebellion's success. On the eve of St George, Henry appeared in all his finery and celebrated the Fast of the Garter, despite growing rumours of revolt.[8] Reports show that Henry celebrated with all the trappings, as king and as host.[9]

The performances of this first progress of Henry VII and Elizabeth of York gave their new subjects a chance to tell their stories to the new king and queen. Officials offered the king a key to their cities, which represented in many ways the key to their hearts and loyalty. In return, the royals demonstrated the strength of the dynasty and its promise that the years of war and bloodshed were behind them. The king knew his first progress was about more than sharing stories with his people. There is evidence that

Henry understood the political implications of a strong showing in the heartland of Yorkist support.[10]

Henry VII would surely have considered his three-month tour of the north of England a success. He had made important steps in consolidating support for his reign and his family. Three months later, he would celebrate another essential component of the dynasty he envisioned: the birth of his son, Arthur. The first year of his reign had put the dynasty on solid ground. The king's visit to the north was part of that success. The pageantry of this first Tudor progress set the stage for the years of progresses to follow. Henry's progresses, built on the success of his first one, contributed to his success in consolidating the country around his reign.

1 Over the Top International Event
The Field of Cloth of Gold in 1520 was a defining example of using royal excess to celebrate royal success. The courts of Henry VIII and Francis I met to celebrate a treaty between Henry and Francis and reset the troubled relationship between England and France. It was as if Henry had recognised the limitations to his goal of making magnificent war and decided to make magnificent peace instead. Everything about the event appealed to the pride of the two kings at the centre, and Henry and Francis spared no effort to outdo the other. Peace could be as noble a goal as victory in battle if it was created and celebrated in the right way.[11]

The site was south of the village of Andres, about halfway between the English castle at Guines and the French castle at Ardes. One of the main concerns of the English was to construct a temporary palace in the field, a marvelous structure that Henry VIII intended as a bold statement: he was so wealthy and powerful he could create a lavish structure for a temporary event. When completed, it was 238 square feet. The walls were built on stone foundations and were 8 feet high. There was a cornice at the top surmounted by a frieze decorated in Italian style and featuring four brick towers.[12] Inside, there were apartments for Cardinal Wolsey, King Henry VIII, and Queen Katherine of Aragon and their courts. Together, the interior and exterior were intended to impress all who saw it with Henry's personal wealth and splendor. It was hung with tapestries and linens. Historian and author Glenn Richardson estimates the cost of constructing and furnishing the temporary palace to be about £10,000.[13]

The activities were likewise carefully constructed to allow the two kings to show off. To eliminate the politically disastrous question of which monarch would hold precedence at official feasts, Queen Claude of France hosted Henry VIII and Queen Katherine hosted Francis I. The dinnerware for the three main feasts was gold for the kings and gold-plated silver for the queens. All the tableware was the best available. The English brought some of the furnishings from England to allow them to show off the best of court trappings. The finest and rarest food was served, featuring around fifty different dishes over the three courses and including swans and peacocks, cooked and redressed in the plumage and decorated in gold; venison and other meat pies; porpoises and fish; and a dolphin. There were also pears and fruit jellies, candied orange peels, wafers, and gingerbread. The subtleties, small sculptures crafted from sugar and marzipan, represented religious scenes.[14]

Not everyone was impressed with the event and its outcome. Bishop Fisher noted the changeable nature of the two kings who, despite the grand display of friendship, were at war within a couple of years. Fisher also pointed out that participation was costly and plunged some courtiers into poverty.[15] But the events of the Field of Cloth of Gold laid the foundation of Henry and Francis's relationship from 1527 onward. It reinforced England's relationship with the Continent. It was echoed in the fall of 1532 when Henry travelled to France once more to meet with Francis and secure his support for the break with Rome and marriage to Anne Boleyn. It did not bring permanent peace; competition and battles between the two men continued until they made their final peace agreement in 1546. Both kings died the next year.

Was the Field of Cloth of Gold successful? It depends how you define success. As historian Glenn Richardson put it, 'It was literally and metaphorically a war game which depended on spectacle for success. It was a very conspicuous piece of royal Renaissance "self-fashioning," of ostentatious material display and political theatre, designed to present the power of monarchy in a dynamic and compelling way.'[16]

1 Missed Meeting for Henry and 1 Big Problem for Catherine Howard
Although the journey to France for the Field of Cloth of Gold was a unique event, it was common for Henry VIII and his court to go on progress

during the summer. Like his father, Henry VIII often travelled to areas that had proven problematic so he could reinforce the absolute nature of his reign and power.

Henry VIII's 1541 progress headed north and planned to reach York by September. There are two reasons given for this destination: to demonstrate to anyone associated with or supportive of the Pilgrimage of Grace and Percy rebellions that the king's control was absolute and to meet his nephew James V of Scotland and potentially resolve ongoing difficulties. A more personal reason was to show off his young wife, Catherine Howard, with whom the king was besotted.

The king and his court left London on 30 June with a huge entourage. Although local areas provided some of the food and lodging for the royal court, Henry's councilors made sure the king lacked nothing while the court was on the road. The French ambassador estimated that 4,000 to 5,000 horses and 200 tents were part of the procession.[17] The itinerary included Enfield, St Albans, Dunstable, Ampthill, Northampton, Gainsborough, Pontefract, Hull, and York, as well as other stops along the way. The council had to be ready to shift plans on a moment's notice. The king was not afraid to deviate from the planned schedule. He was extremely worried about getting plague or any other disease, so he didn't hesitate to cancel a visit or extend a stay. After all, it was his travelling party. The areas that formerly supported rebels made it clear they were ready to make amends and support the king. When the king processed grandly through the area, he 'received the humble submission of the people for their offence, with various sums of money offered by the principal towns, as a sort of propitiatory tribute for forgiveness'.[18]

The king was received with great pomp in the north: 'the town of Stanford gave the king 20 pounds, and Lincoln presented 40 pounds, and Boston 50 pounds, that part which is called Linsey gave 300 pounds … and the Church of Lincoln gave 50 pounds.'[19] At York 200 gentlemen and 4,000 yeomen and serving men met the king, 'which on their knees made a submission, by the mouth of Sir Robert Bowes, and gave to the king 600 pounds'. Other local leaders describe their support in similar words. If part of Henry's goal was to reinforce his reign over the north, according to Hall, he succeeded.

But there were still sore points. Trouble with Scotland was an ongoing theme of Henry VIII's reign. The English king experienced early success thanks to the efforts of Katherine of Aragon and her leadership during the Battle of Flodden back in 1513. But there were ongoing squabbles. In 1541, needed James V to break with Rome and not provide a stronghold for the French and Catholicism on England's northern border. Unwilling to commit to Henry's request, James did not to appear at the arranged meeting with Henry in York. Henry headed south, disappointed over the failed meeting with James V and troubled by a report that his son Edward had contracted malaria. Terrified of losing his only legitimate heir, Henry rushed to Hampton Court.[20]

It turned out Edward was fine, but Henry's stay in Hampton Court still became a tragedy for the king. It was there that the accusations about Catherine Howard came to light. After celebrating his marriage, the king received a note from Cranmer raising concerns about the queen's behavior in her youth. When an investigation proved the accusations true, Henry was broken hearted and furious. He renounced his young queen and vowed never to see her again. Catherine was confined in her rooms at Hampton Court and interrogated about Mannox and Dereham. There is a legend that she managed to break free from the guards and run screaming toward the king, begging for mercy. According to legend, her ghost haunts the corridor of Hampton Court Palace.

For Henry, the progress that had begun with so much potential and celebration, ended in disaster. The same was true of his fifth marriage. After Catherine's execution on 13 February 1542, Henry would wait more than a year before marrying again. He would never regain the bravado he displayed during the heyday of his marriage to Catherine Howard early in the progress.

2 Youthful Progresses of Edward VI

Although Edward is sometimes thought to have been of generally poor heath, contemporary descriptions of his activities indicate this was not the case. He enjoyed vigorous sports such as hunting and fencing. Just as Henry VII had kept his son and heir away from dangerous activities, Henry VIII did the same with Edward. However, unlike his father, Edward became king at such a young age that he continued to be subject to the protectiveness of a council. An Italian visitor observed that Edward seemed to enjoy hunting as an excuse to be able to ride more than the council would otherwise allow.[21]

Edward enjoyed the trappings of royalty as well as physical activity. His court was an extravagant one, with the number of servants increasing over the reign. The young king loved music, and his court was full of performers such as John Fowler, Peter and Philip van Wilder, and a children's choir.[22] Edward appreciated performance, and this was also true of the two progresses Edward VI took in 1550 and 1552.

We have a contemporary record of the 1552 progress: Edward's own account. He wrote to his friend and servant Barnaby Fitzpatrick in August to describe the events of the summer. While Barnaby had been fighting in France, Edward reported 'we have been occupied in killing of wild beasts, in pleasant journeys, in good fare, in viewing of fair countries, and rather have sought hot to fortify our own than to spoil another man's'.[23] The progress continued to Petworth and then the home of Sir Anthony Browne, where they had a great feast. The journey continued to Warblington and Waltham, where the king enjoyed 'both good hunting and good cheer'.[24]

Although it seems the progress was focused on pleasure, Edward also used his time in Portsmouth to review the status of the bulwarks and noted the need for an upgrade, writing 'We find the bulwarks chargeable, massy, well-rampaired; but ill-fashioned, ill-flanked, and set in unmeet places, the town weak in comparison of that it ought to be.' Edward had plans for improvement, 'For the more strength thereof we have devised two strong castles on either side of the haven, at the mouth thereof.' The progress then went to Southampton. The king commented favourably on the work the people of the town had done in sprucing up the town and it walls and praised the handsome town and the citizens that 'made great cheer, and many of them kept costly tables'.[25]

The 1552 progress was Edward's first (and only) major cross-country journey through the south. Some have wondered about a possible association with the king leaving London and the controversies surrounding the publication of the second prayer book, but that does not seem to be the case. There were troubles associated with the publication of the second book, forcing Cranmer to do some strategic negotiating in the privy council, but the king's progress seems to have been unaffected by this.[26]

Edward had inherited his father's sense of magnificence. Whether in London or on the road, Edward presented a dazzling display of royal opulence to reinforce his authority. His inventory includes books and daggers decorated with gold and diamonds. He added fine jewels to his father's collection, notably purchasing 'The Three Brothers' ornament, which included three large rubies, a large diamond, and a great pearl.[27] He was enthusiastic about personal display and dressed in the finest clothes and jewels available. His short reign didn't include the politically focused progresses that had marked the reigns of his father and grandfather, but he did take the opportunity to display his royal image to his people.

2 Become 1: Mary's Marriage Progress

Of all the Tudor monarchs, Mary I made the least use of royal progresses as a tool to promote herself and her authority to her people. In fact, Mary's most successful 'progress' happened before she was crowned. When Jane Grey was proclaimed queen of England, Mary's journey to East Anglia and Kenning Hall, to Framlingham Castle in Suffolk, and finally to London was an extraordinary progress that enabled her to raise enough support to claim the crown. She gathered military strength and cheering crowds in villages along the way. On 29 July 1553, Mary rode triumphantly into and through London.[28] She was not yet crowned queen, and it was not an official progress – more of a successful coup. Still, it had the feel of demonstrating her power and authority to her subjects, who showed their loyalty in return.

A year later, Mary took a short progress in conjunction with her marriage to Philip II. Once parliament ratified the marriage treaty, Mary went ahead with her plans to celebrate the wedding. She opted for a 'destination wedding' in Winchester because of fears of protests in London. Her choice of husband was not popular with the people, and the Wyatt rebellion had proven the level of unrest that was possible. In June, detailed plans were created by Renard to guide Philip about his behaviour when coming to England. It included these instructions:

- Item, when his Highness enters the kingdom, he will be well-advised to caress the nobility and be affable, show himself often to the people, prove that he wishes to take no share in the administration, but leave it all to the council …

- Item, it will be well to show a benign countenance to the people and lead them to look for kindness, justice, and liberty.
- Item, as his Highness knows no English it will be well to select an interpreter and have him among his attendants so that he may converse with the English ...
- Item, for his Highness's greater safety it might be arranged with the nobles who are coming with him that they should bring soldiers dressed in their liveries instead of pages and lackeys, in order that they may be of use if necessity arises ...
- Item, let his Highness, on landing, be openly armed.
- Item, let the vessels remain near the ports ... [29]

In other words, this marriage was a political one, for all Mary's protestations of the great love she had for her husband. It was unpopular, and every element was carefully managed for the public display.

The ceremony was planned for Winchester Cathedral, which was the episcopal seat of Bishop Gardiner. Mary even commissioned a special suit for Philip to wear when he entered the city. On 16 June, Mary and the court left Richmond for Winchester.

Philip arrived on 19 July, was graciously greeted and presented with the Order of the Garter. The earl of Arundel offered a household of 350 for Philip's use, but Philip had brought his own, which caused some tension. Philip and Mary sent messages and gifts to each other, and a couple of days later Philip road to Winchester. Upon arrival he went to the cathedral for prayer and then to the dean's house to meet the queen.[30]

The first wedding of an English queen regnant was celebrated 4 August 1554. It was designed to reinforce the hopes of the union. Philip was dressed grandly, covered in gold and pearls, set off by the Order of the Garter emblem on his leg and the St George collar and a splendid diamond at his neck. Mary was dressed in silver cloth with a rich collar, embellished with gold and jeweled adornment. The diamond Philip had given her was at the centre of the jewelry she wore.[31]

After spending time in Winchester, Mary and Philip's progression returned to London. On 3 August the royal couple stopped at Windsor so Philip could be installed as head of the Order of the Garter. Philip, referred to as 'the king', held a chapter of the order and the couple lodged several days at Windsor Castle.³² On 11 August, the couple went to Richmond as final preparations were made for their entry into London. A week later, they entered London, greeted by the lord mayor and followed by the nobility of England and Spain. The lord mayor gave Mary the mace, and she and Philip entered the city with two swords of state between them.

Mary's wedding celebration and journey would be the only progress of her reign. Although the event was as much about the wedding as the progress, it included the same elements: desire to dress to impress the people, need to deal with politics, interactions with foreign dignitaries, and the logistics of transporting the government through the kingdom.

1 Queen with Many Progresses

Unlike her two predecessors, Elizabeth fully embraced the value of making regular progresses from the beginning of her reign. Just six months after her coronation in January 1559, she embarked on a progress to Kent and Surrey. She left London 17 July for Dartford, visiting Lord Henry Cobham at Cobham Hall. He welcomed her warmly. A few days later, she left and stopped at Gillingham and Otford on her way to Eltham Palace. Next the earl of Arundel hosted her at Nonsuch, and a few days later she was off to Hampton Court. Then she was off to visit her archbishop of Canterbury, Matthew Parker, at Croyden. Then Lord Edward Fiennes de Clinton, the lord admiral, welcomed her to his home in Surrey. All along the way, the queen was entertained with plays and pageants. The lord admiral had even built a banqueting house for the visit where he presented a masque and his best food and drink.³³

Other early progresses followed similar patterns, with nearby stays, loyal hosts, extensive and expensive entertainments from individuals and villages, and the warmth of loyal support. The lack of progress in 1562 is likely because of a smallpox epidemic at court, the same one that nearly killed the queen that October. But other years saw the queen visiting towns and manors so that she could see and be seen by a cross-section of her subjects. There were always cheering crowds and ringing bells. There were always magnificent displays by the court and eager presentations and petitions by loyal subjects.

19 Days at Kenilworth

As queen, Elizabeth lived in a world where religion and politics were intertwined, when her actions were constantly watched and evaluated, and where the struggle for power occurred on all levels. Progresses were opportunities to bring together various people from the court, from the council, and from the country and play out power struggles in a variety of ways. The collision of religion, politics, and personal desire played out in fascinating ways in one of the most famous episodes of Elizabeth's reign: the progress to Robert Dudley's Kenilworth in 1575. It occurred at a time of worries about the succession, Spanish and Catholic tensions in the Netherlands, divisions in Elizabeth's privy council, and Mary, Queen of Scots, encouraging Catholic rebellions.

In the midst of this tension, the royal court headed to Kenilworth. Dudley viewed the visit as an ideal opportunity to advance his personal and political ambitions. The entertainment was on a scale that had never been seen before. The event was described as producing 'the splendor far exceeded what had anywhere else been given', with Dudley exerting 'his whole munificence in a manner so splendid, as to claim a remembrance even in the Annals of our Country'.[34] Two contemporary accounts describe the planned and actual entertainment that occurred between 9 and 27 of July: 'The Princely Pleasures at the Court at Kenilworth' by George Gascoigne and 'A Letter, wherein part of the entertainment unto the Queen's Majesty' by Robert Laneham (or Langham). The two descriptions don't always agree, which some scholars believe indicates that Gascoigne included entertainments that the queen censored because they offended her. By including them in his printed account, Gascoigne was promoting Dudley's story rather than Elizabeth's.[35]

Entertainments during the queen's stay focused on the unique relationship between Elizabeth and Dudley. But for complicated reasons, it seems some of the masques and plays were not performed as planned.[36] Dudley had designed some entertainments to project himself as the rescuer of Elizabeth and as the warrior who could promote the Protestant cause abroad.[37] Elizabeth was fiercely protective of her place on the throne and the power it involved; she did not see herself as needing to be rescued and did not take kindly to entertainments that seemed to portray her as such.[38] The queen also resented Dudley's focus on her need to marry. The need of an heir was a common theme of Elizabeth's reign, but it was not one she welcomed. She had long insisted on her ability to rule on her own. It was a complicated issue, and Elizabeth was not going to watch a performance that stated she needed to marry and share her power with anyone.

In addition to using literary entertainments to convince the queen to marry him, Dudley used portraiture. Studies show that Dudley's home included as many as fifty portraits, including four of himself and the Elizabeth that had been specially commissioned for the progress. Dudley reinforced his special status with the queen; he's the only known courtier to have publicly displayed large portraits of himself and Elizabeth that appeared to be complementary to each other.[39] Just as the entertainments had displayed competition between Dudley's and Elizabeth's interests,[40] the portraits seem to have elements of competition as well. As Elizabeth Goldring points out, the portraits of Dudley emphasise his marital and military ambitions, and these did not always coincide with Elizabeth's.[41] Although this was the first time portraits were part of the overall pageantry presented for the queen, it was not the last. Dudley's use of portraits as part of his display is another way the Kenilworth progress represented an innovation.[42]

The fanciful and elaborate nature of the productions lead some to believe they might have been seen by a young William Shakespeare and provided inspiration for parts of *A Midsummer Night's Dream*. Young Shakespeare was 11 at the time, and his father John was mayor of Stratford. Their home in Stratford was only about twelve miles from the festivities, so it's not out of the question to imagine them in the audience. Laneham's account mentions the castle landscape shifting from dale to hill, and Shakespeare uses the words in combination twice in *Midsummer*. The entertainments included a water pageant featuring a mechanical dolphin and a mermaid accompanied by musical instruments. That seems to be echoed in Act II, scene 1 of the play:

> Since once I sat upon a promontory,
> And heard a mermaid on a dolphin's back
> Uttering such dulcet and harmonious breath
> That the rude sea grew civil at her song,
> And certain stars shot madly from their spheres
> To hear the sea-maid's music.

There is another possible allusion to Shakespeare in the overall failure of the event to win the queen's hand. At least since his wife's death in 1560, Dudley had been hoping to marry the queen. For years he had used pageants and performances to advance his suit, staging productions that warned against foreign marriage and promoted his qualities as a protector, lover, and husband. But ultimately, he failed to win the queen at Kenilworth. In *Midsummer*, Oberon reflects (II.1):

> That very time I saw, but thou couldst not,
> Flying between the cold moon and the earth,
> Cupid all arm'd: a certain aim he took
> At a fair vestal throned by the west,
> And loosed his love-shaft smartly from his bow,
> As it should pierce a hundred thousand hearts'
> But I might see young Cupid's fiery shaft
> Quench'd in the chaste beams of the watery moon,
> And the imperial votaress passed on,
> In maiden meditation, fancy-free.

It's thought the play was written around 1595, when Elizabeth surely would have been happy to think of herself as 'fancy-free'. There's no way to know if Shakespeare actually saw the Kenilworth entertainment, but he certainly would have been able to learn about it from printed accounts. The use of imagery of the progress entertainments and plays such as *Midsummer* reflects the power of plays and pageantry throughout Elizabeth's reign.

1 Final Progress of the Tudor Dynasty

As Elizabeth's rule went into the new century, she began to show some signs of fatigue. Concerned, Robert Cecil (who had replaced his father) urged to remain in or near London. But in the summer of 1602, Elizabeth was determined to go on her annual progress. She enjoyed the change of routine and relished her time outdoors hunting and hawking.

What turned out to be Elizabeth's final progress was cut short because of bad weather and fear of illness. She was gone part of July and August. The key event was her stay at Harefield in Middlesex, hosted by Sir Thomas Egerton, lord keeper of the Great Seal. His estate was transformed into a theatre for the spectacular entertainments. On the first day of the visit, after the queen alighted from her horse, she was met by Time and Place, who stated they would be suspended for the duration of her stay.[43] The dialogue included Time explaining she was there 'to entertain the wonder of this time', and Place followed by stating, 'no place is great enough to receive her'. After a brief discussion, Place delivered the final lines, 'Time, Place, Persons, and all other circumstances do concur altogether in bidding her welcome.'[44]

Place also made clear that the Egertons were the owners of this particular place, while the queen and her court were visitors. A staged disagreement between the bailiff and dairymaid about how the visitors will be welcomed included the line 'I will make way for these strangers', suggesting clearly that Elizabeth is a stranger who must wait to be escorted in.[45] Even so, once the court took up residence at the Egerton home, that location became the court – the court was wherever the queen was. Household and court became one, the centre of the government merged with the people. There was a role for Elizabeth to play at the court and at the household, and she participated actively in entertainments throughout the progress.

The queen's progress to Harefield provides an example of the tremendous cost of hosting these events. Lord Egerton spent nearly £1,300 entertaining Elizabeth over a four-day period. He had to build new ovens and employ more than 120 additional artisans to create the appropriate venue for the visit and accompanying entertainment. Extending staff and even extending buildings was not unusual when hosting the royal court on progress. William Cecil stated he had originally intended his home at Theobalds to be fairly modest but had enlarged it because of Elizabeth's frequent visits. When hosting Elizabeth in 1591, the earl of Hertford had added extensions to his home and erected new pavilions, as well as a temporary kitchen.[46]

Portraiture, which was an element of the 1575 progress to Kenilworth, might also have played a part in the 1602 progress. The famous 'Rainbow' portrait of Queen Elizabeth is thought by scholars some to be a record of the queen's appearance at a masque. The details of the clothing and jewelry are full of symbolism and might have little to do with reality.[47] There are elements of the 1602 progress that make a connection to the portrait.

Lady Walsingham presented the queen the robe of rainbows, with a poem that included several verses that referenced Iris, rain, and rainbows, including:

> But this he saith, that to his feast
> Cometh Iris, an unbidden guest,
> In her moist robe of collars grey,
> And she cometh, she ever stays
> For the space of forty days,
> And more or less rains every day.[48]

Janet Arnold states that the motto 'no sine sole Iris' on the portrait indicates it might have been commissioned by Egerton to commemorate the visit. Perhaps the queen wore the headdress and mantle in one of the masques. Egerton may have given Elizabeth the jeweled serpent, but there is no record of that even though extensive records exist about other gifts from the progress.[49]

Numbers and Progresses

Her Majesty Elizabeth II is reported to have said, 'I have to be seen to be believed.' With omnipresent media coverage, being seen is not much of a challenge for modern royals. In fact, their challenge seems to be finding a moment or two to be truly off camera.

Like the most recent queen, Tudor monarchs had to be seen to be believed. Unlike the current royals, Tudors didn't have the paparazzi to splash royal images across social media. The only social media available was word of mouth and court gossip. To counter rebellions and promote majesty and magnificence, the Tudors had to be seen at court and around the country. Henry VII, Henry VIII, and Elizabeth I made great use of progresses to communicate and connect with their people. These trips were one of the reasons people felt they knew the monarchs, which encouraged support. The progresses contributed to the legends of the Tudors, and they are one of the ways we understand them today.

Chapter Nine

9 Ways the Tudors Changed Everything

The Difference a Dynasty Makes

Elizabeth's final parliament assembled 27 October 1601. The queen was seeking financial support or 'subsidies'. She hoped for a speedy session, but members had grievances they demanded be heard, especially their complaints about Elizabeth's monopoly grants. The queen was concerned by the Commons' demands and about the public demonstration in the lobby. She was worried the seeds of the Essex rebellion might still take root, and she realised that for the first time she would need to capitulate to the wishes of parliament and pacify her ministers. She was pressured into making a proclamation that rescinded the most hated monopolies and agreed to issue no more 'Letters of Assistance'.[1]

Even so, Elizabeth managed to retain a level of control and play her cards to great effect. She refused to relinquish the power to grant monopolies in the future. And she planned to make a speech that recast the relationship between monarch and parliament in her favour. There are different versions of the so-called 'Golden Speech'. She wrote one herself and sent a fair copy to Sir Henry Savile, provost of Eton. Seven copies emerged after the speech was delivered. The one most closely associated with her is the draft she wrote herself, which is held at the British Library.[2]

One version is from the Commons journal of Hayward Townshend, a member for Bishopscastle (held at the Bodleian Library at Oxford). It includes this passage:

> I do assure you there is no prince that loveth his subjects better or whose love can countervail our love. There is no jewel, be it of ever so rich a price, which I set before this jewel – I mean your loves ... There will never queen sit in my seat with more zeal to my country, care to

my subjects, and that will sooner with willingness venture her life for your good and safety, than myself.³

Another version comes from the papers of Sir Thomas Egerton, privy councilor, lord keeper of the Great Seal, and Master of the Rolls from 1596 to the queen's death. It is held at the Huntington Library in California. This version includes this passage:

> I accept with no less joy than your loves can desire to offer such a present and more esteem it than any treasure or riches (for that we know to prize), but loyalty, love, and thanks I count invaluable. And though God hath raised me high, yet this I count the glory of my crown – that I have reigned with your loves ... The zeal of which affection tending to ease my people and knit their hearts unto us, I embrace with a princely care. For above all earthly treasure, I esteem my people's love, more than which I desire not to merit ... And though you have had and may have many mightier and wise princes sitting in this seat, yet you never had not shall have any that will love you better.⁴

These words are spoken to reinforce the relationship the queen had developed over a lifetime. The older members of parliament would have seen her grow up, surviving the dangers in the reigns of Edward and Mary to take and hold the throne. The younger members might have had trouble remembering any other monarch. Elizabeth had been on the throne more than forty years, and those years had all been spent in London with them.

It was a far cry from the time Henry Tudor, a relative unknown, had come over with a band of mercenaries to fight for the crown and then explain why he deserved it. Over the 118 years of the Tudor reign, things had changed. Or had they? Did the Tudors really change things in lasting ways?

Let's find out. Let's roll the numbers!

The Story of 9 Ways the Tudors Changed Everything

The numbers tell us the Tudors weren't just fascinating, glamorous, violent, charismatic, passionate, and tyrannical They were also change makers. In ways small and large, the Tudors really did make lasting change. Here are nine ways they did it.

3 Meals: The Tudors and Breakfast
Did the Tudors 'invent' breakfast? Many historians believe very few people ate breakfast during medieval times, attributing the widespread popularity of breakfast to the Tudors. But out understanding might be affected by who kept the records. Breakfast was most often eaten by those who started work early, in need of food early in the morning to get them through hours of labour before others were out of bed. These folks tended not to be the ones leaving written records. By later Elizabethan times, the habit of eating breakfast was more widely practiced at court.

Early in his reign, Henry VIII, along with the rest of his court, ate his first meal of the day around 10:30 or 11 in the morning, and sometimes as late as noon. Known as 'dinner', this was the most substantial meal of the day. Breakfast, a meal that 'broke the fast' and was eaten earlier, was not common except for labourers, small children, pregnant or breastfeeding women, and people who were sick.[5]

Why did labourers, especially those on farms, eat breakfast? During the reign of Henry VIII, parliament passed a law in 1515 that required craftsmen and labourers to be working by 5 am between March and September. That was hours before dinner was served. The workers needed some food to keep up the strict pace of work that was required. The law also specified they should not take longer than half an hour for breakfast.[6] About twenty years later, diplomat and scholar Thomas Elyot concluded that he thought breakfast was necessary and healthy for larger portions of the population. He disagreed with the theory that adult men should wait until dinner. By the time Elyot was writing, dinner was eaten later, which contributed to the need for an earlier meal. Additionally, according to Elyot, in a cold and damp climate like England, a person needed the morning meal.[7]

As Elizabeth's reign went on, breakfast became more common among a larger portion of the population. Those at court were more likely to eat soon after rising, although the early association of breakfast with workers made some view breakfast as less desirable. It was modest compared with the rest of the meals eaten during the day, frequently consisting of fish or meat along with manchet bread.[8] For example, Robert Laneham described his morning at starting at 7 o'clock, with the first activity of the day a trip to the chapel and then a breakfast of manchet and a bowl of ale.[9]

Choices for breakfast varied based on status, as it did for all other meals. The gentry grew their own wheat for white bread, producing high quality of white flour that would become a manchet loaf. Next was 'cheat' bread or wheaten bread, which was yellow or grey. The darker bread had more bran and less pure wheat and was rough and dry. The least appealing options would be using flour made from rye, barley, or grounds peas, beans, oats, or lentils.[10]

Tudors also considered the quality of the food eaten at breakfast. Andrewe Boorde, a physician writing during the 1550s, cautioned that the breakfast of bacon and fried eggs might be acceptable for a labourer but was not healthy for a gentleman. A gentleman should have his eggs poached.[11] Elizabethans also selected foods that they believed would improve their health, for example adding sage to breakfast in hopes it would sharpen the brain.[12]

By the end of the dynasty, breakfast was an important meal in the Tudor court. If you enjoy a good breakfast, thank a Tudor.

1 Toilet: The First Flush in England

One of the lesser-known inventions of Tudor England was the first flushing toilet in the country. The notion of privacy while answering nature's call was foreign to most in Tudor times – in fact, privacy in general was unusual in a period of crowded homes and beds for most people. However, there were some notable developments over the period if you were at court.

One of these was the 'Great House of Easement' at Hampton Court Palace. Even though it was described as offering 'malodorous communal facilities' for lower-ranking courtiers,[13] this was only in comparison with the more appealing 'ensuite toilets' made available to premiere courtiers in their chambers. The House of Easement was a toilet block, originally situated by the river near the main gatehouse providing twenty-eight seats.[14]

The one-time facility was converted into grace-and-favour apartments in the nineteenth century. The British cultural television programme *One Foot in the Past* reconstructed what it might have looked like by examining the existing structure and the closed sewers still in place under Hampton

Court Palace. It turns out the views were pretty good for those visiting the facilities, looking out over the east and west fronts of the palace. The courtiers sat on an oak plank, did their business, and watched over the comings and goings of the court. Not so glamorous as the ensuite toilets, and certainly nothing compared to the king's or queen's velvet covered close stool. Still, using the House of Easement would have been far preferable to cleaning it, which fell to the king's gong scourers. They typically faced four-weeks' worth of the court's visits.[15]

Later in the dynasty, John Harington seems to have invented the flushing toilet. Harington, Queen Elizabeth's godson, described and offered images of his invention in *An Anatomy of the Metamorphosed Ajax*, published in 1596. Harington offers a step-by-step process for building and installing the unit. He even includes a safety warning regarding children and the sluice: 'bind it down with a vice pin, so as without the key it will not be opened'.[16] He also includes diagrams, although the inclusion of fish swimming in the basin seems a bit optimistic.[17] There is some thought this might not be the very first toilet – archeological research at Eltham has uncovered a flushing garderobe and sluice from the reign of Henry VIII. Still, Harington's contraption is the one that made it to the monarch's lodgings, in this case Queen Elizabeth's at Richmond.[18] For whatever reason, the invention did not catch on, and it would be many years before flushing toilets came into wide use.

Even so, the Tudors could flush!

6 Permanent Outdoor Theatres
In the final years of the Tudor dynasty, London's streets were teeming with people wealthy enough to spend time and money on entertainment. It was the perfect time for a permanent structure for playgoing, an alternative to blood sports like bear baiting or public executions. Noblemen were becoming patrons of theatre companies, providing financial and legal support, and often giving companies cast-off clothing for costumes as well.

Theatre going changed forever when Richard Burbage established London's first purpose-built playhouse in 1576. It was constructed about a mile outside of the city's jurisdiction and named The Theatre. The name might seem unimaginative today, but in its time, it was literally *the* theatre – the only building dedicated to viewing plays. The Theatre was an open-air amphitheatre, featuring three tiers of galleries for the viewers.[19] The next year, the Curtain was built by a rival acting company. It was named for the plot of land it occupied – there was no curtain across the stage.[20] For the first time, rather than viewing travelling productions or temporary staging in inn-yards or in grand homes (or even at court), the public could go to a theatre to enjoy a play.

The Rose Theatre followed, built by Philip Henslowe in 1587. It was originally smaller than the Theatre or the Curtain, but Henslowe enlarged it in 1592. The Swan was built on the Bankside of the Thames near the Rose in 1595. It was the largest of the playhouses in London at the time. There is a sketch of the Swan Theatre that is associated with the diary of Johannes de Witt who describes the London amphitheatre and draws a picture of the Swan to accompany his description. In 1597, Burbage and his company broke the lease on the theatre and, while the owner was away, dismantled the structure. They used the material to build The Globe, which opened in 1599.

The city authorities tended to be suspicious about plays, players, and everything associated with them.[21] The idea of large crowds, public discussions, mingling of different levels of society represented a perceived threat to city order. There was also the question of labourers and apprentices taking time away from their jobs or worship to go to the theatre in the afternoon. Tensions continued with authorities as theatres became more and more popular. Londoners and visitors squeezed themselves into the theatres, which were located near the brothels, bear pits, and other pleasure spots west of London Bridge. Crime, poverty, drink, sex, and theatre were embedded into this part of city life at the edges of and at odds with the moral and ordered life of religious and civic leaders.[22]

The least expensive way to attend a play was standing around the stage, jostling against others and the sellers of food, drink, and more personal entertainment (remember the brothels were in the neighbourhood). The more you were willing to pay, the more comfortable your experience became, with nobles paying for roomy chambers with cushioned seats.[23] The most expensive seats were right on the stage, where those who wanted to show off their appearance could position themselves to be seen by the crowds. In the round amphitheatres, the crowd often became restless or participated in the play, making comments, throwing food, engaging with the actors.

The appearance of purpose-built theatres during Tudor times shaped the entertainment of London forever. Do you enjoy going to the theatre? That's thanks to the Tudors as well.

200,000 People Living in London in 1600

Despite the plague, starvation, and infant and childhood mortality, the population throughout Europe grew over the Tudor dynasty. The European population increased from 67 million in 1500, fifteen years after Henry VII took the throne, to 89 million in 1600, three years before the death of Elizabeth I.[24] The same was true in England. By the time Henry VII took the throne in 1485, England was beginning to recover from the devastating effects of the plague and poor harvests. The population began to grow steadily over the course of the reigns of the Tudors, reaching about 4 million by the end of Elizabeth's reign. The population of Wales doubled over the Tudor period as well, from about 500,00 to 1 million.[25] The rate of population growth in England outpaced that on the Continent as a whole.

The population grew even more dramatically in London. When Henry VII came to London to take the throne, the city had a population of about 50,000 people. By the end of the sixteenth century, the population of London had quadrupled to 200,000.[26] This despite high rates of death from recurring bouts of plague. The growth in people reflected the growth in the status and importance of the city, from a small capital of a nation struggling to emerge from years of civil war to an important economic and political centre. The physical city expanded as well. At the beginning of the Tudor period, most of the population lived within the city walls that had been erected during the medieval period. By 1600, less than half the population lived within the walls, with most people living in the sprawling areas outside the city centre.[29]

People from all over England were coming to London for economic reasons, seeking greater opportunities or education in the city. Foreigners were also coming into London as the city grew and offered more chances to make a fortune. As religious persecution increased across Catholic Europe, many fled to England for religious reasons and ended up in London. The government was eager to take advantage of the economic advantages associated with an influx of people. They brought skills the English merchants and artisans lacked, and they opened up new trade opportunities.[28] But at the same time, the sheer number of people crowding into the city created significant shortages in food and lodging, leading to broken laws and street crime. The reality for thousands of those living in London was a desperate quest for survival, crowded into small apartments. The city teemed with life, an exciting opportunity for those who could afford it, but a devastating game for those caught up in the crush. And over the reign, people kept coming. By the time Elizabeth died, about half the entire urban population of England lived in London.[30]

The increased stature of London on the European stage, driven in part by the increase in people from all over the world calling it 'home', also brought attention to the city's relationship with the monarchy. Generally speaking, the Tudors and London had a politically stable relationship. The monarchs enjoyed a solid degree of support with city leaders, and there was a good level of participation at the local government level. In addition, the elite living in London shared many of the city's commercial interests. The city and the Tudor government needed and benefitted from each other, and with some exceptions, things went well.[30] Elizabeth, in particular, used London as her stage and enjoyed the brighter and brighter spotlight it offered as her reign progressed. As she never travelled outside of England and seldom ventured far from the capital city, Elizabeth developed and promoted her international reputation with London's help.

London became one of the centres of Europe and the world during the Tudor dynasty.

1 Central Location for Commerce: The Royal Exchange

In the sixteenth century, London Bridge was the only way to walk across the Thames, the bridge that connected Southwark and its less predictable life with the centre of power. The City of London represented wealth, mercantile prowess, and self-government. Over the Tudor dynasty it became one of the most important cities in Europe, and the centre of the walled city was the site Thomas Gresham chose to build his mercantile and economic centre: the Royal Exchange.

The Royal Exchange was similar to a stage, not for costumed players but for merchants and investors and Gresham himself, who saw the project as a means of securing the approval and support of Elizabeth I. It was an ambitious project that allowed Gresham to position himself in a way that would last beyond his lifetime, to leave a permanent mark on the city. It also was an attempt to position London alongside such economic powerhouses throughout Europe and attract merchants and traders from around the world. The architecture was reminiscent of the Bourse in Antwerp, Europe's leading merchant centre.[31] The building design epitomised London's goal of becoming a major player in international trade.

The City donated 100,000 bricks for the building, and additional stone and workers were imported from Holland.[32] The site was cleared, and on 7 June 1566, Gresham laid the foundation stone.[33] An early drawing shows an open courtyard, the spot where trading would take place, which according to contemporary engravings was paved and looked like a knot garden. The yard was surrounded by columned arcades. There were entrances at Lombard Street and Cornhill. Everything was impressive in style and in scope. It's estimated the space could have held 4,000 people. The first gallery was for drapers and cloth merchants. The upper gallery housed as many as 150 stalls offering expensive merchandise. The third gallery was patterned after Antwerp marts where merchants and retailers set up stalls.[34]

To gain the title 'Royal Exchange', Gresham needed the queen's approval. She officially opened the establishment in early 1571. Gresham was afraid there weren't enough active shops to impress the royal visitor, so he paid for candles to be burning in empty spaces and kept moving goods around to make it appear there was plenty of action. The queen arrived on 23 January with her nobles. She dined with Gresham, then entered the Exchange on the south. She reviewed all three galleries and was pleased to see the 'finest wares in the City'. The queen was satisfied and called for a herald and a trumpet so the site could be 'proclaimed the Royal Exchange'.[35]

The Royal Exchange was a centre of London commerce. The Exchange was also an important social space. One of its most important and enduring characteristics was that it was a public, open to all. As such, it attracted merchants and shoppers from around the world, as well as others who came not to shop but to catch up on the latest news. Information had a value all its own. The crowded marketplace was ideal for those wishing to call attention to themselves and their goods, and for those who wanted to gather information quietly – in essence hiding in plain sight. In fact, even those spying on the queen might find an opportunity for intelligence gathering. In 1574, one of the duke of Alba's agents was spotted at the Royal Exchange dressed as a merchant.[36]

The original building was destroyed by the Great Fire of London in 1666, and a second complex was built on the site. The second version of the Royal Exchange was burned in 1838 by a fire caused by an overheated stove. The third building, which stands today, adheres to the original design. Queen Victoria reopened it in 1844. It is the traditional place where some royal proclamations are read by a court herald, including the accession of King Charles III in September 2022. It's now a retail centre with shops and restaurants. If you look along the side walls, you can spot a statue of the first 'royal' associated with the Royal Exchange, Queen Elizabeth I herself.

Modern commerce and early versions of shopping malls – brought to you by the Tudors.

1 Iconic Kingly Image (Thanks to Henry and Holbein)

Throughout history, portraits have always been about more than a representation of a person's looks. They also show the power, authority, wealth, prestige, ambitions, taste, and learning of the subject. The royal portrait is a special kind of portraiture, carefully curated to promote the subject as grand and all-powerful. Portraits included details of the clothing and surroundings of the monarch, along with symbols that would have been very powerful at the time. Portraits during the Tudor reign also showed more about the homes and properties of the sitters, giving clues about the lives of the royal figures. And it is during the Tudors that we see the emergence of family portraits, a way to emphasise the security of the dynastic line.

Portraits were strategically used to proclaim the legitimacy of the Tudor dynasty. Over the sixteenth century, the works of Nicholas Hilliard, Lucas Horenbout, Lavina Teerlinc, William Scrots, Antonis Mor, Hans Eworth, Steven van der Meulen, George Gower, Robert Peake the Elder, Marcus Gheeraerts the Younger, and more visited and lived in England to paint the members of the Tudor regime. The first known portrait of the Tudors was a portrait of Henry VII painted in 1505. From then until the reign of Elizabeth I, royal portraits graced the halls of the Tudor court, demonstrated loyalty in noble homes throughout England and Europe, and were sent abroad as part of potential marriage arrangements and as gifts to build alliances. The history of portraiture throughout the reign is significant, with a shift to more realistic images and at the same time a deliberate focus on propaganda. But perhaps the pivotal portraiture pairing was that of Henry VIII and the image of Tudor royalty created by his court painter, Hans Holbein the Younger.

Holbein visited the English court from his home in Basel, Switzerland in the 1520s and returned there in the early 1530s. He watched the rise of Anne Boleyn, the fall of his friend Thomas More, and then Anne's own fall. He painted More and Cromwell, and he may have drawn or painted Anne Boleyn – there are drawings by him in the Royal Collection, but some find the identification of the sitter as Anne problematic.[37] He certainly painted the king's next two wives: Jane Seymour and Anne of Cleves. And he created the iconic version of Henry VIII that has gone down in history.

No ruler in history did a better job establishing visual recognition than Henry VIII.[38] Holbein's creations of Henry VIII have made him the most easily recognisable monarch to people in Britain and abroad. Holbein created a mural celebrating the Tudor dynasty for the privy chamber at Whitehall Palace. It was the most prestigious commission he was given and represented the pinnacle of his career.[39] The painting includes Elizabeth of York and Henry VII in the background, part of the dynasty but certainly not at the centre. In the centre is an altar, next to which stand Henry VIII and his current wife, Jane Seymour. The altar contains a question: which of the two kings was supreme, Henry VII or Henry VIII. Not wanting to leave anything to change, Henry VIII seems to have written the answer himself:

> The former often overcame his enemies and the fires of his country and finally gave peace to its citizens. The son, born indeed for greater tasks, from the altar removed the unworthy, and put worthy men in their place. To unerring virtue, the presumption of the popes has yielded. And so long as Henry the Eighth carries the scepter in his hand, Religion is renewed, and during his reign the doctrines of God have begun to be held in his honor.[40]

In addition, as if to dare anyone to disagree, Holbein creates a new perspective between his representation of Henry and the viewer. The initial plan, which we can still see in the cartoons for the portrait of Henry VIII at the National Portrait Gallery, show the king in three-quarters profile. For the finished painting, the king's head is shifted so it looks straight out, meeting the eyes of his viewers directly. It was reported to have intimidated those who encountered it, which is easy to imagine.[41] The king is painted standing, his legs spread wide and his shoulders an astonishing breadth. A small copy of the mural was created by Flemish artist Remigius van Leemput for Charles II in 1688. Ten years after that piece was created, Whitehall Palace was destroyed by fire and the original mural was lost.

Even though the original mural was lost, the image of Henry VIII created for that portrait remains. Numerous other portraits of the king follow that pattern: Henry staring straight ahead, hands of hips, taking the Superman pose centuries before Superman. The stance is also echoed in portraits of Edward VI, in an attempt to cast him in his father's image.[42] Holbein's composition became the definitive image of Henry VIII throughout the sixteenth century, and it remains so today. It is the one image of Henry VIII that is universally recognisable in a moment's glance.

We owe early depictions of recognisable royalty (not to mention the Superman pose) to the Tudors.

800 (approximately) Monasteries Dissolved in the Reign of Henry VIII

As part of the break with Rome, Henry VIII oversaw the seizure and dissolution of monasteries, abbeys, nunneries, and friaries. This would have significant and life-changing effects on individuals and families all over the country. For years, monasteries and other religious institutions had provided religious instruction, places of retreat, and support in times of sickness or economic downturns. They were a mainstay of the nation's culture. Between 1534, when the Act of Supremacy started the process, and 1540, more than 800 monasteries were closed.[43]

As far as the political and economic implications of the Reformation go, it was the dissolution of the monasteries that marked a turning point in English history. The shift of land ownership from church to crown represented the most dramatic overhaul since the invasion of William the Conqueror in 1066. The religious houses of England represented a great deal of wealth, land, and stability. After a series of spending sprees, the decision to destroy the monastic structure of England allowed Henry to make a historic land grab and bring the power associated with money to the crown.

The king worked in waves, starting with the First Act of Suppression in 1536, which focused on smaller monasteries. The unprecedented nature of the event made for confusion about its implementation. A lease for land in St Margaret's parish in Southwark provides a powerful example of this. The lease for land of the Fraternity of Our Blessed Lady to a waterman (on condition he not use the property for brothels) includes a note on the back questioning if the fraternity still own the property and have the right to make the lease.[44]

The actions were based on a narrative that clergy had become corrupt, and the church in Rome had far exceeded its rights by receiving money from English monasteries. Royal commissioners travelled throughout England, Wales, and Ireland to assess the wealth and property of individual monastic houses. The 1536 Act of Suppression targeted small monasteries, and the Second Suppression Act of 1539 followed up with larger monasteries and religious houses. By 1540, the rate of seizure and dissolution averaged fifty a month.

Everything about the landscape of England, from trade to farming to charity to architecture to culture, was transformed by these actions. The dissolution of the monasteries created a lasting change to all levels of English society. The king became much wealthier and used his new-found wealth to bolster his accounts and negotiate with powerful members of the nobility. Nobles were able to purchase or were gifted monastic properties, which they frequently turned into grand homes. Monastic life was turned upside down.[45] Some monastic treasures were preserved, but entire libraries and collections of historic treasures were lost or looted.

One of the lasting outcomes was the loss of social support for vulnerable citizens of London. The most vulnerable members of society, the poor, elderly, sick, and needy were left destitute as the safety net they had relied on disappeared. In 1582, John Howes published a description of how Edward VI asked the Lord Mayor of London to address the deficit associated with the dissolved Greyfriars monastery regarding orphans. The Lord Mayor assembled a committee that identified 300 fatherless children and 350 poor men who were overburdened with support of their children. The committee raised funds and put collection boxes in parish churches throughout London. Ultimately, they appointed a staff of fifty to offer a grammar school with a teaching staff, barber, tailor, and handyman at Christ's Hospital. This was a life-saving resource for many, but the need outstripped the resources available.[46]

The dissolution of the monasteries can be considered one of the most revolutionary events of the Tudor dynasty, a comprehensive and rapid change to society.[47] Why do wealthy families lie in homes called things like 'Downton Abbey'? Ask a Tudor.

4 English Translations of the Bible

It was illegal to publish or own an English language version of the Bible in the early years of Henry VIII's reign. However, the king began to rethink the restrictions as the Reformation went on, and by the mid-1530s, more and more people were expecting to be able to read the Bible in English. Thomas Cromwell was a long-time advocate for the publication of the English Bible, grasping the religious and political implications of a Bible-based religion. He was in contact with Miles Coverdale, a convert to Lutheranism who was eager for an English translation.[48]

Miles Coverdale translated and published the first complete bible in English, using an earlier English translation by religious scholar William Tyndale as a source. It was first printed in Antwerp in 1535, then two editions were published in London in 1537.[49] The title page included illustrations by Holbein of Henry VIII flanked by King David and St Paul, and the text and it was dedicated to the king. Although it lacked the royal imprimatur, Henry supported the printing and distribution.[50] It included the Old Testament, New Testament, and Apocrypha.[53] The 1539 folio edition carried the royal license and was the first officially approved Bible translation in English. Cromwell and Cranmer felt the Coverdale Bible was not enough. The upper house of the Convocation of Canterbury petitioned the king to authorise a Bible in English.[52] Cromwell's goal was to have an English Bible in every church in English, available for anyone who wished to read it. More than 9,000 copies of the Great Bible were printed between 1538 and 1541.

The Great Bible included a woodcut title page that made clear the leadership structure in England. Henry VIII receives the word directly from God and then passes it to his leaders: Cranmer and the bishops, and

Cromwell and the nobles.⁵³ The structure of society is reflected here: the king directly under God, his chosen servants interceding between him and his people. Throughout the crowds shown in the woodcut, people cry out 'Vivat Rex', and 'God save the king.' The king is presented as God's representative on earth in matters spiritual and temporal. The king himself authorised these images for both printings. The woodcut embodied the message of the Reformation: the king was divine and supreme.⁵⁴ When it was reprinted in 1541, Cromwell had fallen from favour and the space where his seal had previously been is blank.⁵⁵ It was a not-so-subtle reminder that the king was in charge, and if you ran afoul of the king, you ran afoul of God.

Toward the end of Henry's reign, he became concerned about the widespread reading of the Bible, so he restricted its use. Under Edward VI, these restrictions were lifted. When Mary I took the throne, she restored England's allegiance to Rome. The only Bible published her reign was the Whittingham New Testament printed in Geneva in 1557. William Whittingham, Miles Coverdale, and others created the first edition of what is referred to as the 'Geneva version', which is the earliest English language Bible printed with verse divisions. Notes indicate that the New Testament is a revision of Whittingham's 1557 New Testament, while the Old Testament and Apocrypha were based primarily on the Great Bible.⁵⁶

The Geneva Bible was imported into England during Elizabeth I's reign, despite the queen's objections to the Genevan version of Reform. It was first printed in England in 1576.⁵⁷ The language was forceful and vigorous, which appealed to some readers. The Church of Scotland adopted the Geneva Bible, which signaled a shared language of worship between England and Scotland.⁵⁸ The Geneva Bible remained the most popular translation through the mid-seventeenth century, and it was favoured by the Puritans.⁵⁹

One of the queen's primary objections to the Geneva Bible were the marginal notes provided to help people with their study. Elizabeth and her ministers, particularly her chosen church officials, saw many of these comments as challenging the authority of the monarchy and her role within the church. Therefore, the queen instructed the Church of England to publish an update of the Great Bible in 1568. This would become the second officially authorised English language Bible.⁶⁰ After its initial publication, it was revised twice during Elizabeth's reign, in 1572 and 1602.

Elizabeth's first archbishop of Canterbury, Matthew Parker, spearheaded the translation of the 'Bishop's Bible'. Parker had a special connection to Elizabeth, as he had been Anne Boleyn's chaplain. According to legend, Anne had asked him to care for her daughter. Parker created a special presentation copy for Queen Elizabeth's personal use. In 1568, he explained to William Cecil that he had arranged for a book to be bound to be presented to Elizabeth.[61] However, his health did not allow him to present the volume himself, so he asked Cecil to present it along with a letter asking her to accept his gift.[62]

The King James Bible is the most famous and widely used English translation of the Bible, but the tradition of having the Bible available in the English language started with the Tudors.

1 New (and Changing) 'State' Church, and Some Other Options
Elizabeth's reign would determine the final iteration of Tudor religion. Henry VIII's break with Catholicism and more specifically the pope represented concern about his dynasty more than his soul, and the king remained opposed to significant reform. Edward VI enacted dramatic reform measures, establishing a new form a worship that was required in church across the country. His attempt to put Jane Grey on the throne was a sign of his commitment to religious reform. Mary I fulfilled her promise to return England to the fold of Rome, and she put her husband Philip in charge of the religious policies that would do so. Mary hoped Elizabeth would reign as a Catholic, but she was skeptical.

When Elizabeth took the throne, her council, her subjects, and the world watched to see how she would set up religion in her regime. The religious conflicts began quickly, with Marian bishops trying to hold onto power while reform leaders hurried back from exile on the Continent. Elizabeth's first proclamation about religious was cautious, and she and Cecil learned from the bitter divisions over religion during Mary's reign.[63] They wanted the people on their side. Although Elizabeth likely did not say she did not wish to make windows into men's souls, the phrase does seem to reflect her intention. For the first decade of her reign, the approach worked. But as time went on, conflicts came.

For one thing, the length of the queen's reign meant that Catholics were dying off and the rising population was being raised in Elizabeth's church. Organised opposition to her religious policy began in the 1560s and was propelled into the spotlight with the arrival of Mary, Queen of Scots, in 1568, the Northern Rebellion in 1569, and the pope's 1570 excommunication of Elizabeth and invitation to English Catholics to rebel against her. While she held her ground against the Catholics trying to remove her from power, Elizabeth also resisted the attempts of Puritans trying to push reform further than she was willing to go.

The English religious landscape was very different at the end of the Tudor regime, and some of the changes instituted by the Tudors remain hundreds of years later. The two versions of the Book of Common Prayer issued in the reign of Edward VI represented a move toward the establishment of the Protestant religion. It helped the spread of literacy and is recognised for its superior writing and use of idiom, imagery, and rhythm. It was revised again in the sixteenth and seventeenth centuries, and the 1662 version, with a few changes, has influenced the liturgy of most English-speaking Protestant churches. Elizabeth's religious policies were messy, but they attempted to allow loyalty to the crown to prevail as a qualifying factor in royal favour. Her determination to keep loyal Catholics in her court meant most English Catholics remained loyal to the queen.

At the end of Elizabeth's reign, the Church of England was there to stay. There would be more religious turmoil over the years, but the monarchy and national religion would not be Catholic again. Elizabeth I's religion would be echoed in the reign of another Elizabeth. Just as Elizabeth I did, HM Queen Elizabeth II held the titles of 'Defender of the Faith' and 'Supreme Governor of the Church of England'.

The English Reformation during the Tudor regime had a lasting impact on the religion, culture, and society of the nation. The consolidation of religious power and the monarchy and elimination of the monasteries meant that worship and issues such as poverty became the focus of the state rather than the church. Changing religious ideas had an impact on not just the appearance of churches but on homes as well, as the art people hung on their walls looked very different in the years after reform. The break with Rome and Catholic Europe affected the economic status of the country and especially of London as merchants established new trade partners and routes and explored the new world.⁶⁴ The lives of people throughout England and Europe were reimagined because of the Reformation.

Numbers and Lasting Change

The Tudors weren't attempting to make decisions that would create lasting change or be remarked on by people living hundreds of years later. They were attempting to hold onto the throne, keep the country secure from enemies, generate and gather wealth, and keep things going in the next generation. Still, their actions created long-term changes.

From small things like the popularity of breakfast and first attempt at a flushing toilet in England to larger issues like the burgeoning of London's population, changes in trade and the economy, and huge upheavals association with religious change, the Tudors changed everything. The England at the end of Elizabeth's reign in 1603 was entirely different from the England Henry Tudor convinced to accept him as King in 1485. The Tudors made decisions and created a reality that led to lasting change in England and beyond.

Chapter Ten

Top 10 Tudor Secrets and Surprises

The Tudor reign lasted from 1485 to 1603, nearly 120 years. Over that time, religion, culture, economics, daily life, and international relations changed. It is the most famous of the English royal dynasties, full of larger-than-life characters and fascinating events. There are books and movies and television program. But do we know it all? Can the Tudors still surprise us?

The End of the Tudor Dynasty

In 1602 Robert Cecil, who had replaced his father as the queen's chief minister, held an entertainment for Elizabeth that included a shrine to Astraea, the virgin goddess of Greek mythology associated with purity and justice. In Cecil's case, the goddess was a representation of Elizabeth herself.[1] Elizabeth was keen to be represented as an icon, a replacement for the Virgin Mary as the Virgin her people could worship.

The reality was a queen who was not an idol but an ageing woman who had outlived most of her closest friends and, for many people, her usefulness as a monarch. She still had moments of energy and spirit, as when she energetically danced galliards with the duc de Nevers or walked briskly nearly every the morning.[2] The Tudor monarchy was a personal monarchy, and the queen well understood the importance of her lively presence and what it represented to her people. She had carefully crafted an image of herself as powerful and magnificent from the first days of her reign, and she was determined to maintain it.

Elizabeth's refusal to name an heir had been based on her belief that even her loyal subjects were turn their eyes and hearts to the 'rising sun' of the next monarch. In late 1602, that was beginning to happen. She had enjoyed generally good health for most of her reign, but the new year saw her becoming more frail. As she had always feared, her councilors turned to the king of Scots, looking to him as the rising sun.[3] Some went north to attempt to gain the favour of James, and even those who remained in England were in frequent communication with him. Feeling she was losing the love of her people, Elizabeth began to lose heart. John Harington visited the court and tried to bring some joy to the queen with poetry, but she said she was unable to enjoy his verses.[4]

In 1603, Elizabeth retreated to Richmond and withdrew from court. On 15 March, Noel de Caron wrote that her recovery was doubted.[5] The Queen was declining steadily, plagued by guilt over Mary, Queen of Scots, and devastated by the death of her friend and servant Katherine, Countess of Nottingham. But the slight recovery did not last. Giovanni Scaramelli, the Venetian secretary, said she allowed grief to overcome her.[6] For days she refused to lie down, but eventually she accepted the counsel of Katherine's widow, the lord high admiral who encouraged her to go to bed.[7]

There was a serious worry with trouble her throat that the doctors feared might choke her, but they had been able to treat it.[8] Elizabeth briefly rallied on 23 March. She asked her ministers to care for the peace of the realm. She lifted her hand to her head when the lord high admiral asked if she wished the king of Scots to succeed her. This was taken as agreement. That night, surrounded by only her ladies, the queen died.[9]

It was the end of the dynasty. The Tudor story was over. There was nothing left. Thanks to the printing press, increased literacy, and an explosion of portraits, as well as the survival of numerous buildings related to the time, we know more about the Tudors than about previous dynasties. Can the Tudors still surprise us? Is there more to learn?

Let's find out. Let's roll the numbers!

The Top 10 Tudor Surprises

The numbers tell us that the Tudors can continue to surprise us. Here are the Top 10 surprising numbers about the Tudor dynasty.

2 Bookends of the Dynasty: Margaret Beaufort and Elizabeth I

Why have I chosen Margaret Beaufort as the beginning of the dynasty? After all, Henry VII was the first Tudor monarch. But Henry never would have become king, and it's almost certain he would not have been able to hold his throne without the efforts of his formidable and dedicated mother, Margaret Beaufort.

Henry VII's Chapel at Westminster Abbey is a fitting tribute to the dynasty, with a soaring ceiling and elaborate memorials to Henry VII and Elizabeth of York and to Elizabeth I (who shares her elaborate memorial with her sister Mary). But right there among Henry VII's family celebration is a memorial with a tribute from Erasmus that reads, 'Margaret of Richmond, mother of Henry VII, grandmother of Henry VIII.' She has been described as Henry VII's 'devout and rather awesome mother',[10] a fitting tribute. Margaret Beaufort was the great-granddaughter of John of Gaunt, son of Edward III. It was through her that Henry Tudor claimed the throne.

Margaret Beaufort became a single mother at age 13 and spent the rest of her life protecting and promoting the future of her son. She managed to play successfully on both sides of the Wars of the Roses, favoured in the court of her Lancastrian relative Henry VI, but also highly regarded in the Yorkist courts of Edward IV and Richard III. She collaborated with Elizabeth Woodville to help place Henry Tudor and Elizabeth of York on the English throne. Of course, that paints her with the negative attribution of 'ambitious', something not admired in women of the time. She's even been accused of killing Edward V and his brother in the Tower of London. Margaret's life is one of contradictions: war and peace, gain and loss, life and death. She survived and eventually thrived, seeing her son and her grandson become kings of England. She truly was a 'queen in all but name'.[11]

Elizabeth's lasting popularity, which actually increased during the Stuart reign, is demonstrated by Shakespeare's play *Henry VIII*, a nostalgic celebration of Elizabeth. The play ends with the birth of Elizabeth, which in the world of the play is something to be celebrated more than it was at the time. Here's some of Cranmer's speech (*Henry VIII*, Act V, scene 5):

> This royal infant – heaven still move about her! –
> Though in her cradle, yet now promises
> Upon this land a thousand blessings,
> Which time shall bring to ripeness, she shall be –

> But few now living can behold that goodness –
> A pattern to all princes living with her,
> And all that shall succeed.

According to this 'prophecy', Elizabeth would be not only the one to bring the land a 'thousand blessings' but also a pattern to the men who follow her. It's a far cry from the early description of a woman's reign as 'monstrous regiment'.

Elizabeth had managed to shatter expectations of female rule. As she had early wished, the description of her reign would contain the phrase, 'a queen, having ruled 44 years and 4 months, lived and died a virgin'. The accession of King James VI of Scotland, who would become James I of England, was probably greeted with joyful shouts and likely sighs of relief. The new king came with sons, seeming to eliminate the possibility of female rule for the foreseeable future. It looked like Elizabeth's reign would fade into oblivion. However, James turned out to be less effective and less popular than anticipated. Elizabeth and the Tudors, with their focus on royal magnificence, were missed. I want to thank Dr. Tracy Borman for calling my attention to this Stuart-era couplet:

> A Tudor! A Tudor! We've had Stuarts enough,
> None ever reign'd like old Bess in her ruff.[12]

3 or 5: Katherine of Aragon's Place in Tenure as Queen Consort

In 1328, Philippa of Hainault married King Edward III. This would become one of the most successful royal partnerships of medieval England. She would become the second-longest queen consort with thirty-nine years in the position. Queen Charlotte, wife of George III, is the longest-serving queen consort, having held the position for fifty-seven years. Marguerite of Anjou, the queen consort of the Henry VI, served twenty-six years. Queen Mary, wife of George V, was queen consort for twenty-five years. Henrietta Maria, wife of Charles I and his queen consort until his execution, held the position for twenty-four years.

Where does Katherine of Aragon fit in? As with so much of her life, the way you count her time as queen consort depends on how you view her marriage to Henry VIII. If you were to ask Katherine herself, she would say she was queen consort from her marriage to her death in 1536, giving her a tenure of twenty-seven years. Officially, however, her marriage to Henry VIII was declared null and void in 1533, which would reduce her tenure to twenty-four years. She's either in third place in terms of tenure, between Philippa of Hainault and Marguerite or she's tied for fifth with Henrietta Maria at twenty-four years, coming in after Marguerite of Anjou and Queen Mary.

In any case, it's a good reminder that Katherine of Aragon was by far Henry VIII's longest wife and Tudor England's longest serving queen consort. She had a considerable impact on Henry, the Tudors, and the history of royal wives.

6 'Other' Marriages

Henry VIII's six marriages set the standard for most-married monarch of all time. But some of his siblings had their share of trips to the altar as well.

Henry VIII's older brother Arthur married Katherine in a grand celebration on 14 November 1501. The marriage was a huge victory for Henry VII and the new dynasty, and Katherine's parents were among the great leaders of Europe. Arranging a marriage with the daughter Ferdinand and Isabella of Spain represented approval of the dynasty and opened potential trade agreements and an alliance against France. Katherine came to England in early October 1501 and was welcomed in style. Henry VII wanted all of London to rejoice with him. The ceremony was held in St Paul's Cathedral, which had been redesigned. A raised platform was built to allow more people to see the bride process to the church, accompanied by her young brother-in-law, Prince Henry. A fountain of wine flowed by the west door of St Paul's, helping promote the celebration.[13]

The question of the wedding night is a complicated one, but it didn't seem like such a budding controversy at the time. Arthur is said to have boasted about his exploits in the marriage bed, and many of the courtiers at the time believed the couple had consummated the marriage. At the time, everyone believed there was plenty of time to work things out if there had been a bit of trouble. No one could have imagined that Arthur would die on 2 April 1502, ending the short marriage and plunging the Spanish alliance and Katherine's life into chaos and uncertainty. It was the first marriage of Henry VII's children, and it had not ended well.

Margaret Tudor was the next of Henry VII's children to marry. She was just 13 years old when she went to Scotland. Henry VII had been contemplating the marriage for several years as a means of settling the ongoing disputes with the Scots. The marriage between the 30-year-old James IV of Scotland and the 13-year-old Margaret Tudor was celebrated on 8 August 1503. Their first child was born in 1507. The couple ultimately had six children, but only one survived infancy: James, born in 1512.

Margaret saw the dangers of Scotland's war with England, asking her husband why the French were more important 'than the cries of your little son and mine'. [14] The war with England ended in disaster for Scotland. James was killed at the Battle of Flodden on 9 September 1513. Margaret was left a widow and pregnant at age 23, and Scotland was left with an infant king. Margaret was recognised as regent until she entered into a secret marriage in 1514 that would prove her political undoing. Archibald Douglas, the earl of Angus, was pro-English like Margaret. The pro-French members of the council acted quickly and summoned the duke of Albany to become governor of Scotland in Margaret's place. The council also demanded that she turn over her young sons. Margaret returned to Henry VIII's court, but Angus decided to make peace with Albany.[15]

Margaret was determined to divorce Angus, a move that (ironically) Henry VIII strongly disapproved of. She was granted an annulment from Angus in 1527 on the grounds of his precontract with Lady Janet Douglas. Once Margaret obtained the annulment, she married her lover, Henry Stewart in 1528. By 1536, she had tired of Stewart, who proved to be more determined to sleep with other women and spend Margaret's money than Angus had been. She eventually reconciled with him and died at Methven Castle on 18 October 1541. Not a happily ever after story.

Henry VII's youngest daughter Mary didn't equal their marital scandals of her siblings, but she did manage a couple of trips down the aisle. Mary was sent to France in 1514 as part of the peace treaty with French King Louis XII. Mary's marriage to Louis, when she was just 18 and he 52, wasn't expected to be a long one, but it ended more quickly than anticipated when Louis died on 1 January 1515. Mary was now a young widow, and Henry VIII likely expected to make another political marriage for her. But when Mary returned to England, but she was not alone. While still in France, she married a second time. Her husband was the man who had been sent to bring her back to England, who happened to be one of her brother's closest friends: Charles Brandon, Duke of Suffolk.

Brandon later explained to Wolsey, 'The Queen would never let me in rest till I had granted her to be married, and so, to be plain with you, I have married her heartily.' He went on to explain he'd been so hearty in the marriage he feared she was already pregnant.[16] Technically, this was treason, but Henry VIII decided to make the best of it. The couple were married again in England on 13 May 1515 in the presence of the king and court. Mary remained with Brandon until her death in 1533 at age 37. Her two daughters, Frances and Eleanor, married and had daughters who were named in Henry VIII's succession.

Margaret Tudor and her marriages gave us Mary, Queen of Scots, and Henry, Lord Darnley. Mary Tudor's marriage gave us three Grey sisters: Jane, Katherine, and Mary. So not only did Margaret and Mary Tudor jazz up the marital exploits of the second Tudor generation, but they also produced heirs who would spice up the third!

5,000 Calories, Mostly in 2 Meals

Food was a huge part of the Tudor court. Royal meals were often a public affair, with food being as much about presentation as about taste. The wealthier the household, the more exotic and finely displayed the food. Tudor courtiers enjoyed a wide variety of food, with the bulk of the diet consisting of meat. In addition to fresh venison and beef, there were plenty of other dishes for courtiers, including geese and chickens, pigeons and pheasants, capons, swan, various sauces, pastries, tartes, gingerbread, and fritters.[17] The highest nobility and the royals were also treated to exotic food such as citrus fruit, almonds, and spices and sugar. Imported food was only available to the very wealthiest. What you ate and served to guests was a public statement of wealth and status.

When was all this food eaten? For the first part of the dynasty, the meals started with dinner, which was served around 11:00 in the morning. Henry VIII loved to hunt in the morning, so he would have worked up quite an appetite. He was given the choice of anything he desired, and a dinner might include roasted game, meat pies, and possibly conger eel or porpoise.[18]

The Tudors believed that the stomach was a sort of cauldron, and proper digestion was critical for health and fertility, something very important to

Henry VIII. That belief dictated the order in which food was served and eaten. Physicians recommended beginning a meal with foods that took a long time to digest, such as beef, peas, and other ingredients commonly found in soup. Soup was a popular first course because it provided 'juice' in the cauldron. Meat would be next. Henry was especially fond of meat, and he ordered a 'flesh day' requiring that meat be compulsory for his courtiers. After all the meat, diners rested with a bit of wine or ale before moving on to salad and seasonal fruit. Vegetables were cooked and eaten as 'sallats', dressed with vinegar, oil, and sugar. At the end of the meal, cheese was served to close the stomach and seal in the food. It's no wonder the king easily got through 5,000 calories a day!

Henry VIII had come to the throne as a tall, athletic, vigorous young man, and he remained so in the early years of his life. Consuming such meals did not take a serious toll on his health when he spent his days hunting, riding, jousting, dancing, playing tennis, and competing in other sports. But after his serious jousting accident in 1536, he was no longer able to be so physically active. Even though he could hunt, he aged quickly from that point on, and the French ambassador described him as stout rather than athletic by 1541. Henry's armor, which we wore until late in his life, had to be made to his exact measurements, giving us a good indication of his size. Between 1536 and 1541, his waist increased from 37 inches to 54 inches.[20] By 1546, Henry was morbidly obese. He could barely get around and had to be helped or even carried from room to room. He had an early form of a chairlift to help him get up and down stairs. An ulcer on his leg continued to fester, and his clothing orders reflected desire for comfort rather than desire to project royal power.[21] By the time he died, he was huge, with some estimates that he weighed around 400 pounds.

Henry VIII is often portrayed as absolutely rotund – and he was probably even bigger than we imagine.

56 Years After the Wars of the Roses, the Final 'Yorkist Pretender' Was Executed

The first Tudor king claimed that by marrying Elizabeth of York, he had effectively ended the Wars of the Roses and put an end to the York versus Lancaster battles. This was premature, as Lambert Simnel and Perkin Warbeck made a claim for the House of York. But after Henry VII successfully defeated both attempts, it would seem that the Yorkists might be finished once and for all.

Not quite. In fact, it was fifty-six years after Bosworth that the final Yorkist was executed. Margaret Pole was the daughter of George, Duke of Clarence, brother of Edward IV and Richard III. Margaret was married to Richard Pole, a Tudor supporter. She became friends with Katherine of Aragon, joining the household of Princess Mary. When Henry VIII annulled his marriage to Katherine, Margaret remained loyal to her friend. Even so, she managed to stay on stable terms with Henry VIII for a few years, until her son Reginald was publicly critical of Henry VIII and Anne Boleyn.[22]

Margaret denounced her son's actions and was allowed to return to Henry's court after Anne Boleyn's fall. But her time in the king's favour didn't last. Margaret was arrested in November 1538 when it was proven her son Geoffrey had been in communication with Reginald. She was sent to the Tower of London, where she lived well, as wealthy people often did. She was allowed by maintain her status by paying for servants and good food. It was probably a surprise when, without much explanation or even a clear charge, she was told on 27 May 1541 that she would be executed within an hour. The execution was arranged so quickly that the regular executioner was not on duty. Instead, a young and inexperienced man was asked to perform a stunning task: execute one of the most noble women in the country, the niece of two kings. He was not up to the task, and it took several blows to remove her head. The final member of the Yorkist regime that had so challenged Henry VII was hacked to death.[23] It was a violent ending for the person considered to represent the final Yorkist claim to the throne.

Henry VII is often described as a paranoid king. He wasn't the only one. Henry VIII saw a 68-year-old woman as a threat to his hold on the throne and was concerned enough about to order her execution. The spectre of the House of York lasted long into the Tudor reign.

1 Tudor Monarch Left a Diary
Did you know a Tudor king kept a diary? Edward VI began keeping a diary when he became king. The entries for the first two years, 1547 to 1549, provide a chronicle of Edward's memories of past events. At first, he writes about himself primarily in the third person. This shifts in 1550, when he

begins to write in the first person. At that point it becomes more like a traditional diary, with entries that describe the events of individual days. The final entry is from November 1552. This is the only autobiographical record from Plantagenet, Tudor, or Stuart England.[24] It shows us details of the Tudor court, Edward and his counsellors, and the inner workings of the court. But it gives us little personal or emotional insight.

Edward demonstrates he is aware of the complexities of his position as king ruling with a protectorate. He describes how always guarded, allowed 'not half a quarter of an hour alone'.[25] He was suspicious of the people around him, and he was aware of the level of his vulnerability. He seemed to see himself as a symbol of the monarchy and of the country, rather than a preteen boy. He writes with emotion about a time in July 1549 that 'because there was a rumor that I was dead, I passed through London'.[26] It helps us see that it took a specific effort for Edward to be seen by the people, something that happened regularly with Henry VIII but apparently less often for the boy king.[27]

The entries reveal an apparent lack of regret for the fate of those who worked against him or against his realm. For example, Edward seemed to have been close to his uncle Edward Seymour, Duke of Somerset, who was ousted as protector in 1549. Somerset was able to return to the council, but in 1551 he was sent to the Tower and accused of treason. He was executed in January 1552. At that same time, Edward was enjoying the most expensive revels of his reign. Between Seymour's trial in December and execution in January, there was a procession through London that included a mock beheading of Somerset. It's not clear if the king was amused by this, but his record of the execution in his journal is cold.[28] The king simply wrote, 'The Duke of Somerset had his head cut off upon Tower Hill between eight and nine o'clock in the morning.'[29] We don't know what Edward would have been like had he grown to rule on his own, but his diary entries point to not so much to a precious teen as a tyrant in the making.

7, as in 007: John Dee and James Bond

James Bond is the hero of twelve novels and two short stories about the British Secret Service. The stories have become one of the longest running and highest grossing film series of all time in the US. But what does Bond creator Fleming have to do with the Tudors?

John Dee was a scientist, geographer, astrologer, mathematician, and possibly spy in the court of Elizabeth I. He chose the date of her coronation. Dee was one of the most learned men of his day. He helped the queen's explorers as they went on their voyages and was devoted to the queen and used horoscopes to help her root out potential threats and rivals.[30] Before he came into royal service, Dee attended Cambridge University. He entered St John's College and graduated in 1546. He then became an original fellow of Trinity College, where his clever stage effects for a production of Aristophanes's *Peace* earned him a reputation as a magician. He travelled around Europe, studying and lecturing. He worked with other mathematicians and astrologers. He sought out William Cecil, who used Dee as one of his agents, making use of his travels around the world. When he wrote to Cecil or Elizabeth from abroad, he signed with a symbol. Some think he used '00' as a symbol for eyes or as a code for 'your eyes only'. He also used the number 7, which has been interpreted as a lucky or sacred number. This means he signed 007.[31]

It is possible that author Ian Fleming was inspired by the life of John Dee when he created the James Bond series. And John Dee (not Sean Connery) may have very well been the original 007.

2 Hours of Prep Time for Elizabeth I Every Morning
In sixteenth-century England, clothing was one of the most immediately ways to communicate wealth and status. It was immediately apparent to all, and it was known to be regulated (although not always successfully) by law. The Tudors were interested in maintaining and projecting their royal status, and elaborate appearance in a stunning wardrobe was one of the ways they did so. This reached its height in the reign of Elizabeth I, who was skilled in the art of projecting an image of royalty and magnificence.

Elizabeth could have coined the phrase 'dress to impress'. Certainly no one understood it better. The sheer size of the queen's wardrobe is an indicator of the importance she put on dressing the part of royal monarch. Giovanni Scaramelli, Venetian secretary in England, wrote that Elizabeth had 6,000 gowns.[32] This number is likely greatly exaggerated, as Elizabeth was known to modify her outfits with different sleeves or other components. Other estimates range from 2,000 [33] to 3,000.[34] In any case, it was a tremendous collection.

It was no small task to get Elizabeth dressed in the mornings, and it took a small army of women to accomplish the tasks. This wasn't merely a matter of a royal expecting to be helped to fasten a dress up the back. Elizabeth literally could not have dressed herself. Each layer of clothing was put on and carefully secured in place with pins or laces. Excavations of Hampton Court Palace have uncovered numerous pins, pointing to the number worn and lost during the reigns of the Tudors.[35] Sometimes the queen's gowns were sewn on the morning, and then unpicked at the end of the day. Then there were the final decorative features – collars, ruffs, cuffs – all of which would be attached. The queen's ladies used laces, buttons, hooks, and ribbons to add the elements.[36]

As the reign went on, Elizabeth used clothing, makeup, and jewels to hide her ageing. Her appearance became less realistic and more iconic, and her dresses were even more ostentatious. This required greater and longer efforts of her ladies, who went through a lengthy ritual every morning. First, they checked the gowns and accessories for poison to keep the queen safe in the face of increasing rebellions. They helped the queen into her smock, having warmed it by the fire to make it as comfortable as possible. Then came the farthingale, the stays, and understockings and silk stockings. The women pinned and laced and sewed multiple layers of clothing and sleeves and ruffs, then helped the queen into her shoes. Her hair, something Elizabeth had been proud of, was dressed grandly in the early years of her reign and later her wigs were dressed even more grandly, with jewels and embellishments.[37] Her makeup also increased as the reign progressed, unfortunately including mercury and antimony, which almost certainly damaged her skin and made her look even older, and possibly lead to headaches, respiratory problems, and organ damage. Dr. Tracy Borman suggests that it's possible Elizabeth's fiery or mercurial temper might have been caused or at least made worse by the mercury in her makeup.[38]

It's no wonder such an ordeal took a good two hours to get the queen ready in the morning!

1 Bath a Month, Whether She Needed it or Not
There are plenty of stories, rumours, and jokes about how bad the Tudors smelled. While it's true that big cities like London, full of animals in the streets and no one cleaning up after them, the odors would be different

from those today. Walking along the streets of London or through the lanes of villages, people of all classes would experience the smells of latrines, burning crops, metal being smelted, leather being conditioned, and clothes being dyed with urine, and food being cooked over the fire. It was the norm, and at the time it was what everyone expected.[39]

People who were living in cities, especially those at court, were exposed to a host of smells all around them. But especially in the upper levels of society, people smelling sweet was something to be desired. This was not accomplished by bathing. Bathing, after all, was a considered a danger in Tudor times. In *This is the Mirror or Glasse of Health*, Thomas Moulton specifically recommends that people not use baths or stoves or sweat heavily, 'for all openeth the pores of a man's body and maketh the venomous ayre to enter and for to infect the blood'.[40]

The royals did bathe occasionally, but it was a different experience that the quick shower we take today. Henry VIII turned bathing into a luxurious experience, with steam baths installed at Richmond, Whitehall, and Hampton Court Palace. He would wear a linen shirt and coif while bathing. The Tudors preferred water strews with herbs and flowers or rose oil rather than with soap.[41] Elizabeth is said to have bathed once a month against the advice of her doctors, who worried she was washing away the oils that would preserve her health and opening her pores up to evil illnesses. She may have taken baths more for pleasure than health or hygienic reasons – her baths were even more luxurious than her father's. She had bathrooms installed with hot and cold water running from oyster shells at Whitehall and the room she bathed in at Windsor was lined with mirrors.[42]

Thomas Elyot's *The Castel of Health*, published in 1541 and offering numerous instructions about eating for good health and keeping the humors in balance, sums up the approach getting clean in the morning: a man should rub himself with a coarse linen cloth, first softly and then with increasing pressure until his flesh is a bit red and swollen. That would ensure 'his body is clensed'.[43] But would that be enough to ward off smell?

Historian Ruth Goodman reports she followed the Tudor approach to getting clean twice. First, she went without bathing for three months while living her normal life in modern society. She reports that no one noticed. Her routine included wearing a fine linen smock every day, over which she wore modern clothes. She wore linen hose as well. She changed the smock and hose daily, and she rubbed herself down every night. She was, in her words, 'remarkably smell free' for the entire time, despite going all that time without a bath or shower. Her second experience was while filming a Tudor-based television series, so she wore Tudor-appropriate outwear as well as underwear. As she was living a farmer's life, she changed her linens less often, and even though there was a bit more of a smell, it was covered nicely by the smells of the cooking she spent her days doing.[44]

In other words, life in Tudor times certainly smelled different from life today, but one bath a month would have been more than enough to keep you sweet smelling.

3 Recent Discoveries about the Tudors

The most powerful thing about history can be that we're learning more from it all the time. As we remain curious and keep asking questions, we find that things we thought we knew might not be accurate after all, and items we believed were lost forever might turn up in unexpected places. There are three powerful recent examples of the ways we continued to be surprised about the Tudors.

Thanks to the work of historian Ruth Richardson, Head of Exhibitions at National Museum Wales (and former Curator of the Royal Ceremonial Dress Collection at Historic Royal Palaces) Eleri Lynn, and Joint Chief Curator of Historic Royal Palaces Tracy Borman, we now believe that one of Queen Elizabeth I's dresses was donated to Bacton Church in honour of Elizabeth's cherished servant Blanche Parry. Parry was from Bacton and retained a strong connection to her birthplace.[45] The cloth was displayed from 1879 to 1904, when Reverend Charles Brothers had it framed because he believed it might have come from one of Elizabeth's dresses. By 2016, the cloth had been associated with the dress worn by Elizabeth I in the 'Rainbow portrait.' It was brought to Hampton Court Palace for restoration, where Eleri Lynn confirmed it had originally been part of a skirt. Two textile experts spent about 2,000 hours conserving the cloth and extraordinary embellishments.[46]

I was lucky enough to visit Hampton Court Palace in 2019 when the altar cloth was on display alongside the Rainbow Portrait. It was an extraordinary way to experience this history and the way that we continue to learn more about the Tudors.

Tudor learning continues. Other discoveries are uncovering the inner workings of the Tudor court related to one of its most famous members, Anne Boleyn. Historian Kate McCaffrey recently uncovered previous erased writing in Anne Boleyn's Book of Hours, which is on display at Hever Castle. The inscriptions provide a history of the provenance of the book following Anne's dramatic fall from favour in 1536. Based on Ms McCaffrey's research, it appears Anne's book was kept safe by a number of family friends who lived near her family home in Kent. Three of these were women who seem to have made a commitment to preserve Anne's memory. It's a fitting thought when linked to the couplet Anne wrote, 'Remember me when you do pray, that hope doth lead from day to day.'[47]

And there's more. Paul Fitzsimmons of Marhamchurch Antiques has an extraordinary sense of the special, and when he purchased what was listed as a 'wooden bird', he thought it might be more than that. He spoke with historian and author Sandra Vasoli, who put him in touch with historian James Peacock of Hampton Court Palace. Soon Dr Tracy Borman was brought into the picture. Fitzsimmons was tipped off by the nature of the bird, which was crowned, holding a sceptre, and accompanied by roses. He knew it was a royal bird. And he was right. The use of Anne Boleyn's falcon emblem, and the fact that the falcon is wearing an Imperial crown, indicate that this was once part of the ceremonial decoration celebrating Anne's coronation and reign. In fact, it may have been displayed at Hampton Court Palace, either in the Great Hall or in Anne's private chambers.[48] Thanks to the generosity of Fitzsimmons, the work of the restoration team, and the commitment of Hampton Court Palace, the falcon – fully restored to its original look and glory – went on public display at Hampton Court Palace in May 2022.

There's always something new to learn and experience with the Tudors!

Numbers and Surprises

There are so many ways the Tudors continue to surprise us. From new insight into existing documents and dresses, to discoveries of carved birds that turn out to be royal emblems, recent work of historians demonstrates that Tudor history is alive and well. I'm so grateful to have been able to speak with Tudor historians about these recent findings, and I look forward to continuing to learn from ongoing research.

We will all continue to be surprised by the Tudors and the numbers that tell their stories.

Notes

Chapter One
1. According to the Royal Shakespeare Company, Henslowe's Diary includes a reference to 'Harey VI' performed on 3 March 1592 at the Rose Theatre.
2. Shakespeare, *Henry VI*, part 1, II.4.
3. Rackin, 'Modern Perspective: *Henry VI, Part 1*', Folger Shakespeare Library website.
4. Carr, *John of Gaunt*, p. 9.
5. Amin, *Beaufort*, pp. 15-16.
6. Ibid, p. 166.
7. Amin, *Beaufort*, p. 38.
8. 'Richard II: Jan 1397', in *Parliament Rolls of Medieval England*.
9. Amin, *Beaufort*, p. 82.
10. Ibid, p. 41.
11. Jones, *Hollow Crown*, p. 149.
12. Amin, *Beaufort*, p. 255.
13. Jones, *Hollow Crown*, p. 211.
14. Ellis, *Three Books of Polydore Vergil*, p. 196.
15. Jones, *Hollow Crown*, p. 278.
16. Penn, *Winter King*, p. 5.
17. Ellis, *Three Books of Polydore Vergil*, p. 202.
18. Penn, *Winter King*, p. 7.
19. Halliwell-Phillipps, *Letters of the Kings of England*, pp. 161-62.
20. 'Henry VII: November 1485', in *Parliament Rolls of Medieval England*.
21. Ibid, November 1485.
22. Penn, *Winter King*, p. 21.
23. Hall, *Union of Two Noble Families*, p. 425.
24. Gardiner, *Letters and Papers*, p. 421.
25. Jones, *Hollow Crown*, p. 327.
26. Ibid, p. 330.
27. Penn, *Winter King*, p. 22.
28. Thomas, *Authority*, p. 70.
29. Amin, *Tudor Pretenders*, p. 78.
30. Ibid, p. 81.
31. Penn, *Winter King*, p.23.

32. Amin, *Tudor Pretenders*, p. 145.
33. Gristwood, *Blood Sisters*, p. 269.
34. Halliwell-Philipps, *Letters of the Kings*, vol. 1, p. 172.
35. Amin, *Tudor Pretenders*, p. 252.
36. Hooker, 'Notes on Organization', p. 19.
37. Penn, *Winter King*, p. 29.
38. Amin, *Tudor Pretenders*, p. 268.
39. Ibid, p. 300.
40. Ibid p. 306.
41. BL Cotton Titus D. IV f.12v.
42. Johnston, 'Catherine of Aragon's Pomegranate', pp. 153-54.
43. Hunt, *Drama of Coronation*, p. 34.
44. Ibid, p. 36.
45. Bergeron, 'Elizabeth's Coronation Entry', p. 6.
46. Brietenberg, 'Iconic Representation', p. 1.
47. Ibid, p. 11.
48. Hunt, *Drama of Coronation*, p. 165.
49. TNA, E 156/43.

Chapter Two
1. Stone, *History of Mary I*, p. 507.
2. Ibid, p. 513.
3. Loades, *Mary Tudor*, pp. 241-44.
4. Stone, *History of Mary I*, p. 519.
5. Whitelock, *Elizabeth's Bedfellows*, p. 327.
6. Castor, 'Empress Matilda'.
7. Spenser, *White Ship*, p. 175.
8. Ibid, p. 178.
9. Borman, *Crown and Sceptre*, p. 34.
10. Lewis, *Stephen and Matilda's Civil War*, p. 111.
11. Castor, *She Wolves*, pp. 100-01.
12. Lewis, *Stephen and Matilda's Civil War*, p. 64.
13. Levine, 'Spiritual and Temporal', p. 121.
14. *The Act of Succession 1534*.
15. Wilson, *Lion's Court*, p. 370.
16. *The Second Succession Act 1536*.
17. *Statues of the Realm*, pp. 655-60; Lipscomb, *King is Dead*, p. 29.
18. *The Third Succession Act of King Henry VIII's Reign*.
19. *Statues of the Realm*, pp. 955-56.
20. Lipscomb, *King is Dead*, p. 30.
21. Lewis, *Stephen and Matilda's Civil War*, p. 34.
22. Hunt, *Coronation*, p. 125.
23. Whitelock, *Elizabeth's Bedfellows*, p. 187.

24. *CSP Spain*, September 1553, pp. 21-30.
25. *CSP Spain*, October 1553, pp. 1-5.
26. Hunt, *Drama of Coronation*, p. 130.
27. Ibid, p. 131.
28. Whitelock, *Elizabeth's Bedfellows*, p. 209.
29. Planche, *Regal Records*, p. 17.
30. Hunt, *Drama of Coronation*, p. 132.
31. Psalms 118:23-24.
32. Somerset, *Elizabeth I*, p. 59.
33. Camden, *History Renowned Princess*, p. 18.
34. Arnold, *Wardrobe*, p. 52.
35. Emmerson and McCaffrey, *Becoming Anne*, p. 12.
36. Richards, 'Mary Tudor as "Sole Quene"?', pp. 904-05.
37. Whitelock, *Elizabeth's Bedfellows*, p. 337.
38. Naunton, *Fragmenta*, p. 9.
39. Marcus, *Collected Works*, p. 51.

Chapter Three
1. Borman, *Private Lives*, p. 171.
2. *LP* Henry VIII, vol. 12 part 2, October 11-15, pp. 309-24.
3. Bovey, 'The Medieval Church'.
4. Moore and Reid, *Manifold Greatness*, p. 18.
5. Chrimes, *Henry VII*, p. 52.
6. Ibid, p. 57.
7. Penn, *Winter King*, p. 116.
8. Cockburn, 'Defender of the Faith'.
9. Lipscomb, *King is Dead*, p. 65.
10. Ryrie, 'From Sacred Scriptures'.
11. Alford, *Edward VI*, p. 6.
12. Hunt, *Drama of Coronation*, p. 84.
13. MacCulloch, *Tudor Church Militant*, p. 89.
14. Ibid, p. 142.
15. Ellis, *Three Books of Vergil*, p. 196.
16. Tallis, *Uncrowned Queen*, p. 143.
17. Griffiths, *Making Tudor Dynasty*, pp. 115-16.
18. Penn, *Winter King*, p. 22.
19. Ibid, p. 71.
20. Borman, *Private Lives*, p. 68.
21. Ibid, p. 180.

Chapter Four
1. BL Harley MS 6798, f. 87 r.
2. BL C.18.e.2(114*).

3. Alford, *Cecil*, p. 28.
4. Nichols, *Chronicle of Queen Jane*, pp. 90-91.
5. Nichols, *Diary of Henry Machyn*, Jan-Mar 1558, pp. 162-69.
6. Alford, *Cecil*, p. 80.
7. Marcus, *Collected Works*, p. 7.
8. Alford, *Cecil*, p. 88.
9. Ibid, p. 101.
10. Wright, *Queen Elizabeth and her Times*, p. 24.
11. I found this quotation in several biographies, the earlies of which is Strickland's *Life of Queen Elizabeth*, p. 627.
12. Values calculated at bankofengland.co.uk.
13. Cole, 'Monarchy in Motion', p. 35.
14. BL Add. MS 35830, vol. 259v.
15. Nichols, *Progresses and Processions*, vol. 1, p. 151.
16. Ibid, p. 206.
17. Keenan, 'Spectator and Spectacle', p. 102.
18. Ibid, p. 86.
19. Nichols, *Life and Times Hatton*, p. 126.
20. Tinniswood, *Behind the Throne*, p. 17.
21. Nichols, *Progresses and Processions*, vol. 1, p. 539.
22. *CSP Spain*, vol. 1, pp. 1-6.
23. *CSP Spain*, vol. 1, pp. 7-21.
24. Borman, *Private Lives*, p. 274.
25. Gristwood, *Elizabeth and Leicester*, p. 78.
26. Ibid, p. 335.
27. Paranque, *Blood, Fire, and Gold*, p. 194.
28. Whitelock, *Queen's Bedfellows*, pp. 185-87.
29. Marcus, *Collected Works*, p. 303.
30. BL Cotton MS, Caligula ff. 17v-18r.
31. Williams, *Rival Queens*, p. 159.
32. TNA MPF 1/366/1.
33. BL Add MS 88966.
34. BL C. 18e. 2(144).
35. Marcus, *Collected Works*, p. 189.
36. Doran, *Elizabeth's Circle*, p. 160.
37. Lambeth Palace MS 4267 f. 19.
38. Borman, *Private Lives*, p. 370

Chapter Five
1. *CSP Spain*, February 1553.
2. Ives, *Jane Grey*, pp. 8-9.
3. Inner Temple, Petyt MS 538, vol. 47, fo. 317.
4. Loach, *Edward VI*, p. 164.
5. Nichols, *Literary Remains*, pp. 568-69.

6. MacCulloch, *Church Militant*, pp. 40-41.
7. Penn, *Winter King*, pp. 341-45.
8. Lipscomb, *King is Dead*, p. 128.
9. *CSP Spain*: 1547, pp. 16-31.
10. Lipscomb, *King is Dead*, p. 133.
11. Nichols, *Literary Remains*, p. 561 note 1.
12. Nichols, *Literary Remains*, p. cxcix; Alford, *Edward VI*, p 81.
13. *CSP Spain*: July 1553, pp. 1-10.
14. Ibid.
15. Ibid.
16. Loach, *Edward VI*, p. 171.
17. Ives, *Lady Jane Grey*, p. 187.
18. Ibid.
19. Hunt, *Legitimacy*, p. 333.
20. Ibid, p. 334.
21. Foxe, *Acts and Monuments*.
22. Ives, *Lady Jane Grey*, pp. 191-92.
23. Whitelock, *Elizabeth's Bedfellows*, p. 181.
24. *CSP Spain*: July 1553, 11-15.
25. Ibid.
26. Tallis, *Crown of Blood*, p. 170.
27. Ibid, pp. 114-15.
28. Whitelock, *Elizabeth's Bedfellows*, p. 181.
29. Stow, *Two London Chronicles*, p. 27.
30. Tallis, *Crown of Blood*, pp. 177-78.
31. TNA, C 82/973.
32. *CSP Spain*: July 1553, pp. 16-20.
33. Whitelock, *Elizabeth's Bedfellows*, p. 182.
34. Tallis, *Crown of Blood*, p. 182.
35. Ibid, p. 183.
36. Hunt, 'Legitimacy, Ceremony, Drama', p. 334.
37. *CSP Spain*: July, 1553, pp. 16-20.
38. Tallis, *Crown of Blood*, p. 184.
39. Ibid, p. 188.
40. Nichols, *Diary of Henry Machyn*, p. 35.
41. Tomlin, 'Proclamation of Lady Jane Grey', p. 3.
42. Ibid, p. 4.
43. Nichols, *Diary of Henry Machyn*, p. 37.
44. Russell, *History of English Government*, p 3.

Chapter Six
1. Borman, *Private Lives*, p. 84.
2. *CSP Spain*, vol. 1, 13 December 1502.
3. Fraser, *Six Wives*, p.39.

4. *CSP Spain*, vol. 1, 15 April 1507.
5. *CPS Spain*, vol. 1, 20 March 1509.
6. Frasier, *Six Wives*, p. 49.
7. Richard Marius, *Thomas More: A Biography*, p. 53.
8. Frasier, *Six Wives*, p. 52.
9. Fraser, *Six Wives*, p. 121.
10. Hall, *Chronicle*, p. 631.
11. Ives, *Anne Boleyn*, p. 37.
12. *CSP Spain*: 21-30 June 1532.
13. *CSP Venice*: October 1532.
14. Gristwood, *Tudors in Love*, p. 115.
15. Ives, *Anne Boleyn*, p. 70.
16. Gristwood, *Tudors in Love*, pp. 150-51.
17. Norton, *Anne Boleyn Papers*, p. 56.
18. Ibid.
19. Fraser, *Six Wives*, pp. 133, 142.
20. *Letters Patent*, Pembroke, National Archives; Ives, *Anne Boleyn*, pp. 158-59.
21. Ives, *Anne Boleyn*, p. 171.
22. Ibid, p. 163.
23. *CSP Spain*: April 1533.
24. Hunt, *Drama Coronation*, p. 45.
25. Ibid, p. 46.
26. Ibid, p. 51.
27. Goldring, *John Nicol's Progresses*, p. 23.
28. Lipscomb, *1536*, p. 53.
29. *CSP Spain*: 17 February 1536.
30. Lipscomb, *1536*, p. 68.
31. Ibid, p. 73.
32. Ives, *Anne Boleyn*, p. 335.
33. Ibid, p. 325.
34. McCaffrey, 'Fit for Two Queens'.
35. Loades, *Six Wives*, p. 149.
36. *LP Henry VIII*, May 1536, 15 May.
37. Wriothesley, *Chronicle*, p. 43.
38. Fraser, *Six Wives*, p. 217.
39. Manners, *Royal Commission*, pp. 309-10.
40. *LP Henry VIII*, October 1536, 24 October.
41. Wriothesley, *Chronicle of England*, p. 68.
42. Ibid, note d.
43. Borman, *Private Lives*, p. 171.
44. *LP Henry VIII*, 24 Oct 1537.
45. Loades, *Six Wives*, pp. 189-90.
46. Wriothesley, *Chronicle of England*, pp. 109-10.

47. Ibid.
48. Strype, *Ecclesiastical Memorials*, p. 554.
49. Ibid.
50. Ibid, p. 555.
51. Ibid, p. 556.
52. *LP Henry VIII*, 6 July 1540.
53. Ibid.
54. Ibid, 11 July 1540.
55. Fraser, *Six Wives*, pp. 326-27.
56. Russell, *Young and Damned*, p. 53.
57. Ibid, p. 59.
58. Borman, *Private Lives*, p. 188.
59. Fraser, *Six Wives*, p. 322.
60. Loades, *Six Wives*, p. 207.
61. *LP Henry VIII*, 3 Sept 1540.
62. Borman, *Private Lives*, p. 191.
63. *LP Henry VIII*, 12 July 1540.
64. Borman, *Private Lives*, p. 193.
65. Fraser, *Six Wives*, p. 344.
66. Borman, *Private Lives*, p. 194.
67. Ibid, p. 195.
68. Borman, *Private Lives*, p. 173.
69. *LP Henry VIII*, 3 November 1537.
70. Borman, *Private Lives*, p. 178.
71. *CSP Spain*: December 1541.
72. *LP Henry VIII*, 16 January 1541.
73. Fraser, *Six Wives*, p. 358.
74. Loades, *Six Wives*, p. 221.
75. *LP Henry VIII*, 15 January 1543.
76. Borman, *Private Lives*, p. 205.
77. Fraser, *Six Wives*, p. 366.
78. Lynn, *Tudor Fashion*, p. 83.
79. Borman, *Private Lives*, p. 207.
80. Lynn, *Tudor Fashion*, p. 83.
81. Frasier, *Six Wives*, p. 389.

Chapter Seven
1. TNA SP 11/4/2 f. 3-3v.
2. Hunt, *Drama Coronation*, p. 2.
3. Legg, *English Coronation Records*, pp. xxi-xxii.
4. Borman, *Private Lives*, p. 71.
5. Hall, *Chronicle*, pp. 507-09.
6. Sharpe, *Selling Tudor Monarchy*, p. 111.

7. Legg, *English Coronation Records*, p. 198.
8. Hall, *Chronicle*, pp. 422-23.
9. Hunt, *Drama Coronation*, pp. 17-18.
10. Ibid, p. 77.
11. Loach, *Edward VI*, p. 37.
12. Hunt, *Drama Coronation*, pp. 84-85.
13. Gristwood, *Blood Sisters*, p. 251.
14. Nichols, *Privy Purse*, p. lxxi.
15. Ibid, p. lxxii.
16. Gristwood, *Blood Sisters*, p. 252.
17. Nichols, *Privy Purse*, p. lxxiv.
18. Gristwood, *Blood Sisters*, p. 252.
19. Nichols, *Privy Purse*, p. lxxiv.
20. Hunt, *Drama Coronation*, p. 39.
21. *LP Henry VIII*, 31 May 1533.
22. Ives, *Anne Boleyn* p. 174.
23. *LP Henry VIII*, 31 May 1533.
24. Ives, *Anne Boleyn*, p. 177.
25. Ibid, p. 178.
26. *CSP Venice*: 7 June 1533.
27. Emmerson and McCaffrey, *Becoming Anne*, p. 10.
28. Ives, *Anne Boleyn*, p. 179.
29. Hunt, *Drama Coronation*, p. 42.
30. Hunt, 'Reformation', p. 63.
31. *CSP Spain*: Sept. 19, 1553.
32. *CSP Spain*: Oct. 3, 1553.
33. Hunt, 'Reformation', p. 65.
34. *CSP Spain*: Sept. 13, 1553.
35. Hunt, 'Reformation', p. 67.
36. Ibid, p, 68.
37. Arnold, *Wardrobe*, p. 52.
38. Somerset, *Elizabeth I*, p. 70.
39. Borman, *Elizabeth's Women*, p. 192.
40. Hunt, *Drama Coronation*, p. 146.
41. Kewes, 'Godly Queens', p. 50.
42. Hunt, 'Reformation', p. 70.
43. Emmerson and Ridgway, *Boleyns of Hever*, p. 113.
44. Somerset, *Elizabeth I*, p. 72.
45. Hunt, 'Reformation of Tradition', pp. 16-17.

Chapter Eight
1. Somerset, *Elizabeth I*, p. 372.
2. Meagher, 'First Progress Henry VII', p. 46.

3. Hall, *Chronicle*, p. 426.
4. Mulryne, 'Court Festivals'.
5. Meagher, 'First Progress Henry VII', p. 48.
6. Cavell, 'Memoir of the Court', p. 147.
7. Meagher, 'First Progress Henry VII', p. 50.
8. Sharpe, *Selling Tudor Monarchy*, p. 54.
9. Cavell, 'Memoir of the Court', p. 150.
10. Ibid, p. 151.
11. Richardson, *Cloth of Gold*, p. 7.
12. Ibid, p. 224.
13. Ibid, pp. 56, 66.
14. Solly, 'When Henry VIII and Francis I'.
15. Richardson, *Cloth of Gold*, p. 178.
16. Ibid, p. 208.
17. *LP Henry VIII*, August 1541.
18. Madden, 'Henry VIII Entry', p. 4.
19. Hall, *Chronicle*, p. 842.
20. Borman, *Henry Men Made Him*, p. 450.
21. Borman, *Private Lives*, p. 225.
22. Alford, *Edward VI*, p. 58.
23. Nichols, *Literary Remains*, p. 80.
24. Ibid, p. 81.
25. Ibid.
26. MacCulloch, *Church Militant*, p. 101.
27. Loach, *Edward VI*, pp. 137-39.
28. Borman, *Henry Men Made Him*, p. 245.
29. *CSP Spain*: June 1554.
30. Whitelock, *Elizabeth's Bedfellows*, p. 249.
31. Streckfuss, 'Spes Maxima', p. 148.
32. *CPS Spain*, vol. 13, 1554-58.
33. Nichols, *Progresses and Processions*, p. 74.
34. Ibid, pp. 418-19.
35. Frye, p. 92.
36. Goldring, *Nichol's Progresses*, p. 172.
37. Frye, *Elizabeth I Representation*, p. 62.
38. Ibid, p. 92.
39. Goldring, *Nichol's Progresses*, p. 164.
40. Frye, p. 62.
41. Goldring, *Nichol's Progresses*, p. 177.
42. Ibid, p. 188.
43. Archer, *Progresses Pageants*, p. 10.
44. Nichols, *Literary Remains*, vol. 3, p. 590.
45. Archer, *Progresses Pageants*, p. 11.

46. Somerset, *Elizabeth I*, p. 376.
47. Arnold, *Wardrobe*, p. 81.
48. Nichols, *Progresses and Processions*, vol. 3, pp. 592-95.
49. Arnold, *Wardrobe*, pp. 83-84.

Chapter Nine
1. Guy, *Elizabeth Later Years*, pp. 354-55.
2. Ibid, p. 356.
3. *Marcus, Collected Works*, pp. 337-40.
4. Ibid, pp. 340-41.
5. Borman, *Private Lives*, p. 112.
6. Mortimer, *Time Traveler*, p. 120.
7. Goodman, *Be a Tudor*, p. 86.
8. Borman, *Private Lives*, p. 304.
9. Mortimer, *Time Traveler*, p. 120.
10. License, *Woodsmoke and Sage*, p. 264.
11. Goodman, *Be a Tudor*, p. 87.
12. Mortimer, *Time Traveler*, p. 217.
13. MacDonald, *Lavatorial Luxury*.
14. Borman, *Private Lives*, p. 129.
15. MacDonald, 'Historians Recreate Lavatorial Luxury'.
16. Harington, *Metamorphosis*, p. 8.
17. Ibid, p. 12.
18. Thurley, *Houses Power*, p. 371.
19. Playhouses, British Library website.
20. Picard, *Elizabeth's London*, p. 222.
21. Ibid.
22. Alford, *London*, p. 23.
23. Picard, *Elizabeth's London*, p. 223.
24. Ogden, 'Changes Population', p. 182.
25. Goodman, *Be a Tudor*, p. ix.
26. Picard, *Elizabeth's London*, p. xxii.
27. *Open City: London*, Folger Shakespeare Library website.
28. Picard, *Elizabeth's London*, p. 144.
29. Goodman, *Be a Tudor*, p. x.
30. Archer, 'Government of London', p. 19.
31. *Open City: London*, Folger Shakespeare Library website.
32. Ibid.
33. Stow, *Survey of London*, Cornehill warde.
34. Alford, *London's Triumph*, pp. 108-09.
35. Stow, *Survey of London*, Cornehill warde.
36. Alford, *London's Triumph*, p. 112.
37. Moyle, *King's Painter*, p. 283.

38. Sharpe, *Selling Tudor Monarchy*, p. 130.
39. Moyle, *King's Painter*, p. 314.
40. Sharpe, *Selling Tudor Monarchy*, p. 136, using J. Rowlands.
41. Moyle, *King's Painter*, p. 316.
42. Cooper, *Tudors to Windsors*, p. 42.
43. *Open City: London*, Folger Shakespeare Library website.
44. Ibid.
45. Wooding, 'Reform, Wrath, and Ruin'.
46. Picard, *Elizabeth's London*, pp. 199-201.
47. Bernard, 'Dissolution of Monasteries', p. 390.
48. Wilson, *Lion's Court*, p. 137.
49. 'Coverdale Bible', British Library website.
50. Wilson, *Lion's Court*, p. 167.
51. 'Coverdale Bible', Museum of the Bible website.
52. Ibid.
53. 'Coverdale Bible', British Library website.
54. Sharpe, *Selling Tudor Monarchy*, p. 144.
55. Moore, *Manifold Greatness*, p. 34.
56. Moule, *Historical Catalogue*, p. 61.
57. Ibid, p. 88.
58. Moore, *Manifold Greatness*, p. 36.
59. Ibid, p. 164.
60. 'Great Bible', Museum of the Bible website.
61. The Folger Shakespeare Library in Washington, DC holds a copy of the Bishop's Bible, bound in red velvet and decorated with embossed clasps with the queen's initials, that it thought to be this presentation copy. I have seen it there, and it is a magnificent artifact of the Tudor English translations of the Bible.
62. *Manifold Greatness*, Folger Shakespeare Library website.
63. Wilson, *Brief History Reformation*, p. 351.
64. 'Reformation: Shattered World, New Beginnings', University of London website, pp. i-2.

Chapter 10
1. Brigden, *New Worlds*, p. 355.
2. Gristwood, *Tudors in Love*, p. 339.
3. Camden, *Most Renowned Elizabeth*, Book IV, p. 659.
4. Borman, *Private Lives*, p. 369.
5. *CSP Elizabeth*: March 1603.
6. *CSP Venice*: March 20, 1603.
7. Borman, *Private Lives*, p. 371.
8. *CSP Elizabeth*: March 15, 1603.
9. Borman, *Private Lives*, p. 371.

10. Tallis, *Margaret Beaufort*, p. xxxi.
11. Ibid, p. xxxiv.
12. Borman, *Crown and Sceptre*, p. 249.
13. Cunningham, 'Prince Arthur'.
14. Gristwood, *Tudors in Love*, p. 115.
15. Ibid, pp. 125-26.
16. Gristwood, *Tudors in Love*, p. 122.
17. License, *Woodsmoke and Sage*, pp. 252-53.
18. Hampton Court, 'Tudor Food', Historic Royal Palaces website.
19. Borman, *Private Lives*, pp. 115-16.
20. Lipscomb, *King is Dead*, p 12.
21. Borman, *Private Lives*, pp. 216-17.
22. Lynch, 'Outliers: Margaret Pole'.
23. Jones, *Hollow Crown*, p. xxxii.
24. Westfall, 'Boy Who Would Be King', p. 273.
25. Brigden, *New Worlds*, p. 181.
26. Ibid.
27. Westfall, 'Boy Who Would Be King', p. 271.
28. Ibid, pp. 282-83.
29. Nichols, *Literary Remains*, p. 390.
30. Borman, *Private Lives*, p. 313.
31. 'Original 007?', Cambridge University.
32. *CSP Venice*: 10 July 1603.
33. Arnold, *Wardrobe Unlocked*, p. 174.
34. Sharpe, *Selling the Tudors*, p. 412.
35. Lynn, *Tudor Fashion*, p. 149.
36. Borman, *Private Lives*, p. 318.
37. Ibid, pp. 320-21.
38. Ibid, p. 360.
39. License, *Woodsmoke and Sage*, p 195.
40. Moulton, *Mirror or Glass of Health*.
41. Borman, *Private Lives*, p. 124.
42. License, *Woodsmoke and Sage*, p. 203.
43. In Goodman, *How to be a Tudor*, p. 19.
44. Goodman, 'Getting Clean'.
45. Lynn, *Tudor Fashion*, p. 168.
46. Richardson, 'Bacton Altar Cloth', p. 54.
47. McCaffrey, 'Hope from Day to Day'.
48. Gershon, 'Wooden Falcon'.

Bibliography

Abbreviations
BL (British Library)
CSP (Calendar of State Papers)
LP (Letters and Papers)
TNA (The National Archives UK)

Primary Sources
Acts of the Privy Council of England, vol. 3, 1550–1552. Originally published by Her Majesty's Stationery Office. London: 1891.
Calendar of Cecil Papers in Hatfield House: Volumes I-2, 1506–1582. Originally published by Her Majesty's Stationery Office. London: 1883.
Calendar of State Papers, Foreign. Elizabeth: July 1561, 11-20. Originally published by Her Majesty's Stationery Office London: 1866.
Calendar of State Papers, Spain (Simancas), Volume 1, 1558–1567. Ed. by Martin A.S. Hume. Originally published by Her Majesty's Stationery Office. London: 1892.
Calendar of State Papers, Venice. Originally published by Her Majesty's Stationery Office. London: 1867.
Camden, William. *The History of the Most Renowned and Victorious Princess Elizabeth, Late Queen of England*. Fourth Edition. London: 1688.
Dasent, John Roche, ed. *Acts of the Privy Council of England*, Volume 1, 1542–1547. Originally published by Her Majesty's Stationery Office. London: 1890.
Drawing of Darnley's murder created for William Cecil Birds-eye view of the Darnley murder scene, February 1567. TNA, MPF 1/366/1.
Drawing of the Arms of Dauphin Francis and Mary, Mary Queen of Scots, England and Scotland, July 1559. BL, Cotton S, Caligula Bx ff. 17v-18r.
Edward VI's Devise for the Succession. Inner Temple, Petyt MS 538, vol. 47, fo. 317.
Elizabeth I's Tilbury Speech, BL, Harley MS 6798, f. 87r.
Elizabeth I's instructions for Sir Nicholas Throckmorton, 27 July 1567. BL, Add MS 88966.
Elizabeth to Queen Mary I, 17 March, 1554. TNA, SP 11/4/2. ff.3-3v.
Ellis, Sir Henry. *Three Books of Polydore Vergil's English History, Comprising the Reigns of Henry VI, Edward IV, and Richard III*. London: 1744

Excommunication of Elizabeth, SDN Pi Papae V. Sententia declaratoria Elisabeth praetensam Angliae Reginam, Rome 1570. BL, C. 18.e.2(114*).

Foxe, John. *Book of Martyrs (or Acts and Monuments)*. Philadelphia: 1881.

Gardiner, James. *Letters and Papers Illustrative of the Reigns of Richard III and Henry VII* (2 volumes). London: 1861–63.

Given-Wilson, Chris, Paul Brand, Seymour Phillips, Mark Ormrod, Geoffrey Martin, Anne Curry, and Rosemary Horrox, eds. *Parliament Rolls of Medieval England*. Woodbridge: 2005. https://www.british-history.ac.uk/no-series/parliament-rolls-medieval?page=2.

Goldring, Elizabeth, Faith Eales, Elizabeth Clarke, and Jayne Elisabeth Archer, eds. *John Nichol's Progresses and Public Processions of Queen Elizabeth I, Volume V.* Oxford: 2014.

Hall, Edward. *Chronicle Containing the History of England During the Reign of Henry IV and the Succeeding Monarchs, to the End of the Reign of Henry VIII.* Carefully collated with the editions of 1548 and 1550. London: 1809.

Hall, Edward. *The Union of the Two Noble and Illustre Families of Lancastre and Yorke.* 1548 Edition. London: 1809.

Halliwell-Phillips, James. *Letters of the Kings of England*, Volume 1. London: 2009.

Harington, John, *The Metamorphosis of Ajax.* Chiswick: 1819.

Harrington, John, *An Anatomy of the Matamorpho-sed Ajax.* London: 1596.

Haynes, Samuel, *A Collection of State Papers Relating to Affairs in the Reigns of King Henry VIII, King Edward VI, Queen Mary, and Queen Elizabeth from the Year 1542 to 1570.* London: 1740.

'Henry VII: November 1485, Part 1'. *Parliament Rolls of Medieval England.* https://www.british-history.ac.uk/no-series/parliament-rolls-medieval/november-1485-pt-1.

Historical Memorials, *Ecclesiastical and Civil, of Events under the Reign of Queen Mary I.* Vol III. London: 1721.

Howes, John, *A brief note of the order and manner of the proceedings in the first erection of the Three Royal Hospitals of Christ, Bridewell, and St Thomas the Apostle* (at the charge of Septimus Vaughan Morgan). London: 1904.

Hume, Martin A. Sharp, trans. *Chronicle of King Henry VIII of England, being a Contemporary Record of some of the Principal Events of the Reigns of Henry VIII and Edward VI.* London: 1889.

Legg, L.G. Wickham, ed. *English Coronation Records.* London: 1901.

Lelandi, Joannis. *Antiquarii de rebus Britannicus Collectanea*, volume IV. London: 1770.

LP, Foreign and Domestic, Henry VIII, Volume 7, 1534, Ed. James Gairdner. London: Her Majesty's Stationery Office, 1883.

LP, Foreign and Domestic, Henry VIII, Volume 12 Part 2, June–December 1537. Originally published by Her Majesty's Stationery Office, London, 1891.

Letters Patent relating to Anne Boleyn, Countess of Pembroke. 22 April 1509–24 March 1603. TNA, E 156/43/2.

Madden, Frederic. 'Account of King Henry VIII's Entry into Lincoln in 1541'. Letter to Henry Ellis, Esq. *Archaeologia*, Vol. XXIII. London: 1831.
Manners, Charles, Duke of Rutland. *Royal Commission on Historical Manuscripts*. London: 1888.
Marcus, Leah S. Janel Mueller, and Mary Beth Rose. *Elizabeth I: Collected Works*. Chicago: 2000.
Mary Queen of Scots to William Cecil, Tutbury, 23 May 1570. TNA SP 53/5. f. 72.
Moulton, Thomas. *This is the Myrror or Glasse of Health*. London: c. 1539.
Naunton, Sir Robert. Fragmenta Regalia: *Memoirs of Elizabeth, her Court and Favourites*. London: 1824.
Nicolas, Harris. *Memoirs of the Life and Times of Sir Christopher Hatton, K.G.* London: 1847.
Nichols, J.G., ed. *The Diary of Henry Machyn, Citizen and Merchant-Taylor of London, 1550–1563*. Camden Society: 1848.
Nichols, John Gough, ed. *The Chronicle of Queen Jane, and of Two Years of Queen Mary, and especially of the Rebellion of Sir Thomas Wyatt*. Camden Society: 1850.
Nichols, John Gough. *Literary Remains of King Edward VI*. 2 Volumes. London: 1857.
Nichols, John. *Privy Purse Expenses of Elizabeth of York*. London: 1830.
Nichols, John. *The Progresses and Public Processions of Queen Elizabeth*, Volumes 1-3. London: 2018 (orig. 1788).
Norton, Elizabeth. *The Anne Boleyn Papers*. Gloucestershire: 2013.
Poems on the coronation of King Henry VIII of England (1509–1547) and Queen Katherine of Aragon (d. 1536.) BL, Cotton Titus D. IV f.12v.
Privy Council Letter to Henry Grey, 6th Earl of Kent, ordering the enactment of the warrant for the execution of Mary Queen of Scots, 3 February 1587. BL Add Ms 48027.
Proclamation of Lady Jane Grey as Queen of England, 1553. Renascence Editions. University of Oregon: 2001.
'Richard II: January 1397'. *Parliament Rolls of Medieval England*. https://www.british-history.ac.uk/no-series/parliament-rolls-medieval/january-1397.
Sententia declaratoria contra Elisabeth praetensam Angliae Reginam, Rome, 1570. BL, C.18.e.2. [114*].
Stone, J.M. *The History of Mary I, Queen of England as found in the Public Records, Dispatches of Ambassadors, in Original Private Letters, and Other Contemporary Documents*. London: 1901.
Stow, John, *A Survey of London*. Reprinted from Text of 1603. Oxford: 1908.
Stow, John. *Two London Chronicles from the Collections of John Stow*. Camden Society: 1910.
Strype, John. *Ecclesiastical Memorials: Relating Chiefly to Religion and the Reformation of it, and the Emergencies of the Church of England under Henry VIII, Edward VI, and Mary I*. Volume 1. Oxford: 1822.
The Act of Succession 1534, Parliamentary Archives. HL/PO/PU/1/1533/25H8n22. https://ukparliament.shorthandshories.com/succession.

The Second Succession Act 1536, Parliamentary Archives. HL/PO/PU/1/1536/28H8n7. https://ukparliament.shorthandshories.com/succession.

The Third Succession Act of King Henry VIII's Reign, Parliamentary Archives. HL/PO/PU/1543/35H8n1. https://ukparliament.shorthandshories.com/succession.

Queen Regent's Prerogative Act 1554. Parliamentary Archives. 1 Mar Session 3, c1. https://ukparliament.shorthandshories.com/succession.

William Cecil to Sir Nicholas Throckmorton, 14 July 1561. BL, Add. MS 35830, fol. 159v.

Wingfield, Robert. *Life of Queen Mary I.* BL Add MS 48093.

Wright, Thomas, ed. *Queen Elizabeth and her Times, a Series of Original Letters selected form the inedited Private Correspondence of the Lord Treasurer Burghley, the Earl of Leicester, the Secretaries Walsingham and Smith, Sir Christopher, and most of the distinguished persons of the Period.* Volume 1. London: 1838.

Wriothesley, Charles, *A Chronicle of England During the Reigns of the Tudors, from AD 1485 to 1559,* volume 1. London: 1875.

Secondary Sources

Alford, Stephen, *London's Triumph: Merchant Adventurers and the Tudor City.* London: 2017.

Alford, Stephen. *Edward VI.* London: 2014.

Amin, Nathen. *Henry VII and the Tudor Pretenders: Simnel, Warbeck, and Warwick.* London: 2020.

Amin, Nathen. *The House of Beaufort.* London: 2017.

Archer, Ian W. 'The Government of London, 1500–1650'. *The London Journal,* volume 26 (2001), issue 1, pp. 19-28.

Archer, Jayne Elisabeth, Elizabeth Goldring, and Sarah Knight. *The Progresses, Pageants, and Entertainments of Queen Elizabeth I.* Oxford: 2007.

Arnold, Catherine. *Globe: Life in Shakespeare's London.* London 2015.

Arnold, Janet. *Queen Elizabeth's Wardrobed Unlocked.* London: 2015.

Baetjer, Katharine, 'Portrait Painting in England, 1600–1800'. *Heilbrunn Timeline of Art History,* October 2003. http://metmuseum.org/toah/hd/bpor.

Bailey, Alfred. *The English Crown: A Historical Sketch.* London: 1879.

Bedworth, Candy, 'Power and Propaganda – The British Royal Portrait'. *Daily Art Magazine,* 21 April 2022. http://dailyartmagazine.com/british-royal-portrait/.

Bell, Aryn Elizabeth. 'Elizabeth I and the Policy of Marriage: The Anjou Match, 1572–1582'. University of North Dakota, *UND Scholarly Commons,* Jan. 2013. http://commonsund.edu/cgi/viewcontent.cgi?article=23988context=thesis.

Bell, Doyne C. *Notices of the Historic Persons Buried in the Chapel of St Peter ad Vincula in the Tower of London.* London: 1877.

Bergeron, David M. 'Elizabeth's Coronation Entry (1559): New Manuscript Evidence'. *English Literary Renaissance,* Volume 8, No. 1, (Winter 1978), pp. 3-8.

Bernard, G.W. 'The Dissolution of the Monasteries,' in *History* (Vol. 96, No. 4 (324), October 2011), pp. 390–409.

Borman, Tracy. *Crown and Sceptre*. London: 2020.
Borman, Tracy. *Elizabeth's Women*. London: 2009.
Borman, Tracy. *Private Lives of the Tudors*. London: 2016.
Bovey, Alixe. 'The Medieval Church: From Dedication to Dissent'. *The Middle Ages*. 30 April 2015. http://bl.uk/the-middle-ages/articles/church-in-the-middle-ages-from-dedication-to-dissent.
Breitenberg, Mark. "'…the hold opened": Iconic Representation and Interpretation in "The Quenes Majesties Passage"', in *Criticism*, Volume 28, No. 1 (winter 1986), pp. 1-25.
Brigden, Susan. *New Worlds, Lost Worlds*. London: 2000.
Bryson, Alan, 'Remembering the Field of Cloth of Gold', *Medieval Manuscripts Blog*. 7 June 2020. http://bl.uk/digitisedmanuscripts/2020/06/thefieldofclothofgold.
Butlin, R.A. and R.A. Dodgshon. *An Historical Geography of Europe*. Oxford: 1999.
Castor, Helen. 'Empress Matilda, daughter of Henry I: A Queen in a King's World.' *History Extra*, 10 September 2020. https://www.historyextra.com/period/medieval/matilda-daughter-of-henry-i-a-queen-in-a-kings-world/.
Castor, Helen. *She Wolves: The Women Who Ruled England Before Elizabeth*. London: 2011.
Cavell, Emma. *A Memoir of the Court of Henry VII*. University of Tasmania. October 2001. http://eprints.utas.edu/19121/1/whole_CavellEmma2002_thesis.pdf.
Cavendish, Richard. 'The First Book of Common Prayer'. *History Today*, volume 49, issue 1, January 1999. http://historytoday.com/archive/first-book-common-prayer.
Chrimes, S.B. *Henry VII*. Yale: 1977.
Cockburn, Calum. 'Defender of the Faith," *Medieval manuscripts*. 21 July 2020. https://blogs.bl.uk/digitisedmanuscripts/2020/07/defender-of-the-faith.html.
Cole, Mary Hill, 'Monarchy in Motion: An Overview of Elizabethan Progresses', *The Progresses, Pageants, and Entertainments of Queen Elizabeth I*, pp. 27-45.
Coverdale Bible. https://www.bl.uk/collection-items/coverdale-bible
Coverdale Bible. https://collections.museumofthebible.org/artifacts/10847-coverdale-bible.
Cooper, Taryna, ed. *Tudors to Windsor: British Royal Portraits*. London: 2018.
Cunningham, Sean, 'Prince Arthur, Catherine of Aragon, and Henry VIII: A Story of Early Tudor Triumph and Tragedy'. *History Extra*, 25 February 2021. http://historyextra.com/period/tudor/prince-arthur-catherine-katherine-aragon-king-henry-viii-marriage-death-brother.
Doran, Susan. 'Henry VIII and the Reformation'. *Discovering Sacred Texts*. 23 Sept 2019. https://www.bl.uk/sacred-texts/articles/henry-viii-and-the-reformation.
Dunn, Jane. *Elizabeth and Mary*. New York: 2004.
Durkan, John. James, 'Third Earl of Arran: The Hidden Years'. *The Scottish Historical Review*, Volume 65, No. 180, Part 2 (Oct. 1986), pp. 154-166.
Emmerson, Owen and Claire Ridgway. *The Boleyns of Hever Castle*. 2021.

Emmerson, Owen and Kate McCaffrey. *Becoming Anne: Connections, Culture, Court*. Hever Castle: 2022.
The Elizabethan Court Day by Day. http://folgerpedia.folger.edu/The-Elizabethan-Court-Day-by-Day.
Fraser, Antonia. *The Six Wives of Henry VIII*. London: 1993.
Frye, Susan. *Elizabeth I: The Competition for Representation*. Oxford: 1996.
Gershon, Livia, 'Wooden Falcon Sold for $101 Originally Belonged to Anne Boleyn'. *Smithsonian Magazine*, 9 November 2021. http://smithsonianmag.com/smart-news/wooden-falcon-once-sold-for-101-was-anne-boleyns-180979033.
Goodman, Ruth. 'Getting Clean, the Tudor Way'. *The New Republic*, February 15, 2016.
Goodman, Ruth. *How To Be a Tudor*. London: 2015.
The Great Bible. https://collections.museumofthebible.org/artifacts/6573-the-great-bible.
Griffiths, R.A. 'Henry Tudor: The Training of a King'. *Huntington Library Quarterly*, Volume 49, no. 3, Tudor History Issue (Summer, 1986), pp. 197-218.
Griffiths, Ralph and Roger Thomas. *The Making of the Tudor Dynasty*. Stroud: 2005.
Gristwood, Sarah. *Blood Sisters: The Women Behind the Wars of the Roses*. London: 2013.
Gristwood, Sarah. *Elizabeth and Leicester*. London: 2008.
Gristwood, Sarah. *Game of Queens*. London: 2017.
Gristwood, Sarah. *Tudors in Love*. London: 2021.
Guy, John. *Elizabeth: The Later Years*. New York: 2016.
Halsted, Caroline. *Life of Margaret Beaufort, Countess of Richmond and Derby, Mother of King Henry VII, and Foundress of Christ's and St John's College, Oxford*. London: 1845.
Hooker, Jams. 'Notes on the Organization and Supply of the Tudor Military under Henry VII'. *Huntington Library Quarterly*, vol. 23, no. 1, 1959, pp. 19-31.
Hunt, Anna and Anna Whitelock. *Tudor Queenship: The Reigns of Mary and Elizabeth*. New York: 2010.
Hunt, Alice. 'Legitimacy, Ceremony and Drama: Mary Tudor's Coronation and Republica'. *Interludes and Early Modern Society: Studies in Gender, Power and Theatricality*. 2007. https://doi.org/10.1163/9789401205894_016.
Hunt, Alice. 'The Reformation of Tradition: The Coronations of Mary and Elizabeth'. *Tudor Queenship: The Reigns of Mary and Elizabeth*, pp. 63-80.
Hunt, Alice. *The Drama of Coronation: Medieval Ceremony in Early Modern England*. London: 2008.
Ives, Eric. *Lady Jane Grey: A Tudor Mystery*. London: 2009.
Johnson, Lauren. *Shadow King*. London: 2019.
Johnston, Hope. 'Catherine of Aragon's Pomegranate, Revisited', in *Transactions of the Cambridge Bibliographical Society*, Vol. 13, No. 2 (2005), pp. 153-173.
Jones, Dan. *Hollow Crown*. London: 2015.

Keenan, Siobhan. 'Spectator and Spectacle: Royal Entertainments at the Universities in the 1560s', in *The Progresses, Pageants, and Entertainments of Queen Elizabeth I*, pp. 86-103.

Keene, Jessica L and Amanda E. Herbert. 'The Tudors are Trending: An English Dynasty Continues to Dominate Popular Culture'. *Perspectives on History, the newsmagazine of the American Historical Association*, Sept. 16, 2020. https://www.historians.org/research-and-publications/perspectives-on-history/october-2020/the-tudors-are-trending-an-english-dynasty-continues-to-dominate-popular-culture.

Kewes, Paulina. 'Godly Queens: The Royal Iconographies of Mary and Elizabeth'. In *Tudor Queenship: The Reigns of Mary and Elizabeth*. New York: 2010.

Kyle, Chris R. 'Monarch and Marketplace: Proclamations as News in Early Modern England'. *Huntington Library Quarterly*, Volume 78, No. 4 (Winter 2015), pp. 771-787.

Levine, Mortimer. 'Henry VIII's Use of His Spiritual and Temporal Jurisdictions in His Great Causes of Matrimony, Legitimacy, and Succession'. *The Historical Journal*, vol. 10, no. 1. Cambridge: 1967, pp. 3–10.

Levine, Mortimer. 'A Parliamentary Title to the Crown in Tudor England'. *Huntington Library Quarterly*, vol. 25, no. 2, University of California Press, 1962, pp. 121–27. https://doi.org/10.2307/3816567.

Lewis, Matt. *Henry II and Eleanor of Aquitaine: Founding an Empire*. London: 2021.

Lewis, Matt. *Stephen and Matilda's Civil War*. London: 2021.

License, Amy. *Woodsmoke and Sage: The Five Senses, How the Tudors Experienced the World*. Cheltenham: 2021.

Life at the Tudor Court: The Place to See and be Seen. www.hrp.org.uk/hampton-court-palace.

Lipscomb, Suzannah. *1536: The Year that Made Henry VIII*. New York: 2016.

Lipscomb, Suzannah. *The King is Dead: The Will of Henry VIII*. London: 2015.

Loach, Jennifer. *Edward VI*. Yale: 1999.

Loades, David. *Mary Tudor*. London: 2012.

Lynch, Alex. 'Outliers: The Death of Margaret Pole'. *Historic Royal Palaces Blog*, 10 December 2019. https://blog.hrp.org.uk/outliers-the-death-of-margaret-pole/.

Lynn, Eleri. *Tudor Fashion*. Historic Royal Palaces: 2017.

MacCulloch, Diarmaid. *Tudor Church Militant: Edward VI and the Protestant Reformation*. London: 2001.

MacDonald, Marianne. 'Historians recreate Henry VIII's velvet world of lavatorial luxury'. *Independent*. 8 July 1995.

Manifold Greatness: The Creation and Afterlife of the King James Bible. https://folgerpedia.folger.edu/Manifold_Greatness:_The_Creation_and_Afterlife_of_the_King_James_Bible

McCaffrey, Kate E. 'Hope from Day to Day: Inscriptions Newly Discovered in a Book Owned by Anne Boleyn'. *Times Literary Supplement*, 21 May 2021.

https://www.the-tls.co.uk/articles/inscriptions-discovered-in-a-book-owned-by-anne-boleyn-essay-kate-e-mccaffrey.

McCaffrey, Kate. 'A Book Fit for Two Queens'. The Morgan Library & Museum Blog. 2021. https://www.themorgan.org/blog/book-fit-two-queens.

Meagher, John C. 'The First Progress of Henry VII'. *Renaissance Drama New Series,* Volume 1, (1968), pp. 45-73.

Moore, Helen, and Julian Reid, eds. *Manifold Greatness: The Making of the King James Bible.* Oxford: 2011.

Mortimer, Ian. *Time Traveler's Guide to Elizabethan England.* London: 2012.

Mortimer, Ian. 'Tudor Chronicler or Sixteenth-Century Diarist? Henry Machyn and the Nature of His Manuscript'. *The Sixteenth Century Journal.* Volume 33, No. 4 (Winter 2002), pp. 981-998.

Moule, Horace Frederick and Thomas Herbert Darlow, eds. *Historical Catalogue of the Printed Editions of Holy Scripture in the Library of the British and Foreign Bible Society Library.* 1903.

Moyle, Franny. *The King's Painter: The Life and Times of Hans Holbein.* London: 2021.

Mulryne, J.R. 'Court and Civic Festivals in Tudor and Early Stuart England'. *British Library Treasures in Full.* https://www.bl.uk/treasures/festivalbooks/stuartengland.html.

Ogden, P.E. 'Changes in Population and Society, 1500 to the Present'. *An Historical Geography of Europe.* R.A. Butlin and R. A. Dodghson, eds. Oxford: 1998.

Open City: London, 1500–1700. https://folgerpedia.folger.edu/Open_City:_London,_1500%E2%80%931700

Paranque, Estelle. *Blood, Fire, and Gold: The Story of Elizabeth I and Catherine de Medici.* London: 2022.

Penn, Thomas. *Winter King.* London: 2018.

Picard, Liza, *Elizabeth's London.* New York: 2003.

Planche, J.R. *A Chronicle of the Coronations of the Queens Regnant of England.* London: 1838.

'Playhouses'. *Treasures in Full, Shakespeare in Quarto.* https://www.bl.uk/treasures/shakespeare/playhouses.html

Rackin, Phyllis. 'A Modern Perspective: *Henry VI, Part 1*'. *Shakespeare's Works.* https://shakespeare.folger.edu/shakespeares-works/henry-vi-part-1/henry-vi-part-1-a-modern-perspective/ .

Reformation: Shattered World, New Beginnings. University of London, Senate House Library, 2017. https://reformation.senatehouselibrary.ac.uk/sites/default/files/downloads/Reformation%20exhibition%20catalogue_0.pdf

Richards, Judith M. 'Mary Tudor as "Sole Quene"?: Gendering Tudor Monarchy'. *The Historical Journal,* Volume 40, No. 4 (Dec 1997), pp. 895-924.

Richardson, Glenn. *The Field of Cloth of Gold.* Yale University: 2014.

Richardson, Ruth E. 'The Bacton Altar Cloth: A Dress Fit for a Tudor Queen?' *Current Archaeology,* Issue 357, Dec. 2019, pp. 52-55.

Rickert, Edith. 'Political Propaganda and Satire in A Midsummer Night's Dream'. *Modern Philology*, Aug. 1923, Vol. 21, No. 1 (Aug. 1923), pp. 53-87.
Russell, Gareth. *Young and Damned and Fair: The Life of Catherine Howard*. London: 2016.
Russell, John. *An Essay on the History of the English Government and Constitution from the Reign of Henry VII to the Present Time*. London: 1865.
Ryrie, Alec. 'From Sacred Scriptures to the People's Bible'. *Discovering Sacred Texts*, British Library. 23 Sep 2019. https://www.bl.uk/sacred-texts/articles/from-sacred-scriptures-to-the-peoples-bible.
Samton, Alexander. 'Changing Places: The Marriage and Royal Entry of Philip, Prince of Austria, and Mary Tudor, July-August 1554'. *The Sixteenth Century Journal*, Vol. 36, No. 3 (Fall 2005), pp. 761-784.
Sharpe, Kevin. *Selling the Tudor Monarchy*. Yale University: 2009.
Snook, Edith. 'Jane Grey, "Manful" Combat, and the Female Reader in Early Modern England'. *Renaissance and Reformation*, Volume 32, No. 1 (Winter 2009), pp. 47-81.
Solly, Meilan, 'When Henry VIII and Francis I Spent $19 Million on an 18-day Party'. *Smithsonian Magazine*. 23 June 2020. https://www.smithsonianmag.com/history/five-hundred-years-ago-henry-viii-and-francis-i-spent-19-million-18-day-party-180975116.
Somerset, Anne. *Elizabeth I*. London: 2003.
Spenser, Charles. *White Ship: Conquest, Anarchy, and the Wrecking of Henry I's Dream*. London: 2021.
Streckfull, Corinna, 'Spes maxima nostra: European Propaganda and the Spanish Match'. *Tudor Queenship*, pp. 146-252.
Stone, Jean Mary. *Mary I: Queen of England*. London: 1901.
Strickland, Agnes. *Life of Queen Elizabeth*. London: 1906.
Strong, Roy C. 'The Popular Celebration of the Accession Day of Queen Elizabeth I'. *Journal of the Warburg and Courtauld Institutes*, Vol. 21, No. 1-2 (Jan-Jun 1958), pp. 86-103.
Tallis, Nicola. *Uncrowned Queen: The Fateful Life of Margaret Beaufort*. London: 2019.
'The Original 007'. *Cambridge University News*. 3 November 2008. https://www.cam.ac.uk/news/the-original-007.
Thomas, Paul. *Authority and Disorder in Tudor Times, 1485–1603*. Cambridge: 1999.
Thurley, Simon, *Houses of Power: The Places that Shaped the Tudor World*. London: 2017.
Tiniswood, Adrian. *Behind the Throne*. London: 2018.
Tomlin, Rebecca and Louise Horton. 'Proclamation of Lady Jane Grey'. *Society of Antiquaries*. https://www.sal.org.uk/wp-content/uploads/2019/10/Proclamation-of-Lady-Jane-Grey-object-in-depth.pdf.
Tudor Food and Eating. https://www.hrp.org.uk/hampton-court-palace/history-and-stories/tudor-food-and-eating.

Turnham, Anna and Andrea Clarke. 'Celebrating the New Year Elizabethan Style'. *Medieval manuscripts blog*. 1 January 2022. https://blogs.bl.uk/digitisedmanuscripts/2022/01/celebrating-the-new-year.html.

Watkins, Sarah-Beth. *Margaret Tudor, Queen of Scots: The Life of King Henry VIII's Sister*. London: 2017.

Westfall, Suzanna. 'The Boy Who Would be King: Court Revels of King Edward VI, 1547–1533'. *Comparative Drama* Volume 35, No. 3-4, (Fall/Winter 2001–2), pp. 272-292.

Whitelock, Anna. *Elizabeth's Bedfellows: An Intimate History of the Queen's Court*. London: 2013.

Williams, Kate. *Rival Queens: The Betrayal of Mary Queen of Scots*. London: 2019.

Wilson, Derek. *A Brief History of the English Reformation*. London: 2012.

Wilson, Derek. *In the Lion's Court*. London: 2003.

Wood, Margaret. 'My Devise for the Succession'. *In Custodia Legis*. 10 July 2014. https://blogs.loc.gov/law/2014/07/my-devise-for-the-succession/.

Wooding, Lucy. "Reform, Wrath, and Ruin: The Devastating End of Tudor Monasticism'. *Times Literary Supplement*. 10 December 2021. https://www.the-tls.co.uk/articles/the-dissolution-of-the-monasteries-james-g-clark-book-review-lucy-wooding/.

Index

Acts of Succession, 22-24
   Act of Succession 2013, 33
Act of Supremacy, 142
Anna of Cleves, Queen of England
   annulment of marriage, 92
   marriage to Henry VIII, 91
   politics of marriage, 42, 90
Arthur, Prince of Wales
   birth, 10, 41, 104
   death, 82
   marriage, 42, 82

Bacton Church altar cloth, 162
Beaufort, John, 5
Beaufort, Margaret, 6, 5, 28, 37, 40-41, 68, 104, 150-51
Bible
   Bishop's Bible, 146
   Geneva Bible, 145
   Great Bible, 38, 144-45
   King James Bible, 146
   translated into English, 144-46
Blanche of Lancaster, 4
Book of Common Prayer, 39, 46, 147
Boleyn, Anne, Queen of England
   birth of Elizabeth, 86
   coronation, 86, 106-108
   courtly love, 84
   courtship by Henry VIII, 84-85
   falcon emblem found, 163
   marriage to Henry VIII, 85-86
   marquess of Pembroke, 85
   pregnancy, 107
   trial and execution, 87
Boleyn, Thomas, 84
Bosworth, Battle of, 7, 112

Brandon, Frances, 67, 78
Burbage, Richard, 153

Cecil, Robert, 55, 128, 149
Cecil, William, Lord Burghley
   death, 55
   named Elizabeth's first minister, 53
   relationship with Elizabeth, 51
   service before Elizabeth's reign, 52
   service to Elizabeth, 32, 51, 54, 56, 146, 159
   threatened to resign, 54
Chapuys, Eustace, 86, 96, 195
Charles V, Holy Roman Emperor, 71, 76, 83, 86, 88, 96
Claude, Queen of France, 119
Coverdale, Miles, 144
Cranmer, Thomas, 34, 39-40, 86, 144
Cromwell, Thomas, 91, 141, 144
Culpepper, Thomas, 94, 121
Curtain Theatre, 136

Dee, John, 159
de la Pole, John, Earl of Lincoln, 12
Dereham, Francis, 93, 121
Dissolution of the monasteries, 142-44
Douglas, Margaret, 78-79
Dudley, John, Earl of Northumberland, 47, 71-72, 76, 80
Dudley, Robert, Earl of Leicester
   Amy Robsart Dudley's death, 56, 60
   courtship of Elizabeth 1, 49, 56, 126
   Elizabeth's progress to Kenilworth, 60, 125-28

Edward III, King of England, xiv
Edward IV, King of England, xiv, 3, 6, 8, 40, 44, 105, 151

Edward V, King of England, xiv, 13, 36, 103
Edward VI, King of England
  birth, 89
  christening, 34
  coronation, 103-104
  death and 'Devise for the Succession', 20, 67, 69-70, 80
  diary, 157-58
  health, 66, 121
  length of reign, 46
  progresses, 121-23
  religious views, 39-40, 45-46, 104
Elizabeth, Princess of England
  birth and christening, 86
  infancy and early childhood, 51
  imprisoned during Mary's reign, 99
  legitimacy, 75
Elizabeth I, Queen of England
  accession, 26
  Anne Boleyn in coronation procession, 17, 110-14
  as Tudor rose, 27
  clothing and appearance, 159-60
  coronation, 27-28, 99-100, 108, 110-12
  courtly love, 65
  courtships, 30
  death, 51, 150
  'Golden Speech' to parliament, 131-32
  Kenilworth progress, 125-28
  makeup, 160
  Mary Queen of Scots, 54, 63-64
  parliament 53, 131
  portraits, 127, 129
  portrayals film, movies, stage, 50, 138
  progresses, 55-58, 114-15, 128-30
  progresses, cost, 56-57
  Rainbow portrait, 129-30, 162-63
  relationship with her people, 57-58, 131-32
  religion, 27, 29, 32, 53, 54, 146
  Royal Exchange, 139
  suitors, 58-61
  Tilbury speech, 49-50
  Virgin Queen, 30, 149, 152
Elizabeth of York, Queen of England
  coronation, 104-06
  death, 41
  marriage to Henry VII, 8, 41
  Yorkist heir, 3, 9, 40, 103
Eric XIV, King of Sweden, 59

Feria, Count de, 58
Field of Cloth of Gold, 118-119
Fitzroy, Henry, 83
Flushing toilet, 134-35
Food and eating in Tudor times, 133-34, 155-56
Francis I, King of France, 83, 85, 119

Globe Theatre, 136
Great House of Easement, 134-35
Gresham, Thomas, 138-39
Grey, Lady Jane, Queen of England (disputed)
  loses support of council, 76
  place in succession, 22-24, 66-67, 71-72
  proclaimed Queen of England, 73, 75
  signs documents 'Jane the Quene', 75
Grey, Lady Katherine, 78
Grey, Lady Mary, 78

Hall, Edward, 9
Harrington, John, 135
Hatton, Christopher, 57, 59
Hercule Francois, Duke of Alencon then Anjou
  courtship of Elizabeth I, 60-61
Henry IV, King of England, 5, 35, 36
Henry V, King of England, 35, 43
Henry VI, King of England, xiv, 6, 8, 36, 43, 105, 114, 151
Henry VII, King of England
  coronation, 8, 102-03, 112
  death, 68, 83
  founder of dynasty, 1
  length of reign, 36, 46
  marriage to Elizabeth of York, 7-8, 41
  progress 116-118
  religion, 37-38
Henry VIII, King of England
  accession, 36, 68
  and Anne Boleyn, 23, 43, 45, 84-87, 88
  and Anna of Cleves, 90-92

and Catherine Howard, 93-95
and Jane Seymour, 23, 43, 88-89
and Katherine of Aragon, 16, 23, 43, 83-86, 101
and Katherine Parr, 97-98
coronation, 101
early life, 14
death, 68, 98
length of reign, 46
progress to North, 119-121
religious reforms, 38-39, 89
size through reign, 156
time as bachelor, 95-96
Henry, Prince (son of Henry VIII and Katherine of Aragon), 81
Holbein, Hans, 141
Howard, Catherine, Queen of England
Act of Attainder against, 94
accusations, 94, 121
execution, 95
legend of ghostly appearance at Hampton Court Palace, 121
marriage to Henry VIII, 93

Isabella of Castile, Queen of Spain, 82-83

James VI, King of Scotland/James I, King of England, 35, 152
James IV, King of Scotland, 15
John of Gaunt, xiv, 4

Katherine of Aragon, Queen of England
annulment of marriage, 84
childhood, 16
coronation, 101
death, 86
death of Prince Arthur, 82, 101
marriage to Arthur, 42, 153
marriage to Henry VIII, 16, 42, 83
queen of England, 152-53
Knox, John, 19

Mannox, Henry, 93, 121
Margaret of Austria, 84
Margaret of York (Margaret of Burgundy), 12-14
Margaret Tudor
marriage to James IV of Scotland, 154
other marriages, 154
Marguerite of Angouleme, 84
Mary, Princess of England
birth, 82
childhood, 89, 96
gains popular support against Jane Grey, 74
legitimacy, 75
proclaimed Queen of England, 76, 80
response to Jane Grey being proclaimed Queen of England, 72, 73, 80
succession claims, 71
Mary I, Queen of England
coronation, 25-26, 108-10
death, 20
final illness, 19
marriage to Philip of Spain, 31, 109, 123
progress, 123-25
religion, 19, 25, 27, 109
succession and Elizabeth as heir, 20
Mary Stuart, Queen of Scots
and Earl of Bothwell, 62
and Lord Darnley, 62
and Rizzio, 62
Babington plot, 63
Catholic cause, 62
childhood, 96
claims to the English throne, 61
comes to England, 62
imprisonment in England, 62
plots against Elizabeth, 63, 114, 126, 147
Prince James, 62
trial and execution, 63-64
Mary Tudor, Queen of France
descendants: Grey sisters, 28, 78, 155
marriage to Louis XII, 154
marriage to Charles Brandon, 155
Matilda, Empress, Queen of England (disputed), 21-22, 108
More, Thomas, 16, 83, 141

Neville, Richard, Earl of Warwick, 6
Norris, Henry, 87
Northern Rebellion, 147

Parker, Matthew, 146
Parr, Katherine, Queen of England
  death of Henry VIII, 98
  marriage to Henry VIII, 97
  previous marriages, 96
  religion, 97
  stepmother, 97
Parry, Blanche, 162
Philip II, King of Spain
  marriage to Mary I, 31, 109, 123-24
  suitor to Elizabeth I, 58
Pole, Margaret, 157
Pope Alexander IV, 37
Pope Innocent VIII, 37
Pope Julius II, 37
Pope Pius III, 37
Population growth, 137

Queen Regent's Prerogative Act of 1554, 29

Richard II, King of England, xiv, 3, 5, 36, 103, 113
Richard III, King of England, 3, 7, 8, 103, 113, 151
Richard, Duke of York, 13-14
Robsart, Amy, 56, 60
Royal Exchange, 138-40

Seymour, Edward, Duke of Somerset, 68, 89, 158
Seymour, Jane, Queen of England, 88, 89-90, 141, 195
Seymour, Thomas, 89, 97
Shakespeare, William, 1, 127, 151
Stewart, Henry, Lord Darnley, 62
Simnel, Lambert, 11-13
Stanley, William, 14-15
Stoke, Battle of, 12-13
Stuart, Arbella, 79
Swan Theatre, 136
Swynford, Katherine, 4

Theatre, The, 135-36
Tudor, Jasper, 6
Tudor rose, 2, 4, 10-11, 17, 18

Walsingham, Francis, 63-64
Warbeck, Perkin, 11, 13-16
Wars of the Roses, xv, 34, 156
Whitehall family portrait of Henry VIII, 141
Wolsey, Thomas, 38, 118
Woodville, Elizabeth, Queen of England, 9, 40, 151